A guide to Australian Locomotion

2009 edition

A guide book to diesel and electric locomotives running in commercial service today.

Chris Walters, Bernie Baker, Brad Peadon

Published in December 2008 by the Australian Railway Historical Society (New South Wales Division)
67 Renwick Street, Redfern NSW 2016

National Library Card Number and ISBN 978-0-9805106-3-8

Layout and design by Chris Walters
Production assistance—Peter Clark, John Hoyle, Evan Jasper, Rod Milne, Shane O'Neil, Chris Stratton and Darren Tulk
General Manager—Ross Verdich

Front cover: QRNational's freshly repainted CLP13, at Chullora Workshops (Sydney) on Saturday 12 July 2008. Terry McConnell

Back cover: Coote Industrial's NA1874 (still in South Spur livery) and CFCLA's C503 (on hire) pass Wirrappa on Wednesday 10 September 2008. The train was returning east from Mount Christie, having 'dropped' ballast in the section the previous day. Despite the proliferation of former Silverton and South Spur locomotives in Coote Industrial livery, a number of freight and contract services are still operated under the older company banners. Steve Munro

Contents

Glossary of names and abbreviations

AC	alternating current
ACT	Australian Capital Territory
AIS	Australian Iron & Steel
ALCo	American Locomotive Company
ALRC	Australian Locomotive and Railway Carriage Company
AN	Australian National
ANGRMS	Australian Narrow Gauge Railway Museum Society (Woodford, Qld)
ANR	Australia Northern Railroad or Australian National Railways
APC	Australian Portland Cement
ARG	Australian Railroad Group
ARHS	Australian Railway Historical Society
ARTC	Australian Rail Track Corporation
ASC	Aramac Shire Council
ASCR	Australian Sugar Cane Railway (Botanic Gardens, Bundaberg)
ASR	Australia Southern Railroad
ATN	Australian Transport Network
ATT&M	Alexandra Timber Tramway & Museum (Alexandra, Victoria)
AWR	Australia Western Railroad
BBR	Bennett Brook Railway (Whiteman Park, Western Australia)
BCSC	Blue Circle Southern Cement
BHP	Broken Hill Proprietary Limited (known now simply as BHP)
BHPIO	BHP Iron Ore
BHPBIO	BHP-Billiton Iron Ore
BLLPS	Boulder Loop Line Preservation Society (Boulder, WA)
BNSF	Burlington Northern Santa Fe
BPR	Bellarine Peninsula Railway (Queenscliff, Victoria)
BTM	Boyanup Transport Museum (Boyanup, Western Australian)
CFCLA	Chicago Freight Car Leasing Australia
CI	Coote Industrial
CKSTG	Cairns Kuranda Steam Train Group (Cairns, Queensland)
Comeng	Commonwealth Engineering
CR	Commonwealth Railways
CRT	Colin Rees Transport
CSR	Colonial Sugar Refining (known now simply as CSR)
DC	direct current
DSCR	Daylesford Spa Country Railway (Daylesford, Victoria)
DMU	diesel multiple-unit
DOI	(Victorian) Dept of Infrastructure
DOO	driver-only operation
DPU	distributed power unit
DRR	Don River Railway (Don, Tasmania)
DSB	Danske Statsbaner (or Danish State Railways)
DSR&M	Dorrigo Steam Railway & Museum (Dorrigo, NSW)
DVR	Derwent Valley Railway (New Norfolk, Tasmania)
EBR	Emu Bay Railway
EDI	Evans Deakin Industries Ltd, rail portion now Downer-EDI Rail
EE	English Electric
EMB	E M Baldwin & Sons
EMD	Electro-Motive Division of General Motors (now Electro Motive Diesel)
EMU	electric multiple-unit
FA	Freight Australia (previously FV)
FCAB	Ferrocarril de Antofagasta a Bolivia (Chile)
FC	FreightCorp (previously FR)
FMG	Fortescue Metals Group
FNAR	Friends of the North Australian Railway (Adelaide River)
FR	FreightRail (later FC)
FV	Freight Victoria
GDHMM	Gympie & District Historical & Mining Museum (Gympie, Qld)
GATX	General American Transportation Corporation (GE lease company)
GE	General Electric
GEC	General Electric Company (incorporating EE, now part of Alstom—not related to GE)
GM	General Motors
GML	Goldsworthy Mining Limited
GNR	Great Northern Rail
GRPS	Goulburn Roundhouse Preservation Society (Goulburn, NSW)
GTSA	Globe Turbocharger Specialties Australia (known simply as GTSA)
GWA	Genesee Wyoming Australia
HBL	Heggies Bulk Haul
HEP	head-end power
HVRT	Hunter Valley Railway Trust (Branxton, NSW)
HVTR	Hotham Valley Tourist Railway (Pinjarra, WA)
ILRMS	Illawarra Light Railway Museum Society (Albion Park, NSW)
ICTSI	International Container Terminal Services Incorporated

JRW	Junee Railway Workshop
KMR	Kerrisdale Mountain Railway (Kerrisdale, Victoria)
LALG	Lachlan ALCo Locomotive Group
LVR	Lachlan Valley Railway
LVRF	Lachlan Valley Rail Freight
MKA	Morrison Knudsen Australia
MLW	Montreal Locomotive Works
MMM	Mining & Machine Park (Port Hedland, WA)
MNGR	Menangle Narrow Gauge Railway (Menangle Park, NSW)
MPA	Marree Progress Assoc. (Marree, SA)
MRPS	Mornington Railway Preservation Society (Moorooduc, Victoria)
MVHR	Mary Valley Heritage Railway (Gympie, Queensland)
navvy	manual labour/rail maintenance
NR	National Rail
NRM	National Rail Museum (Port Dock, Adelaide)
NREC	National Rail Equipment Corporation
NRR	Northern Rivers Railroad
NSW	New South Wales (state)
NSWGR	NSW Government Railways
NSWRTM	NSW Rail Transport Museum (Thirlmere, Valley Heights, NSW)
NT	Northern Territory
NZ	New Zealand
OGHRM	Old Ghan Heritage Railway & Museum (MacDonnell, NT)
ORH	Office of Rail Heritage (RailCorp)
PBR	Puffing Billy Railway (Belgrave, Victoria)
PCRM	Pine Creek Railway Museum (Pine Creek, NT)
PN	Pacific National
PNQ	Pacific National Queensland
PNT	Pacific National Tasmania
PPL	Patrick PortLink
PRHS	Pilbara Railway Historical Society (Seven Mile, WA)
PRR	Pichi Richi Railway (Quorn, SA)
PTC	Pemberton Tramway Company (Pemberton, WA)
Qld	Queensland (state)
QPSR	Queensland Pioneer Steam Railway (Swanbank, Queensland)
QR	Queensland Railways/Queensland Rail (now known simply as QR)
QRN	QRNational
QVM	Queen Victoria Museum (Launceston, Tasmania)
RAILCO	Ravenshoe and Atherton Insteam Locomotion Company (Atherton and Herberton, Queensland)
RFS	Rail Fleet Services (UGR), Chullora
RHWA	Rail Heritage Western Australia (ARHS WA Division)
RVR	Richmond Vale Railway (Kurri Kurri, NSW)
RTS	Rail Technical Support Group (known simply as RTS)
SA	South Australia (state)
SAR	South Australian Railways
SCT	Specialized Container Transport
SDSRA	Southern Downs Steam Railway Association (Warwick, Queensland)
SGTR	South Gippsland Tourist Railway (Korumburra, Victoria)
SP	Southern Pacific
SRANSW	State Rail Authority of NSW
SRHC	Seymour Rail Heritage Centre
SSR	Southern Shorthaul Railroad
SSRM	Sulphide Street Rail Museum (Broken Hill, NSW)
SSRS	South Spur Rail Services
STC	Silverton Tramway Company
Tas	Tasmania (state)
TGR	Tasmanian Government Railways
TTM	Tasmanian Transport Museum (Glenorchy, Tasmania)
UG	United Goninan (now UGR)
UGR	United Group Rail
UK	United Kingdom
UP	Union Pacific
US	United States of America
Vic	Victoria (state)
VGR	Victorian Goldfields Railway (Maldon, Victoria)
VR	Victorian Railways
WA	Western Australia (state)
WAGR	Western Australian Government Railways
WCWR	West Coast Wilderness Railway (Queenstown/Regatta Point, Tasmania)
WCR	West Coast Railway
WGR	Walhalla Goldfields Railway (Walhalla, Victoria)
YVR	Yarra Valley Railway (Healesville, Victoria)
ZZR	Zig Zag Railway (Lithgow, NSW)

Welcome to Australian Locomotion

The aim of this book is to provide a 'one-stop', clear and concise picture of Australia's modern (diesel and electric) locomotives. If it's out there somewhere, hopefully we've covered it for you. The sheer diversity of locomotion on show in Australia is, however, so eclectic that it is very likely that some hidden 'oddities' have been omitted, whether due to a lack of information, or simply because a few have skipped our notice. If you do indeed come across a locomotive not covered herein, or notice an element of the information that has fallen out-of-date, the authors would enthusiastically encourage, and be very grateful for, any report or update submitted via editor@railwaydigest.com.au.

The locomotives themselves have been sectioned off by 'make'; now this does not always indicate the company responsible for assembly (or rebuild), but by 'technology'. As such, the larger builder catergories are EMD (Electro-Motive Division of General Motors, and more recently Electro Motive Diesel), ALCo (American Locomotive Company), General Electric (GE), English Electric (EE) and Walkers Limited. The less numerous examples of builders such as Comeng (many of whose products are actually covered in the ALCo section) and Tulloch, for example, then follow. Locomotives of the Australian sugar cane industry have their own detailed section, while appendices listing preserved locomotives, up-to-date operator fleet-listings (for cross-referencing), a glossary of abbreviations and of course sources and further reading round off the book.

Although levels of background information have been provided, this book attempts to cover the here and now, and what you will see trackside, and as such can be considered a field guide and 'starting block' for identifying locomotives operating in 2009.

Not what it used to be

Large-scale privatisation of the industry in Australia during the 1990s and 'noughties', wrought upon the country's rail scene a level of change not witnessed since the phasing out of steam power during the 1950s and 1960s. Not coincidentally, this came hard on the heels of an almost unprecedented level of 'first generation' diesel locomotive scrapping, as the industry sought to economise and reduce costs around the nation. Right across Australia, early-generation diesels were torched to 'clear the decks': in NSW it was the 44 and 45 Class, and in South Australia the 930 Class and classic GM1 and GM12 Clyde streamliners. In the south-east, V/Line disposed of T and Y Class in particular, while ANTasrail culled its extensive ZC/1300 Class fleet, obtained at 'bargain' cost from Queensland Rail (QR) only a few years before. In the north, QR itself purged English Electric locomotives of the 1200, 1250, 1270 and 1650 Classes with particular abandon, while Westrail, on the opposite side of the country, sought to rid itself of a multitude of aging locomotives of both Clyde and English Electric heritage. What the current landscape would be like had even a fraction of these units survived into the privatisation era makes for intriguing thinking.

Aside from the decimation of the former State Rail Authority (SRA NSW) electric locomotive fleet (the 46 Class in 1998, and the newer 85 and 86 Class more recently), there has been no repeat of these mass scrappings, and the chance of such occurrences being repeated soon is unlikely. Put simply, there is now a locomotive shortage Australia-wide, and while the rail industry is facing a period of renaissance, surviving locomotives of the 1950s, 60s, 70s and 80s are expected to power on for some time yet.

Which brings us to this book. Although the last ten years have seen a litany of new companies and operators—large and small—entering the industry, sales, mergers, collapses and 'brand changes' have made it nearly impossible to keep up with who owns what, and what runs where. The days of state railway segregation have vanished, and even track gauge is no longer the boundary to operations that it once was.

Preserved locomotives

Locomotives owned by museums and heritage organisations posed an interesting conundrum in terms of how they should be covered. The simple, black and white argument is that these are museum pieces that are no longer part of the scene. However, with each passing year this argument gets thinner; heritage groups have come to realise the benefits of hiring out their locomotives to commercial operators starving for motive power. There are some 'preserved' locomotives that certainly perform regularly in commercial service: the Hunter Valley Railway Trust 44 Class employed by Independent Rail and much of the Seymour Rail Heritage Centre fleet, particularly, spend more time in the service of commercial operators than they do in more heritage-type roles. There are also preservation organisations that have recently begun to adopt a more commercial approach to their business, and while this might irk the purists, it is these groups that may well indicate future directions for heritage rail. However, given that these locomotives are owned (or are in the care of) preservation groups, they have been covered in an index at the rear of the book, listed by original—or in some cases most 'prominent'—owner.

Generally we have restricted the coverage to preserved locomotives of above a certain weight (basically anything bigger than a Malcolm Moore 0-4-0 locomotive), while we've also kept to including locomotives 'easily' accessible to the general public (ie. many locomotives held in private collections, and away from official public access have been omitted). In both cases, this was in an effort to aid overall accuracy rather than precision.

The mission

It should be recorded that—as of press time—the successful bidder for the former Pacific National Tasmania (PNT) operation had yet to be announced. Such an announcement was expected just before Christmas 2008, at which time those locomotives listed in this book as being under PNT ownership will of course revert to this new railway operator ... whomever they may be.

In closing, it is worth mentioning that the 'status' listings in this book are essentially nominal. Many locomotives listed here as 'stored' could return to service at any time, just as those described as 'in service' could be just as quickly withdrawn and stored.

This guide seeks to bring together the locomotives of all of these operators, to assist readers in identifying any locomotive found operating across the country, even the obscure and remote. However, the very nature of recording this ever-changing scene is fraught with risk, and it is quite possible that some of the information within this book might already be out of date (see below). But then, if it was not going to be a challenge, it probably would not have been worth doing.

EMD

1443 at Chullora on Tuesday 20 March 2007.
Bernie Baker

SD70ACe/LC

Builder:	*EMD Ontario, Canada*	Model:	*SD70ACe/LC*
Type:	*Co-Co diesel-electric*	Engine:	*EMD 710G3C-T2 turbo-charged 2-stroke V16*
Traction power:	*3210 kW (4300 hp)*	Length:	*22.64 m*
Weight:	*195.0 tonnes*	Gauge:	*1435 mm*

Above: Then-new SD70ACe/LC locomotives 4319 and 4318 at the Boodarie locomotive facility just south of Port Hedland on Tuesday 24 July 2007. Chris Walters

Commencing in 2005 BHP-Billiton Iron Ore began commissioning a 13-strong fleet (plus one spare-parts unit) of US-built, EMD SD70ACe/LC (the 'LC' denotes 'low clearance') locomotives for its iron ore haulage task. Intended to both cater for a massive upswing of traffic resulting from a surging iron ore demand, while also supplementing an aging General Electric locomotive collection, successive batches have seen the EMD fleet grow and as of press time a further 13 units were on order, with more likely to follow. The second (and subsequent) batch differ from the original 13 units in that they are all fitted with cab modules isolated from the frame (sometimes referred to as the 'whisper' cab) to reduce the effect of noise and vibration on crews.

Road #	Builder's #	Built	Owner	Status	Name/Note
4300	20038540-001	2005	BHPBIO	Stored Nelson Pt	Spare parts package unit
4301	20038540-002	2005	BHPBIO	In service	*Bing*
4302	20038540-003	2005	BHPBIO	In service	*Mooka*
4303	20038540-004	2005	BHPBIO	In service	*Walla*
4304	20038540-005	2005	BHPBIO	In service	*Gillam*
4305	20038540-006	2005	BHPBIO	In service	*Coonarie*
4306	20038540-007	2005	BHPBIO	In service	*Garden*
4307	20038540-008	2005	BHPBIO	In service	*Shaw*

(continued)

Road #	Builder's #	Built	Owner	Status	Name/Note
4308	20038540-009	2005	BHPBIO	In service	*Cowra*
4309	20038540-010	2005	BHPBIO	In service	*Gidgi*
4310	20038540-011	2005	BHPBIO	In service	*Weeli*
4311	20038540-012	2005	BHPBIO	In service	*Poonda*
4312	20038540-013	2005	BHPBIO	In service	*Mindy*
4313	20038540-014	2005	BHPBIO	In service	*Kurrajura*
4314	20058712-001	2006	BHPBIO	In service	-
4315	20058712-002	2006	BHPBIO	In service	-
4316	20058712-003	2006	BHPBIO	In service	-
4317	20058712-004	2006	BHPBIO	In service	-
4318	20058712-005	2006	BHPBIO	In service	-
4319	20058712-006	2006	BHPBIO	In service	-
4320	20058712-007	2006	BHPBIO	In service	-
4321	20058712-008	2006	BHPBIO	In service	-
4322	20058712-009	2006	BHPBIO	In service	-
4323	20058712-010	2006	BHPBIO	In service	-
4334	pending	2008	BHPBIO	pending	-
4335	pending	2008	BHPBIO	pending	-
4336	pending	2008	BHPBIO	pending	-
4337	pending	2008	BHPBIO	pending	-
4338	pending	2008	BHPBIO	pending	-
4339	pending	2008	BHPBIO	pending	-
4340	pending	2008	BHPBIO	pending	-
4341	pending	2008	BHPBIO	pending	-
4342	pending	2008	BHPBIO	pending	-
4343	pending	2008	BHPBIO	pending	-
4344	pending	2008	BHPBIO	pending	-
4345	pending	2008	BHPBIO	pending	-
4346	pending	2008	BHPBIO	pending	-

Above: SD70ACe/LC 4323 working mid-train in Nelson Point Yard at Port Hedland on Sunday 22 July 2007. Chris Walters

SD70ACe

Builder:	*EMD Ontario, Canada*	Model:	*SD70ACe*
Type:	*Co-Co diesel-electric*	Engine:	*EMD 710G3C-T2 turbo-charged 2-stroke V16*
Traction power:	*3210 kW (4300 hp)*	Length:	*22.64 m*
Weight:	*195.0 tonnes*	Gauge:	*1435 mm*

Above: A near-new 4325 at Boodarie on Monday 14 July 2008. Peter Clark

In mid-2008 BHP-Billiton arranged—at short—notice to obtain ten SD70ACe locomotives from the United States, that had actually been intended for North American freight hauler BNSF. Although additional SD70ACe/LC units were on order, with traffic levels continuing to rise, new locomotives were desperately needed by BHP-Billiton. Unlike the other SD70ACe/LC (low clearance) units ordered by the company, these ten ex-BNSF units are standard 'off the shelf' North American SD70ACe locomotives, and have been commissioned in a simplified 'BNSF base' livery of orange. Nine more are on order.

Road #	Original #	Builder's #	Built	Owner	Status
4324	BNSF 9166	20066862-037	2008	BHPBIO	In service
4325	BNSF 9167	20066862-038	2008	BHPBIO	In service
4326	BNSF 9184	20066862-055	2008	BHPBIO	In service
4327	BNSF 9185	20066862-056	2008	BHPBIO	In service
4328	BNSF 9186	20066862-057	2008	BHPBIO	In service
4329	BNSF 9187	20066862-058	2008	BHPBIO	In service
4330	BNSF 9188	20066862-059	2008	BHPBIO	In service
4331	BNSF 9189	20066862-060	2008	BHPBIO	In service
4332	BNSF 9190	20066862-061	2008	BHPBIO	In service
4333	BNSF 9191	20066862-062	2008	BHPBIO	In service
4347	unknown	pending	pending	BHPBIO	In service
4348	unknown	pending	pending	BHPBIO	In service
4349	unknown	pending	pending	BHPBIO	In service
4350	unknown	pending	pending	BHPBIO	In service
4351	unknown	pending	pending	BHPBIO	In service
4352	unknown	pending	pending	BHPBIO	In service
4353	unknown	pending	pending	BHPBIO	In service
4354	unknown	pending	pending	BHPBIO	In service
4355	unknown	pending	pending	BHPBIO	In service

SCT Class

Builder:	*EDI-EMD (Cardiff)*	Model:	*GT46ACe*
Type:	*Co-Co diesel-electric*	Engine:	*EMD 710G3A turbo-charged 2-stroke V16*
Traction power:	*3210 kW (4300 hp)*	Length:	*22.00 m*
Weight:	*134.0 tonnes*	Gauge:	*1435 mm*

Above: SCT004 and SCT009 at Wirappa on Monday 8 September 2008. Steve Munro

The SCT Class are new EMD/Downer-EDI Rail AC-traction locomotives employed by Specialized Container Transport (SCT) on their transcontinental freight services between Perth in Western Australia and Goobang (Parkes) in New South Wales and Melbourne (Victoria). By the end of August 2008 all fifteen of the class had entered service and completely revolutionised SCT's locomotive rostering.

During late October 2008, the first of a series of near-identical GT46ACe locomotives was completed at Cardiff, and it has been reported that these new units will be available for lease under a new division of Downer-EDI Rail during 2009.

Road #	Builder's #	Built	Owner	Status
SCT001	08-1725	2007	SCT	In service
SCT002	08-1726	2007	SCT	In service
SCT003	08-1727	2007	SCT	In service
SCT004	08-1728	2007	SCT	In service
SCT005	08-1729	2007	SCT	In service
SCT006	08-1730	2007	SCT	In service
SCT007	08-1731	2008	SCT	In service
SCT008	08-1732	2008	SCT	In service
SCT009	08-1733	2008	SCT	In service
SCT010	08-1734	2008	SCT	In service
SCT011	08-1735	2008	SCT	In service
SCT012	08-1736	2008	SCT	In service
SCT013	08-1737	2008	SCT	In service
SCT014	08-1738	2008	SCT	In service
SCT015	08-1739	2008	SCT	In service

90 Class

Builder:	*EMD (Canada)/EDI (Cardiff)*	Model:	*GT46CWM*
Type:	*Co-Co diesel-electric*	Engine:	*EMD 710G3A turbo-charged 2-stroke V16*
Traction power:	*2860 kW (3840 hp)*	Length:	*22.00 m*
Weight:	*165.2 tonnes*	Gauge:	*1435 mm*

Above: 9033 and 9034 (two of four additional 90 Class units built during 2005 for PN) lead 9024 through Tighes Hill (on the approach to Port Waratah) with a loaded coal train on Friday 24 March 2006. Stephen Carr

The initial 31-member fleet of the 90 Class revolutionised Hunter Valley coal haulage when introduced by FreightRail (under lease from the Ready Power consortium) in 1994, before becoming part of the Pacific National-owned operation during 2002. Immediately prior to this, the 90 (and 82) Class were sold to FreightCorp (as FreightRail had become known) before the FreightCorp/National Rail sale later that year (see page 35). During late 2005, four additional locomotives were assembled for Pacific National by Downer-EDI Rail at Cardiff Workshops, although the 90 Class haulage task (Hunter Valley coal) has not changed in the 14 years since the first members of the class were introduced.

Road #	Builder's #	Built	Owner	Status	Name
9001	918266-3/94-1373	1994	PN	In service	*Ernest Henry*
9002	918266-2/94-1374	1994	PN	In service	*Michael Wendon*
9003	918266-1/94-1375	1994	PN	In service	*Matthew Ryan*
9004	918266-4/94-1376	1994	PN	In service	*Kevin Nichols*
9005	918266-5/94-1377	1994	PN	In service	*Kevin Barry*
9006	918266-6/94-1378	1994	PN	In service	*Murray Rose*
9007	918266-7/94-1379	1994	PN	In service	*Dunc Gray*
9008	918266-8/94-1380	1994	PN	In service	*Ralph Doubell*
9009	918266-9/94-1381	1994	PN	In service	*Lionel Cox*
9010	918266-10/94-1382	1994	PN	In service	*John Devitt*
9011	918266-11/94-1383	1994	PN	In service	*Kevin Gosper*

(continued)

Road #	Builder's #	Built	Owner	Status	Name
9012	918266-12/94-1384	1994	PN	In service	*Neil Brooks, Peter Evans, Mark Kerry & Mark Tonelli*
9013	918266-13/94-1385	1994	PN	In service	*Michael Diamond*
9014	918266-14/94-1386	1994	PN	In service	*Peter Antonie, Stephen Hawkins*
9015	918266-15/94-1387	1994	PN	In service	*Duncan Armstrong*
9016	918266-16/94-1388	1994	PN	In service	*Herb Elliot*
9017	918266-17/94-1389	1994	PN	In service	*Andrew Cooper, Nicholas Green, Michael McKay, James Tonkin*
9018	918266-18/94-1390	1994	PN	In service	*John Konrads*
9019	918266-19/94-1391	1994	PN	In service	*Dean Lukin*
9020	918266-20/94-1392	1994	PN	In service	*Russell Mark*
9021	918266-21/94-1393	1994	PN	In service	*Ian O'Brien*
9022	918266-22/94-1394	1994	PN	In service	*Clint Robinson*
9023	918266-23/94-1395	1994	PN	In service	*Robert Windle*
9024	918266-24/94-1396	1994	PN	In service	*John Winter*
9025	918266-25/94-1397	1994	PN	In service	*Todd Woodbridge, Mark Woodford*
9026	918266-26/94-1398	1994	PN	In service	*David Theile*
9027	918266-27/94-1399	1994	PN	In service	-
9028	918266-28/94-1400	1994	PN	In service	-
9029	918266-29/94-1401	1994	PN	In service	-
9030	918266-30/94-1402	1994	PN	In service	-
9031	918266-31/94-1403	1994	PN	In service	*Australian Men's Hockey Team*
9032	05-1692	2005	PN	In service	-
9033	05-1693	2005	PN	In service	-
9034	05-1694	2005	PN	In service	-
9035	05-1695	2005	PN	In service	-

Above: 9028, 9004 and 9023 at Mt Thorley Saturday 9 August 2008. Wayne Trowbridge

Q Class

Builder:	*Clyde-EMD (Forrestfield)*	Model:	*GT46C*
Type:	*Co-Co diesel-electric*	Engine:	*EMD 710G3B turbo-charged 2-stroke V16*
Traction power:	*2860 kW (3840 hp)*	Length:	*22.00 m*
Weight:	*133.5 tonnes*	Gauge:	*1435 mm*

Above: Newly repainted Q4015 shines beneath the yard lights at Forrestfield on Saturday 22 March 2008. Q4015 was lead locomotive on one of the trains involved in the Scadden (Esperance Line collision) on Monday 8 September 2008, while Q4005 and Q4009 were trailing units. While Q4009 returned to service within a few weeks of the accident, both Q4005 and Q4015 were expected to require extensive repair work and were undergoing evaluation and assessment at Forrestfield as this book closed for press. It was expected that both would be out of service for some months as a consequence. Evan Jasper

Obtained during 1997/1998, ostensibly as a replacement for the majority of Westrail's aging, standard-gauge L Class fleet, the nineteen Q Class units have instead ended up working side-by-side with their predecessors due to an upswing in the standard-gauge traffic demand. Used primarily on grain and mineral haulage, the Q Class—which introduced Clyde's 'self steering' radial-steer bogie to Australian rails—is now frontline standard-gauge power for the QR-owned Australian Railroad Group (ARG) in Western Australia, although their ventures east across the Nullarbor have been rare (special events and trial periods only). Despite a couple of serious collisions and derailments, investment in the repair and rebuild of the effected units indicates their worth, and the Q Class are likely to be at the forefront of the state's standard-gauge traffic task for some time to come.

Road#	Original #	Builder's #	Built	Owner	Status
Q4001	Q301	97-1454	1997	ARG	In service
Q4002	Q302	97-1455	1997	ARG	In service
Q4003	Q303	97-1456	1997	ARG	In service
Q4004	Q304	97-1457	1997	ARG	In service
Q4005	Q305	97-1458	1997	ARG	Repairs
Q4006	Q306	97-1459	1997	ARG	In service
Q4007	Q307	97-1460	1997	ARG	In service
Q4008	Q308	97-1461	1997	ARG	In service
Q4009	Q309	97-1462	1997	ARG	In service
Q4010	Q310	97-1463	1997	ARG	In service
4011	Q311	97-1464	1997	ARG	In service
Q4012	Q312	97-1465	1997	ARG	In service
Q4013	Q313	97-1466	1997	ARG	In service
Q4014	Q314	97-1467	1997	ARG	In service
Q4015	Q315	97-1468	1997	ARG	Repairs
Q4016	Q316	98-1469	1998	ARG	In service
Q4017	Q317	98-1470	1998	ARG	In service
Q4018	Q318	98-1471	1998	ARG	In service
Q4019	Q319	98-1472	1998	ARG	In service

Above: Q306 at Forrestfield on Saturday 25 March 2006. Although examples of the Q Class remain in the older ARG orange and black livery, all nineteen have now been renumbered, with Q306 presently known as Q4006. Bernie Baker

V Class

Builder:	*EDI-EMD (Cardiff)*	Model:	*GT46C*
Type:	*Co-Co diesel-electric*	Engine:	*EMD 710G3B turbo-charged 2-stroke V16*
Traction power:	*2860 kW (3840 hp)*	Length:	*22.00 m*
Weight:	*134.0 tonnes*	Gauge:	*1435 mm*

Above: V544 leads former FreightCorp 82 Class units 8202 and 8229 on No. 6FP1 empty coal, away from the Northern Power Station at Stirling North near Port Augusta, on Saturday 14 June 2008. This train is now the regular duty for V544 in Pacific National service. Daven Walters

Based on the design of the Westrail Q Class and ordered as an insurance replacement for G Class units (see page 45) G517 and G518 (which were both destroyed in a head-on collision at Ararat on 26 November 1999), V544 spent its first few years of service for Freight Australia (and then Pacific National) working SCT trains between Melbourne, Adelaide and Perth as part of an ongoing 'hook and pull' contract that ended once SCT procured its own locomotive fleet. During 2007, the locomotive was removed from these duties and transferred onto Leigh Creek coal services based out of Port Augusta, South Australia, where it normally works with a pair of ex-FreightCorp 82 Class locomotives (see page 35).

Road #	Builder's #	Built	Owner	Status	Name
V544	01-1603	2002	Pacific National	In service	*Tim Fischer*

FQ Class

Builder:	*EDI-EMD (Port Augusta)*	Model:	*GT46C*
Type:	*Co-Co diesel-electric*	Engine:	*EMD 710G3B turbo-charged 2-stroke V16*
Traction power:	*2860 kW (3840 hp)*	Length:	*22.00 m*
Weight:	*134.0 tonnes*	Gauge:	*1435 mm*

Above: FQ02 (leading ALF22) heads 7AD1 Adelaide to Darwin Freight through Coonamia on Saturday 3 February 2007. FQ01 and FQ02 have been decorated with Indigenous designs to compliment the red FreightLink livery, unlike FQ03 and FQ04, which are both in the standard version of the scheme. Andrew Rosenbauer

Again based on the Westrail Q Class prototype, these four locomotives were built by EDI at Port Augusta and acquired by FreightLink (operators of the Darwin Line on behalf of the Asia Pacific Transport Consortium) for freight haulage on the then new north-south transcontinental railway (although in practice FreightLink trains operate all the way through to and from Adelaide). The four FQ Class locomotives are unable to handle the traffic task on their own, and so are supplemented by a number of (Asia Pacific partner) Genesee Wyoming Australia ALF/CLF/CLP units, in addition to several CFCLA VL Class lease locomotives.

Road #	Builder's #	Built	Owner	Status	Name
FQ01	03-1664	2003	FreightLink	In service	*Kurra Kurraka*
FQ02	03-1665	2003	FreightLink	In service	*Purnu*
FQ03	03-1666	2003	FreightLink	In service	*Wagiman*
FQ04	03-1667	2003	FreightLink	In service	*Aboriginal Stockman*

AN Class

Builder:	*Clyde-EMD (Kelso)*	Model:	*AT46C*
Type:	*Co-Co diesel-electric*	Engine:	*EMD 710G3A turbo-charged 2-stroke V16*
Traction power:	*2860 kW (3840 hp)*	Length:	*22.03 m*
Weight:	*128.0 tonnes*	Gauge:	*1435 mm*

Above: Unique *Ghan*-liveried AN3, stabled at Alice Springs on Sunday 5 June 2005.
Graham Crichton

The last new locomotives ordered by Australian National prior to its sell-off in 1997, the remaining ten AN Class units (AN10 was scrapped following the Hines Hill collision on 14 January 1996) today are 'support' locomotives used on interstate Pacific National steel and intermodal services, usually trailing NR Class GEs (see page 141). The main exception to this rule is AN3, which is commonly used on *The Ghan* passenger service between Adelaide and Alice Springs. Other members of the class can also be found on this train occasionally.

Road #	Builder's #	Built	Owner	Status
AN1	92-1297	1992	Pacific National	In service
AN2	92-1298	1992	Pacific National	In service
AN3	92-1299	1992	Pacific National	In service
AN4	93-1300	1993	Pacific National	In service
AN5	93-1301	1993	Pacific National	In service
AN6	93-1302	1993	Pacific National	In service
AN7	93-1303	1993	Pacific National	In service
AN8	93-1304	1993	Pacific National	In service
AN9	93-1305	1993	Pacific National	In service
AN11	93-1307	1994	Pacific National	In service

14 (ex-MZ III) Class

Builder:	*NoHAB Trollhättan Sweden*	Model:	*JT36C*
Type:	*Co-Co diesel-electric*	Engine:	*EMD 645E3 turbo-charged 2-stroke V20*
Traction power:	*2685 kW (3600 hp)*	Length:	*21.0 m*
Weight:	*125.0 tonnes*	Gauge:	*1435 mm*

Above: 1431 (and 1432) at Blayney on Friday 9 November 2007. Chris Walters

Sixteen of the 20 former DSB (Danish State Railways) MZ III Class locomotives were acquired during 2005 by LVRF for freight haulage in NSW. Delivered in three batches (five in 2006, five in 2007 and six in 2008) most of the class were commissioned (as the 14 Class) following overhaul and modification by Bradken Rail (Braemar). By the time of their arrival, LVRF had become Independent Rail and the class progressively began to appear on the operator's services, working to locations such as Moree, Narrabri and Blayney in addition to frequent use on Minto–Botany and Cooks River trip trains. A number of the final batch were damaged in transit from Denmark during May 2008 and at least two of these (1441 and 1444) are now unlikely to run in Australia without significant rebuilds.

Road #	Builder's #	Built	Owner	Status
1427	2858	1972	Independent Rail	In service
1428	2859	1972	Independent Rail	In service
1429	2860	1973	Independent Rail	In service
1431	2862	1973	Independent Rail	In service
1432	2863	1973	Independent Rail	In service
1433	2864	1973	Independent Rail	Stored
1434	2865	1973	Independent Rail	In service
1435	2866	1973	Independent Rail	In service
1437	2868	1973	Independent Rail	In service
1438	2869	1973	Independent Rail	Stored
1440	2870	1973	Independent Rail	In service
1441	2872	1973	Independent Rail	Stored
1443	2874	1974	Independent Rail	In service
1444	2875	1974	Independent Rail	Stored
1445	2876	1974	Independent Rail	Stored
1446	2877	1974	Independent Rail	Stored

RL Class

Builder:	*RTS (Islington)*	Model:	*AT36C*
Type:	*Co-Co diesel-electric*	Engine:	*EMD 645F3B turbo-charged 2-stroke V16*
Traction power:	*2610 kW (3500 hp)*	Length:	*20.50 m*
Weight:	*132.0 tonnes*	Gauge:	*1435 mm*

Above: RL305 (and RL306) at Broken Hill on Sunday 14 September 2008. Bernie Baker

The RL Class story can be traced back to 1995 and a failed MKA Whyalla project to rebuild a number of former FreightRail 442 Class units with EMD components. MKA folded soon after, and work stopped after the partial rebuild of 44227. NREC, who acquired the former MKA business, eventually restarted the project (with affiliate RTS performing the work at Islington), although ultimately chose to all but withdraw the use of 442 Class components from the project (although 442 Class bogies/pivot castings and traction motors have been re-used under at least some of the new locomotives). RL301 first appeared in late 2005, although it was quite some time before it and six of its sister units slowly entered lease service (initially managed for NREC by CFCLA). Only seven of the proposed ten had materialised by 2008—with these spending most of their time working in South Australia and Victoria—before being sold mid-year to Coote Industrial, with some units then returning to NSW (after an earlier stint in 2006/07) towards the end of that year.

Road #	Built	Owner	Status
RL301	2005	Coote Industrial	In service
RL302	2005	Coote Industrial	In service
RL303	2006	Coote Industrial	Stored/repair
RL304	2006	Coote Industrial	In service
RL305	2006	Coote Industrial	In service
RL306	2007	Coote Industrial	In service
RL307	2008	Coote Industrial	In service
RL308	2008	Coote Industrial	Under construction
RL309	pending	Coote Industrial	Under construction
RL310	pending	Coote Industrial	Under construction

ALF Class

Builder:	*MKA (Whyalla)*	Model:	*JT26C-2M*
Type:	*Co-Co diesel-electric*	Engine:	*EMD 645E3C turbo-charged 2-stroke V16*
Traction power:	*2240 kW (3000 hp)*	Length:	*19.82 m*
Weight:	*128.0 tonnes*	Gauge:	*1435 mm*

Above: ALF19 at Dry Creek (Adelaide) on Monday 6 August 2007. Bernie Baker

Following the split up of the former Australian Railroad Group (ARG) business in 2006, the ALF Class (rebuilt from the former AL Class by Morrison Knudsen Australia during 1994) was allocated between Genesee Wyoming Australia (GWA) and QR, the latter of whom picked up the former ARG Western Australia and NSW business divisions. Of the eight-member ALF Class only ALF25 ended up with QR/ARG and, as had been the case for a number of years prior to the ARG split, it continues to remain based in Western Australia for service on the 1435 mm gauge route from Kwinana/Perth through to Kalgoorlie (and sometimes further east on limestone workings). In 2007 the locomotive was upgraded with ZTR traction control and renumbered as ALZ3208, although its role in the ARG haulage task has not varied as a result. The seven GWA-owned ALF Class units continue to mainly see service in South Australian grain haulage.

Road #	Rebuilt	Builder's #	Built	Owner	Status	Name
ALF18	AL21	94-AN-018	1994	GWA	In service	*City of Port Pirie*
ALF19	AL18	94-AN-019	1994	GWA	In service	-
ALF20	AL24	94-AN-020	1994	GWA	In service	-
ALF21	AL20	94-AN-021	1994	GWA	In service	-
ALF22	AL23	94-AN-022	1994	GWA	In service	-
ALF23	AL25	94-AN-023	1994	GWA	In service	-
ALF24	AL22	94-AN-024	1994	GWA	In service	-
ALZ3208	AL19	94-AN-025	1994	ARG	In service	Formerly ALF25

CLF/CLP Class

Builder:	*MKA (Whyalla)*	Model:	*AT26C-2M*
Type:	*Co-Co diesel-electric*	Engine:	*EMD 645E3C turbo-charged 2-stroke V16*
Traction power:	*2240 kW (3000 hp)*	Length:	*19.58 m*
Weight:	*126.0/134.0 tonnes*	Gauge:	*1435 mm*

Above: CLP13 at Chullora on Saturday 12 July 2008. Terry McConnell

The Australian Railroad Group (ARG) split of 2006 divided the sixteen remaining members of the CLF/CLP Class fleet (themselves 1993 Morrison Knudsen Australia, or MKA, rebuilds of the former CL Class), with five each of the CLF and CLP Classes going to QR/ARG and the remainder to Genesee Wyoming Australia (GWA). Since this time these classic streamlined EMDs have become a fixture on the QRNational intermodal services along the east coast Melbourne–Sydney–Brisbane corridor. Commencing with CLP13 in July 2008, these ten locomotives are slowly being repainted in QRN's yellow, maroon and black livery. The GWA cut of the fleet has generally been focused on South Australian grain haulage, with cross-border visits into NSW and Victoria occurring from time to time. On occasions, one or two of the GWA units have been leased back to ARG to cover locomotive shortages as well. The CLP Class no longer employ the head-end power (HEP) packages that they were equipped with by MKA back in 1993, although their fuel capacity is still greater than that of the CLF units, and as such a slight weight difference (in favour of the CLP) remains between the two.

Road #	Rebuilt	Builder's #	Built	Owner	Status	Name
CLF1	CL2	93-AN-001	1993	ARG	In service	*City of Whyalla*
CLF2	CL11	93-AN-002	1993	ARG	In service	-
CLF3	CL7	93-AN-003	1993	ARG	In service	-

(continued)

Road #	Rebuilt	Builder's #	Built	Owner	Status	Name
CLF4	CL5	93-AN-004	1993	ARG	In service	-
CLF5	CL12	93-AN-005	1993	GWA	In service	-
CLF6	CL6	93-AN-006	1993	GWA	In service	-
CLF7	CL16	93-AN-007	1993	ARG	In service	-
CLP8	CL9	93-AN-008	1993	GWA	In service	*City of Port Augusta*
CLP9	CL13	93-AN-009	1993	ARG	In service	*Wiljakali*
CLP10	CL17	93-AN-010	1993	ARG	In service	*Mirning*
CLP11	CL14	93-AN-011	1993	ARG	In service	*Kaurna*
CLP12	CL15	93-AN-012	1993	ARG	In service	*Ngadjuri*
CLP13	CL3	93-AN-013	1993	ARG	In service	*Nukunu*
CLP14	CL4	93-AN-014	1993	GWA	In service	*Barngarla*
CLP16	CL10	93-AN-016	1993	GWA	In service	*Murunitja*
CLP17	CL8	93-AN-017	1993	GWA	In service	*Arabana*

Above: CLF4 leads X54 into Sandgate with QRNational's 5BM7 Brisbane to Melbourne freight on Friday 3 November 2006. Such duties are regular to the QRN-owned CLF and CLP Class locomotives in 2008. Chris Walters

4000/4100 Class

Builder:	*EDI-EMD (Maryborough)*	Model:	*GT42CU-AC*
Type:	*Co-Co diesel-electric*	Engine:	*EMD 710G3B turbo-charged 2-stroke V12*
Traction power:	*2260 kW (3030 hp)*	Length:	*22.00 m*
Weight:	*120.0 tonnes*	Gauge:	*1067 mm*

Above: 4014 and 4036 haul a loaded coal train through Stowe loop, on the Moura Line on Thursday morning, 19 June 2008. Peter Reading

The 4000 Class were Australia's first narrow-gauge AC-traction locomotives. Initially 38 were ordered by QR and intended for coal haulage (primarily on the Blackwater, Moura and, for a time, Newlands systems), although initially a small number were also employed on the Mount Isa Line alongside the Goninan/GE 2800 Class (see page 150). Gradually all were shifted over to coal haulage service while an additional 11 were acquired during 2004/05, resulting in an eventual total of 49. An increase in this traffic demand yielded a need for yet more 4000-type locomotives, however the design specification had to be altered (notably from Siemens to Mitsubishi inverters), and the result was the 4100 Class, that debuted in late 2007. Fifteen of these newer locomotives were initially ordered, but this was later doubled to 30, with the last expected during 2009. In addition to these, a number of new 83 Class 1067-mm gauge locomotives—based on the 4100 specification—are being built for Pacific National's Queensland coal haulage operation as of late 2008.

EMD

Road #	Builder's #	Built	Owner	Status
4001	99-1484	2000	QRNational	In service
4002	99-1485	2000	QRNational	In service
4003	99-1486	2000	QRNational	In service
4004	99-1487	2000	QRNational	In service
4005	99-1488	2000	QRNational	In service
4006	99-1489	2000	QRNational	In service
4007	99-1490	2000	QRNational	In service
4008	99-1491	2000	QRNational	In service
4009	99-1492	2000	QRNational	In service
4010	99-1493	2000	QRNational	In service
4011	99-1494	2000	QRNational	In service
4012	99-1495	2000	QRNational	In service
4013	99-1496	2000	QRNational	In service
4014	99-1497	2000	QRNational	In service
4015	99-1498	2000	QRNational	In service
4016	99-1499	2000	QRNational	In service
4017	99-1500	2000	QRNational	In service
4018	99-1501	2000	QRNational	In service
4019	99-1502	2000	QRNational	In service
4020	99-1503	2000	QRNational	In service
4021	99-1504	2000	QRNational	In service
4022	99-1505	2000	QRNational	In service
4023	99-1506	2000	QRNational	In service
4024	99-1507	2000	QRNational	In service
4025	99-1508	2000	QRNational	In service
4026	99-1509	2000	QRNational	In service
4027	99-1510	2000	QRNational	In service
4028	99-1511	2000	QRNational	In service
4029	99-1512	2000	QRNational	In service
4030	99-1513	2000	QRNational	In service
4031	99-1514	2000	QRNational	In service
4032	99-1515	2000	QRNational	In service
4033	99-1516	2000	QRNational	In service
4034	99-1517	2000	QRNational	In service
4035	99-1518	2000	QRNational	In service
4036	99-1519	2001	QRNational	In service
4037	99-1520	2001	QRNational	In service
4038	99-1521	2001	QRNational	In service
4039	04-1668	2004	QRNational	In service
4040	04-1669	2004	QRNational	In service
4041	04-1670	2004	QRNational	In service

(continued)

Road #	Builder's #	Built	Owner	Status
4042	04-1671	2004	QRNational	In service
4043	04-1672	2004	QRNational	In service
4044	04-1673	2005	QRNational	In service
4045	04-1674	2005	QRNational	In service
4046	04-1675	2005	QRNational	In service
4047	04-1676	2005	QRNational	In service
4048	04-1677	2005	QRNational	In service
4049	04-1678	2005	QRNational	In service
4101	07-1710	2007	QRNational	In service
4102	07-1711	2007	QRNational	In service
4103	07-1712	2007	QRNational	In service
4104	07-1713	2007	QRNational	In service
4105	07-1714	2007	QRNational	In service
4106	07-1715	2007	QRNational	In service
4107	07-1716	2007	QRNational	In service
4108	07-1717	2007	QRNational	In service
4109	07-1718	2007	QRNational	In service
4110	07-1719	2008	QRNational	In service
4111	07-1720	2008	QRNational	In service
4112	07-1721	2008	QRNational	In service
4113	07-1722	2008	QRNational	In service
4114	07-1723	2008	QRNational	In service
4115	07-1724	2008	QRNational	In service
4116	pending	pending	QRNational	pendng
4117	pending	pending	QRNational	pending
4118	pending	pending	QRNational	pending
4119	pending	pending	QRNational	pending
4120	pending	pending	QRNational	pending
4121	pending	pending	QRNational	pending
4122	pending	pending	QRNational	pending
4123	pending	pending	QRNational	pending
4124	pending	pending	QRNational	pending
4125	pending	pending	QRNational	pending
4126	pending	pending	QRNational	pending
4127	pending	pending	QRNational	pending
4128	pending	pending	QRNational	pending
4129	pending	pending	QRNational	pending
4130	pending	pending	QRNational	pending

Above: Brand new 4103 running light-engine trials at Mount Larcom (near Gladstone) on Thursday 20 September 2007. Peter Reading

Above: 4107 leads a 2250 Class unit through Bajool (between Gladstone and Rockhampton) with a northbound empty coal on Saturday 21 June 2008. 4000 Class units 4006 and 4003 are assisting further back along the train. Steve Munro

PN Class

Builder:	*EDI-EMD (Maryborough)*	Model:	*GT42CU-AC*
Type:	*Co-Co diesel-electric*	Engine:	*EMD 710G3B turbo-charged 2-stroke V12*
Traction power:	*2260 kW (3030 hp)*	Length:	*22.00 m*
Weight:	*120.0 tonnes*	Gauge:	*1067 mm*

Above: PN005 near Bundaberg on Friday 29 June 2008. Chris Miller

Ordered by Pacific National Queensland for their Brisbane–Mackay–Townsville–Cairns corridor intermodal services, thirteen PN Class were constructed by Downer-EDI Rail Maryborough, based on QR's existing 4000 Class. All thirteen locomotives continue in daily service along this route as of late 2008.

Road #	Builder's #	Built	Owner	Status
PN001	04-1679	2004	PN Queensland	In service
PN002	04-1680	2004	PN Queensland	In service
PN003	04-1681	2004	PN Queensland	In service
PN004	04-1682	2004	PN Queensland	In service
PN005	05-1683	2005	PN Queensland	In service
PN006	05-1684	2005	PN Queensland	In service
PN007	05-1685	2005	PN Queensland	In service
PN008	05-1686	2005	PN Queensland	In service
PN009	05-1687	2005	PN Queensland	In service
PN010	05-1688	2005	PN Queensland	In service
PN011	05-1689	2005	PN Queensland	In service
PN012	05-1690	2005	PN Queensland	In service
PN013	05-1691	2005	PN Queensland	In service

S Class

Builder:	*Clyde-EMD (Forrestfield)*	Model:	*JT42C*
Type:	*Co-Co diesel-electric*	Engine:	*EMD 710G3B turbo-charged 2-stroke V12*
Traction power:	*2260 kW (3030 hp)*	Length:	*21.96 m*
Weight:	*118.5 tonnes*	Gauge:	*1067 mm*

Above: S3304 on an alumina train at Calcine on Saturday 23 August 2008. Alex Mackay

Ordered at the same time as (although beaten into traffic by) the standard-gauge Q Class (see page 16), the 11 narrow-gauge S Class locomotives were ordered to modernise Westrail's fleet and cater for an increasing level of mineral traffic in the state's south-west. Indeed the whole class is essentially captive to the Kwinana–Collie/Bunbury route, and rarely appear anywhere else. Despite the influx of refurbished locomotives from Queensland during 2007 and 2008, the S Class remains frontline power on this route.

Road #	Original #	Builder's #	Built	Owner	Status
S3301	S2101	98-1473	1998	ARG	In service
S3302	S2102	98-1474	1998	ARG	In service
S3303	S2103	98-1475	1998	ARG	In service
S3304	S2104	98-1476	1998	ARG	In service
S3305	S2105	98-1477	1998	ARG	In service
S2106	S2106	98-1478	1998	ARG	In service
S3307	S2107	98-1479	1998	ARG	In service
S3308	S2108	98-1480	1998	ARG	In service
S3309	S2109	98-1481	1998	ARG	In service
S3310	S2110	98-1482	1998	ARG	In service
S3311	S2111	98-1483	1998	ARG	In service

VL Class

Builder:	*Avteq (Sunshine)*	Model:	*GT26C*
Type:	*Co-Co diesel-electric*	Engine:	*EMD 645E3C turbo-charged 2-stroke V16*
Traction power:	*2240 kW (3000 hp)*	Length:	*18.34 m*
Weight:	*130.0 tonnes*	Gauge:	*1435 mm*

Above: VL356, VL357 and EL57 at Dynon on Thursday 15 May 2008. Graham Crichton

Based on the Freight Australia/Pacific National XR and XR2 Classes (see next page) the CFCLA VL Class were constructed by Avteq at Sunshine, in western Melbourne, and absorbed quickly into the company's ever-expanding lease fleet. Those so far delivered have been used by El Zorro and QRNational in South Australia and Victoria, while at least three have been employed by FreightLink for intermodal and iron ore trains in the Northern Territory. All twelve are expected to be complete by the end of 2008.

Road #	Built	Owner	Status	Note
VL351	2007	CFCLA	In service	*Dane Hill*
VL352	2007	CFCLA	In service	*Makybe Diva*
VL353	2007	CFCLA	In service	*Comic Court*
VL354	2007	CFCLA	In service	*Van Der Hum*
VL355	2008	CFCLA	In service	*Black Knight*
VL356	2008	CFCLA	In service	*Gatum Gatum*
VL357	2008	CFCLA	In service	*Empire Rose*
VL358	2008	CFCLA	In service	*Vintage Crop*
VL359	2008	CFCLA	In service	*Media Puzzle*
VL360	2008	CFCLA	In service	*Gurners Lane*
VL361	2008	CFCLA	pending	*At Talaq*
VL362	2008	CFCLA	pending	*Efficient*

XR/XR2/XRB Class

Builder:	*FA/PN (Dynon)*	Model:	*GT26C*
Type:	*Co-Co diesel-electric*	Engine:	*EMD 645E3C turbo-charged 2-stroke V16*
Traction power:	*2240 kW (3000 hp)*	Length:	*17.37 m*
Weight:	*124.0 tonnes*	Gauge:	*1435 mm and 1600 mm*

Above: XR551 leads A71 on No. 9556 empty slab steel freight away from Frankston on Monday 5 May 2008. Ross McClelland

One of the success stories of the privatisation period, the rebuild of X38 into a modern, 3000 hp, micro-processor controlled locomotive exceeded the expectations of many observers back in 2002. Such was the success of X38 (later renumbered XR550) that five more X Class rebuilds ensued, and following these, another six were constructed new to the existing design by Freight Australia's South Dynon Workshops (in partnership with a number of sub-contractors and part suppliers). By the time that the first three 'new build' XR2 Class appeared, the former Freight Australia business had been acquired by Pacific National (PN), while the final three units were built as cab-less XRB 'slave' units. The nine XR/XR2 units are used in Rural and Bulk freight services on both the broad and standard gauge within Victoria, although standard-gauge XR555 has in the past ventured as far as Perth on SCT interstate freight services. Operating far more regularly on this transcontinental route are the three XRB locomotives that frequent Pacific National's Melbourne–Perth intermodal services, usually 'sandwiched' between a pair of NR Class units (see page 141). The road number of XR556 was initially left vacant for an intended rebuild of X36, however this is yet to occur.

Road #	X Class #	Built	Owner	Status	Name
XR550	X38	2002	PN	In 1600 mm service	-
XR551	X35	2003	PN	In 1600 mm service	*Norman W DePomeroy*
XR552	X40	2003	PN	In 1600 mm service	-
XR553	X33	2004	PN	In 1600 mm service	-
XR554	X34	2004	PN	In 1600 mm service	-
XR555	X32	2004	PN	In 1435 mm service	-
XR557	new build	2005	PN	In 1600 mm service	-
XR558	new build	2005	PN	In 1600 mm service	-
XR559	new build	2005	PN	In 1435 mm service	-
XRB560	new build	2005	PN	In 1435 mm service	-
XRB561	new build	2005	PN	In 1435 mm service	-
XRB562	new build	2006	PN	In 1435 mm service	-

Above: The three XRB Class units are unique among Australian locomotives in that they are cab-less 'B' units designed to be used only as trailing 'slaves', that can only operate when led by a conventional locomotive (although they are equipped with basic hostler controls for the purpose of being shunted around depots). The three XRB units were also built with larger radiators than the XR/XR2 Class locomotives, while the sound baffle-boards on the XRBs were relocated from the radiator end to the dynamic brake end, compared to the arrangement on the previous XR and XR2 locomotives.

The only other cab-less locomotives to have operated in Australia were three BHP Iron Ore CM40-8M 'rebuild' units (5663, 5664 and 5665; see page 147), however all three were retrofitted with new cabs during 1997. Unlike the first member of the XRB Class (XRB560) XRB561 was built without the traditional steps applied to previous Victorian locomotives. XRB561 is seen here at South Dynon on Tuesday 7 August 2007. Bernie Baker

82 Class

Builder:	*Clyde-EMD (Braemar)*	Model:	*JT42C*
Type:	*Co-Co diesel-electric*	Engine:	*EMD 710G3A turbo-charged 2-stroke V12*
Traction power:	*2260 kW (3030 hp)*	Length:	*22.00 m*
Weight:	*132.3 tonnes*	Gauge:	*1435 mm*

Above: 8241 leads 8245, 8143 and 8168 through Maitland with a down empty coal Friday 22 August 2008. David Porter

Originally numbering 58, three of the 82 Class fleet (delivered for both coal and general freight service—under lease from the Ready Power consortium—during 1994 and 1995) were destroyed when the coal train they were leading collided with the rear of a similar train at Beresfield on 23 October 1997. The three, 8219, 8246 and 8247, were eventually scrapped and thus did not form part of the operational Pacific National fleet when this company acquired the former FreightCorp (who, by then, owned the class outright) and National Rail operations during 2002. Shortly after that, the remaining 55 locomotives were devoted entirely to coal haulage based out of Port Kembla and the Hunter Valley in New South Wales (with two, sometimes three, commonly used on the Stirling North–Leigh Creek coal train in South Australia).

Road #	Builder's #	Built	Owner	Status	Name
8201	94-1308	1994	Pacific National	In service	*Dal Eisenhauer*
8202	94-1309	1994	Pacific National	In service	*Yvonne Braid*
8203	94-1310	1994	Pacific National	In service	*John Mueller*
8204	94-1311	1994	Pacific National	In service	*Ann Paul*
8205	94-1312	1994	Pacific National	In service	-
8206	94-1313	1994	Pacific National	In service	-

(continued)

Road #	Builder's #	Built	Owner	Status	Name
8207	94-1314	1994	Pacific National	In service	-
8208	94-1315	1994	Pacific National	In service	-
8209	94-1316	1994	Pacific National	In service	*Arnold Hannaford*
8210	94-1317	1994	Pacific National	In service	*Bernard Malouf*
8211	94-1318	1994	Pacific National	In service	*Ned Steiger*
8212	94-1319	1994	Pacific National	In service	*Jenny Roberts*
8213	94-1320	1994	Pacific National	In service	-
8214	94-1321	1994	Pacific National	In service	-
8215	94-1322	1994	Pacific National	In service	-
8216	94-1323	1994	Pacific National	In service	-
8217	94-1324	1994	Pacific National	In service	-
8218	94-1325	1994	Pacific National	In service	-
8220	94-1327	1994	Pacific National	In service	*William 'Bluey' Jones*
8221	94-1328	1994	Pacific National	In service	-
8222	94-1329	1994	Pacific National	In service	-
8223	94-1330	1994	Pacific National	In service	-
8224	94-1331	1994	Pacific National	In service	-
8225	94-1332	1994	Pacific National	In service	-
8226	94-1333	1994	Pacific National	In service	-
8227	94-1334	1994	Pacific National	In service	-
8228	94-1335	1994	Pacific National	In service	-
8229	94-1336	1994	Pacific National	In service	-
8230	94-1337	1994	Pacific National	In service	-
8231	94-1338	1994	Pacific National	In service	-
8232	94-1339	1994	Pacific National	In service	-
8233	94-1340	1994	Pacific National	In service	-
8234	94-1341	1994	Pacific National	In service	-
8235	94-1342	1994	Pacific National	In service	*Chris Fydler*
8236	94-1343	1994	Pacific National	In service	-
8237	94-1344	1994	Pacific National	In service	-
8238	94-1345	1994	Pacific National	In service	-
8239	94-1346	1994	Pacific National	In service	-
8240	94-1347	1994	Pacific National	In service	-
8241	94-1348	1994	Pacific National	In service	-
8242	95-1349	1994	Pacific National	In service	-
8243	95-1350	1994	Pacific National	In service	-
8244	95-1351	1995	Pacific National	In service	-
8245	95-1352	1995	Pacific National	In service	-
8248	95-1355	1995	Pacific National	In service	-
8249	95-1356	1995	Pacific National	In service	-
8250	95-1357	1995	Pacific National	In service	-
8251	95-1358	1995	Pacific National	In service	-
8252	95-1359	1995	Pacific National	In service	-
8253	95-1360	1995	Pacific National	In service	-

(continued)

Road #	Builder's #	Built	Owner	Status	Name
8254	95-1361	1995	Pacific National	In service	-
8255	95-1362	1995	Pacific National	In service	-
8256	95-1363	1995	Pacific National	In service	-
8257	95-1364	1995	Pacific National	In service	-
8258	95-1365	1995	Pacific National	In service	-

Above: 8248 leads 8133 north near Wards River, on the lower NSW North Coast Line, with an empty coal train bound for Stratford, on Saturday 14 June 2008. Steve Munro

Goldsworthy/Comalco JT42

Builder:	*Clyde-EMD (Kelso)*	Model:	*JT42C*
Type:	*Co-Co diesel-electric*	Engine:	*EMD 710G3A turbo-charged 2-stroke V12*
Traction power:	*2260 kW (3030 hp)*	Length:	*18.87 m*
Weight:	*129.0 tonnes*	Gauge:	*1435 mm*

Above: R1004 works a loaded bauxite train across the Andoom River on Friday 3 October 2008. This bridge is located at the northern end of the railway, that runs south from the Andoom Bauxite Mine to the Lorim Point export facilities at Weipa, on the western coast of Australia's Cape York. Simon Barber

GML10 was a one-off purchase for Goldsworthy Mining Limited in 1990 and was built at Clyde's Kelso plant, near Bathurst (NSW). However, that company's merger with Mount Newman Mining to form BHP Iron Ore the following year saw GML20 (as it had been renumbered) soon rendered surplus in an otherwise GE-dominated fleet. As such, it was sold to Comalco in 1994 for service on the Weipa (Lorim Point) to Andoom bauxite railway, located on Cape York in far northern Queensland. Although the Weipa/Andoom railway is now a Rio Tinto Aluminium operation, R1004 (as it was subsequently renumbered), has continued to shuttle bauxite along the line ever since. R1004 shares duties with GT26C unit R1001, although two new EDI-EMD JT42C locomotives are under construction (as of late 2008), and are expected to take over most haulage duties on the line in the near future. Former Comalco GT26C unit R1002 now operates for ARG as LZ3120 (see page 49), while a fourth unit, in the form of ex-Canadian National EMD NW2 locomotive 7943 (builder's number 4114 and built in 1946), was scrapped in 1999. Bought in 1976, it had operated for Comalco as R1003 and was used for shunting.

Road #	Original #	Builder's #	Built	Owner	Status
R1004	GML10	90-1277	1990	Rio Tinto, Weipa	In service

DL Class

Builder:	*Clyde-EMD (Kelso)*	Model:	*AT42C*
Type:	*Co-Co diesel-electric*	Engine:	*EMD 710G3 turbo-charged 2-stroke V12*
Traction power:	*2260 kW (3030 hp)*	Length:	*18.51 m*
Weight:	*121.5 tonnes*	Gauge:	*1435 mm*

Above: Freshly overhauled DL42 shines in the late afternoon at Spencer Junction, near Port Augusta on Friday 4 May 2007. Roger Evans

Built between 1988 and 1990 for Australian National, the DL Class was the first EMD locomotive type in Australia to employ the then-new 710 Series engine (although vibration problems with the early, 12-cylinder version of this prime mover have proven a concern with the class). Class leader DL36 has been out of service and in storage at Port Augusta for close to a decade (as of late 2008), but the remaining 13 members of the class (DL37 was scrapped following the Hines Hill collision of 14 January 1996) are now part of the Pacific National fleet, and are employed mostly as trailing, banking and shunt units in New South Wales, Victoria and South Australia, although they have been known to appear in Western Australia from time to time.

Road #	Builder's #	Built	Owner	Status	Name
DL36	88-1244	1988	Pacific National	Stored Port Augusta	* *Peter Morris*
DL38	88-1246	1988	Pacific National	In service	-
DL39	88-1247	1988	Pacific National	In service	-
DL40	88-1248	1988	Pacific National	In service	-
DL41	88-1249	1988	Pacific National	In service	-
DL42	88-1250	1988	Pacific National	In service	-

* *Name plate now removed.*

(continued)

Road #	Builder's #	Built	Owner	Status	Name
DL43	88-1251	1988	Pacific National	In service	-
DL44	88-1252	1989	Pacific National	In service	-
DL45	88-1253	1989	Pacific National	In service	-
DL46	88-1254	1989	Pacific National	In service	-
DL47	89-1255	1989	Pacific National	In service	-
DL48	89-1267	1989	Pacific National	In service	-
DL49	89-1268	1989	Pacific National	In service	-
DL50	89-1269	1990	Pacific National	In service	-

Above: Still wearing remnants of its original coat of Australian National green and yellow, DL43 works a shunt trip at Osborne, near Port Adelaide, on Tuesday 4 September 2007. Lesser duties such as this are one of the few rosters that might earn a DL Class 'lead unit' status in 2009, although during the spring months, when Great Southern Rail's *Indian Pacific* operates as a double-consist, DLs often run as second unit on this service, and due to the required shunt upon arrival at Sydney Terminal, often lead the first half of the train into the platform. Les Coulton

81 Class

Builder:	*Clyde-EMD (Kelso)*	Model:	*JT26C-2SS*
Type:	*Co-Co diesel-electric*	Engine:	*EMD 645E3B turbo-charged 2-stroke V16*
Traction power:	*2240 kW (3000 hp)*	Length:	*19.76 m*
Weight:	*129.0 tonnes*	Gauge:	*1435 mm*

Above: 8180 on a sleeper train at Grafton on Saturday 26 July 2008. Peter Kitcher

Delivered between 1982 and 1986 (with four additional units built in 1991) the former FreightCorp 81 Class fleet remains a vital cog in the Pacific National (PN) haulage task despite most of the class being now well into their third decade. Although the class—which introduced to Australia EMD's Super Series traction control technology on a mass scale (the equipment had been earlier trialled on J26C unit 42220; see page 71)—can be found right around the country (Brisbane, Melbourne, Adelaide and Perth) they remain a particular force in Sydney and NSW, and are involved in grain, intermodal, steel, cement and particularly coal haulage. Presently PN is cycling the class through Downer-EDI Rail's Kelso plant for a round of overhauls that is steadily seeing the fleet repainted in the attractive livery of yellow and blue. Fire damaged 8147 was withdrawn following a fatal level crossing collision at Back Creek (on the Parkes to Stockinbingal line) on 10 March 2007 and is likely to become the first member of the class to be written off. It is currently stored in derelict condition at Lithgow.

Road #	Builder's #	Built	Owner	Status
8101	82-1020	1982	Pacific National	In service
8102	82-1021	1982	Pacific National	In service

(continued)

Road #	Builder's #	Built	Owner	Status
8103	82-1022	1982	Pacific National	In service
8104	82-1023	1982	Pacific National	In service
8105	82-1024	1982	Pacific National	In service
8106	82-1025	1983	Pacific National	In service
8107	82-1026	1983	Pacific National	In service
8108	82-1027	1983	Pacific National	In service
8109	82-1028	1983	Pacific National	In service
8110	82-1029	1983	Pacific National	In service
8111	82-1030	1983	Pacific National	In service
8112	82-1031	1983	Pacific National	In service
8113	82-1032	1983	Pacific National	In service
8114	82-1033	1983	Pacific National	In service
8115	82-1034	1983	Pacific National	In service
8116	83-1035	1983	Pacific National	In service
8117	83-1036	1983	Pacific National	In service
8118	83-1037	1983	Pacific National	In service
8119	83-1038	1983	Pacific National	In service
8120	83-1039	1983	Pacific National	In service
8121	83-1040	1983	Pacific National	In service
8122	83-1041	1983	Pacific National	In service
8123	83-1042	1983	Pacific National	In service
8124	83-1043	1983	Pacific National	In service
8125	83-1044	1983	Pacific National	In service
8126	83-1045	1983	Pacific National	In service
8127	83-1046	1983	Pacific National	In service
8128	83-1047	1983	Pacific National	In service
8129	83-1048	1983	Pacific National	In service
8130	83-1049	1983	Pacific National	In service
8131	83-1050	1983	Pacific National	In service
8132	83-1051	1983	Pacific National	In service
8133	83-1052	1984	Pacific National	In service
8134	83-1053	1984	Pacific National	In service
8135	83-1054	1984	Pacific National	In service
8136	83-1055	1984	Pacific National	In service
8137	83-1056	1984	Pacific National	In service
8138	83-1057	1984	Pacific National	In service
8139	83-1058	1984	Pacific National	In service
8140	84-1059	1984	Pacific National	In service
8141	84-1060	1984	Pacific National	In service
8142	84-1061	1984	Pacific National	In service
8143	84-1062	1984	Pacific National	In service

(continued)

Road #	Builder's #	Built	Owner	Status
8144	84-1063	1984	Pacific National	In service
8145	84-1064	1984	Pacific National	In service
8146	84-1065	1984	Pacific National	In service
8147	84-1066	1984	Pacific National	Stored Lithgow
8148	84-1067	1984	Pacific National	In service
8149	84-1068	1984	Pacific National	In service
8150	84-1069	1984	Pacific National	In service
8151	84-1070	1984	Pacific National	In service
8152	84-1071	1984	Pacific National	In service
8153	84-1072	1984	Pacific National	In service
8154	84-1073	1984	Pacific National	In service
8155	84-1074	1984	Pacific National	In service
8156	84-1075	1984	Pacific National	In service
8157	84-1076	1984	Pacific National	In service
8158	84-1077	1985	Pacific National	In service
8159	84-1078	1985	Pacific National	In service
8160	84-1079	1985	Pacific National	In service
8161	84-1080	1985	Pacific National	In service
8162	84-1081	1985	Pacific National	In service
8163	84-1082	1985	Pacific National	In service
8164	85-1083	1985	Pacific National	In service
8165	85-1084	1985	Pacific National	In service
8166	85-1085	1985	Pacific National	In service
8167	85-1086	1985	Pacific National	In service
8168	85-1087	1985	Pacific National	In service
8169	85-1088	1985	Pacific National	In service
8170	85-1089	1985	Pacific National	In service
8171	85-1090	1985	Pacific National	In service
8172	85-1091	1985	Pacific National	In service
8173	85-1092	1985	Pacific National	In service
8174	85-1093	1985	Pacific National	In service
8175	85-1094	1985	Pacific National	In service
8176	85-1095	1985	Pacific National	In service
8177	85-1096	1985	Pacific National	In service
8178	85-1097	1985	Pacific National	In service
8179	85-1098	1985	Pacific National	In service
8180	85-1099	1986	Pacific National	In service
8181	91-1278	1991	Pacific National	In service
8182	91-1279	1991	Pacific National	In service
8183	91-1280	1991	Pacific National	In service
8184	91-1281	1991	Pacific National	In service

BL Class

Builder:	*Clyde-EMD (Rosewater)*	Model:	*JT26C-2SS*
Type:	*Co-Co diesel-electric*	Engine:	*EMD 645E3B turbo-charged 2-stroke V16*
Traction power:	*2240 kW (3000 hp)*	Length:	*19.82 m*
Weight:	*127.6 tonnes*	Gauge:	*1435 mm and 1600 mm*

Above: BL35 at Dry Creek on Thursday 27 September 2007. Tom Marschall

High horsepower locomotives combining 'box' cabs and a full-width car body were not new to the Australian National (AN) network with eight AL Class locomotives having been delivered during 1976/77. However, following the introduction of the SRANSW 81 Class (from 1982), which incorporated EMD's Dash-2 electrical cabinet and Super Series, AN was impressed with the concept enough to order ten BL Class units from Clyde, which were built at Rosewater, Adelaide during 1983 and 1984. The ten units were initially used on both broad and standard gauge, and continue even today to split between the two, albeit now owned and operated by Pacific National. The three broad gauge examples work steel and grain services in Victoria with the standard gauge units common on mineral and intermodal services along the east coast.

Road #	Builder's #	Built	Owner	Status	Name
BL26	83-1010	1984	PN	In 1435 mm service	*Bob Hawke*
BL27	83-1011	1983	PN	In 1435 mm service	-
BL28	83-1012	1983	PN	In 1435 mm service	-
BL29	83-1013	1983	PN	In 1600 mm service	-
BL30	83-1014	1983	PN	In 1435 mm service	-
BL31	83-1015	1983	PN	In 1435 mm service	-
BL32	83-1016	1984	PN	In 1600 mm service	-
BL33	83-1017	1984	PN	In 1435 mm service	-
BL34	83-1018	1984	PN	In 1600 mm service	-
BL35	83-1019	1984	PN	In 1435 mm service	-

G Class

Builder:	*Clyde-EMD (Rosewater and Somerton)*	Model:	*JT26C-2SS* *JT36C (for 645F3B re-engined units)*
Type:	*Co-Co diesel-electric*	Engine:	*EMD 645E3B turbo-charged 2-stroke V16* *EMD 645F3B turbo-charged 2 stroke V16*
Traction power:	*2240 kW (3000 hp)* *2460 kW (3300 hp)*	Length:	*19.82 m*
Weight:	*127.6 tonnes*	Gauge:	*1435 mm and 1600 mm*

Above: SCT's G514 leads the Seymour Rail Heritage Centre's GM36 on El Zorro empty grain train 5MQ5, through Boggabri on Saturday 14 June 2008. The arrival of the new EDI/EMD-built SCT Class during early 2008 saw the company's nine G Class locomotives subsequently pushed into lease service with operators such as QRNational/ARG, El Zorro and even FreightLink. Stephen Carr

The 33 G Class locomotives were constructed by Clyde between 1984 and 1990, with G511–G525 built at Rosewater (Adelaide) and the remainder at Somerton (Melbourne). G517 and G518 were destroyed in a collision at Ararat on 26 November 1999, not long after the G Class fleet (along with the entire V/Line Freight business) was acquired by Freight Victoria (later known as Freight Australia). Pacific National (PN) now owns the bulk of the G Class, although, was forced to divest itself of a number to other operators (two to CRT/QRNational in late 2004 and nine to SCT in mid 2007) since assuming the fleet from Freight Australia during 2004. Three of PN's G Class units remain on the Victorian broad gauge, with the remainder operating on the standard, and these can be found operating in New South Wales and South Australia in addition to their 'home' state.

G523, G526, G529, G530, G531, G536, G541, and G543 were retrofitted with more powerful EMD 645F3B engines during the period between 2000 and 2002, raising their traction output by 300 hp (although engine swaps may have altered this listing since that time). Many of the standard-gauge PN units were, until early 2008, used on SCT interstate freight services between Melbourne/Parkes and Perth, although the latter company's locomotive fleet expansion has seen this arrangement cease. Five of the standard gauge PN units are now used as 'slave' units on PN's South Coal services in NSW, while others now work throughout Victoria, South Australia and NSW on mineral, grain and container services. The SCT G Class were, for a time, dominant on that carrier's services before the arrival of the new SCT Class units in early 2008. They are now regularly leased to other operators, while QRNational's G516 and G534 are most common on that company's Melbourne–Brisbane corridor services, although they have worked to Perth on occasions.

Road #	Builder's #	Built	Owner	Status	Name/Note
G511	84-1239	1984	SCT	In 1435 mm service	-
G512	84-1240	1984	SCT	In 1435 mm service	-
G513	85-1241	1984	SCT	In 1435 mm service	-
G514	85-1242	1985	SCT	In 1435 mm service	-
G515	85-1243	1985	SCT	In 1435 mm service	-
G516	85-1229	1986	QRN	In 1435 mm service	-
G519	85-1232	1986	PN	In 1435 mm service	-
G520	85-1233	1986	PN	In 1435 mm service	-
G521	85-1234	1986	SCT	In 1435 mm service	-
G522	85-1235	1986	PN	In 1435 mm service	-
G523	86-1236	1986	PN	In 1435 mm service	Re-engined with EMD 16-645F3B
G524	86-1237	1986	PN	In 1600 mm service	-
G525	86-1238	1986	PN	In 1600 mm service	-
G526	88-1256	1988	PN	In 1435 mm service	Re-engined with EMD 16-645F3B
G527	88-1257	1988	PN	In 1600 mm service	-
G528	88-1258	1988	PN	In 1435 mm service	-
G529	88-1259	1988	PN	In 1435 mm service	Re-engined with EMD 16-645F3B
G530	88-1260	1988	PN	In 1435 mm service	Re-engined with EMD 16-645F3B
G531	88-1261	1988	PN	In 1435 mm service	Re-engined with EMD 16-645F3B
G532	88-1262	1988	SCT	In 1435 mm service	-
G533	88-1263	1988	SCT	In 1435 mm service	-
G534	88-1264	1988	QRN	In 1435 mm service	-
G535	88-1265	1988	SCT	In 1435 mm service	Named *Kevin Sheedy Express*
G536	88-1266	1989	PN	In 1435 mm service	Re-engined with EMD 16-645F3B
G537	89-1270	1989	PN	In 1435 mm service	-
G538	89-1271	1989	PN	In 1435 mm service	-
G539	89-1272	1989	PN	In 1435 mm service	-
G540	89-1273	1989	PN	In 1435 mm service	Named *Wycheproof*
G541	89-1274	1989	PN	In 1435 mm service	Named *Birchip* Re-engined with EMD 16-645F3B
G542	89-1275	1989	PN	In 1435 mm service	Named *Warracknabeal*
G543	89-1276	1990	PN	In 1435 mm service	Re-engined with EMD 16-645F3B

C Class

Builder:	*Clyde-EMD (Rosewater)*	Model:	*GT26C*
Type:	*Co-Co diesel-electric*	Engine:	*EMD 645E3 turbo-charged 2-stroke V16*
Traction power:	*2240 kW (3000 hp)*	Length:	*20.73 m*
Weight:	*134.2 tonnes*	Gauge:	*1435 mm*

Above: CFCLA's C508 (badged for South Spur, and with Coote Industrial's NA1874) at Two Wells on Sunday 7 September 2008. Greg O'Brien

Many of the former 1977-vintage V/Line C Class, after a period of storage under National Rail and then Pacific National ownership, were gradually recommissioned by Silverton Rail during 2003 and 2004, with all (including Seymour Rail Heritage Centre's preserved C501—see page 264) finally restored (or being restored) by RTS/NREC as of early 2009 (C509 and C510 were still undergoing overhaul at Islington as of press time). The class are now commonly found on New South Wales container services and New South Wales/South Australia/Victoria infrastructure trains (although the class has also visited Western Australia in recent years), with three now owned by CFCLA and six by Coote Industrial. When C509 and C510 return to service, all ten will be in simultaneous operation for the first time in around 15 years.

Road #	Original #	Builder's #	Built	Owner	Status
C502	C502	76-825	1977	CFCLA	In service
C503	C503	76-826	1977	CFCLA	In service
C504	C504	76-827	1977	Coote Industrial	In service
C505	C505	76-828	1977	Coote Industrial	In service
Cs5	C506	76-829	1977	Coote Industrial	In service
C507	C507	76-830	1977	Coote Industrial	In service
C508	C508	76-831	1977	CFCLA	In service
C509	C509	77-832	1978	Coote Industrial	Overhaul
C510	C510	77-833	1978	Coote Industrial	Overhaul

L Class/Comalco GT26C

Builder:	*Clyde-EMD (Clyde)*	*L251-L273, R1001, R1002*	Model:	*GT26C*
	Clyde-EMD/Comeng	*L274, L275*		
Type:	*Co-Co diesel-electric*		Engine:	*EMD 645E3 turbo-charged 2-stroke V16*
Traction power:	*2240 kW (3000 hp)*		Length:	*19.35 m*
Weight:	*137.0 tonnes (R1001/02 148 tonnes)*		Gauge:	*1435 mm*

Above: 3117 (ex-L274) at Forrestfield on Tuesday 21 February 2006. Bernie Baker

The L Class were both a development of the US EMD SD40 model and Australia's first 3000 hp diesel-electric locomotives. They were acquired by the Western Australian Government Railways in two batches, with the first 23 (L251–L273) coming from Clyde in NSW, and final pair (L274 and L275, financed by Western Mining) following a couple of years later, after being built under sub-contract by Comeng at Rocklea in Brisbane. An additional L Class unit was procured by Westrail in 1994, in the form of Comalco (Weipa) unit R1002, which at 148 tonnes, was somewhat heavier than the standard L, while another unit (L269) was scrapped in 1996. Several L Class were sold off by Westrail in 1998 for use with the short-lived ATN Access operation, and while three of these 'exiles' are still owned by PN, sales and mergers have seen the bulk of the former L Class fleet reunited under QR ownership. Those used in NSW by QR/ARG were known as the 31 Class (except for former Interail units L265 and L271) before their redeployment, while the western-based examples (including the refurbished, lightened former Comalco unit) carry either the L, LQ or LZ classification. The LZ denotes the ZTR traction control package, while the LQ indicates the Q-Tron equivalent (as used on LQ3122—the former L271—and L265). Pacific National's L251, L254 and L270 are also fitted with Q-Tron. The WA-based L Class can essentially be found working almost any standard-gauge roster on the Kwinana–Perth–Kalgoorlie corridor, although they also appear on the Leonora and Esperance Lines radiating out of Kalgoorlie.

Above: L265 (with 2202 and 2201) with a Down empty ARG flour train at Breadalbane on Friday 19 October 2007. Andrew Rosenbauer

In Queensland, R1002's Comalco sister GT26C unit, R1001, is slated for withdrawal shortly, as new owners Rio Tinto have ordered a pair of new JT42C EMDs for the Weipa operation. These units (under construction at Port Augusta) are slated for delivery in late 2008. In the meantime WA-based ARG units LZ3112 and LZ3114 have been sidelined by the Scadden (Esperance Line) collision of 8 September 2008.

Road #	Original #	Builder's #	Built	Owner	Status	Name/Notes
L251	L251	67-541	1967	PN	In service	-
3101	L252	67-542	1967	ARG	In service	*Kurra Kurraka*
LZ3119	L253	67-543	1967	ARG	In service	-
L254	L254	67-544	1968	PN	Stored Port Kembla	*Enterprise 1701E*
LZ3105	L255	67-545	1968	ARG	In service	-
3106	L256	67-546	1968	ARG	In service	-
3102	L257	68-547	1968	ARG	In service	*Wagiman*
LZ3107	L258	68-548	1968	ARG	In service	-
3103	L259	68-549	1968	ARG	In service	*Aboriginal Stockman*
L3108	L260	68-550	1968	ARG	In service	-
3109	L261	68-551	1968	ARG	In service	-
L3110	L262	68-552	1968	ARG	In service	-
LZ3111	L263	68-553	1968	ARG	In service	-
LZ3112	L264	68-554	1968	ARG	Repairs	-
L265	L265	68-555	1968	ARG	In service	*Shoalhaven*
L3113	L266	68-556	1968	ARG	In service	-
LZ3114	L267	68-557	1968	ARG	Repairs	-
L3115	L268	68-617	1968	ARG	In service	-
L270	L270	68-619	1969	PN	In service	-
LQ3122	L271	69-620	1969	ARG	In service	*John Douglas Kerr*
L3116	L272	69-621	1969	ARG	In service	-
3104	L273	69-622	1969	ARG	In service	*Purnu*
LZ3117	L274	73-779	1973	ARG	In service	-
L3118	L275	73-780	1973	ARG	In service	-
R1001	R1001	72-252	1972	Rio Tinto	In service (Weipa)	Ex-Comalco (Weipa)
LZ3120	R1002	72-753	1972	ARG	In service	Ex-Comalco (Weipa)

BHP-Billiton SD40 Series

Builder:	*EMD (USA)*	Model:	*SD40R/SD40-2/SD40T-2*
Type:	*Co-Co diesel-electric*	Engine:	*EMD 645E3 turbo-charged 2-stroke V16*
Traction power:	*2240 kW (3000 hp)*	Length:	*SD40: 20.00 m, SD40-2/SD40T-2: 20.98 m*
Weight:	*166.9 tonnes*	Gauge:	*1435 mm*

Above: Imported SD40R locomotive 3078 shunting a loaded ore rake at Nelson Point on Monday 23 July 2007. Chris Walters

Obtained through GATX (General Electric's US leasing company), BHP-Billiton Iron Ore's SD40R and SD40-2 fleets were obtained at fairly short notice during 2004 to assist in moving large tonnages of ore stemming from a sky-rocketing demand for Australian iron. Three of the SD40R units (3078, 3079 and 3080) are nominally restricted to Nelson Point for tippler shunting at the port, while the remainder of the SD40R and SD40-2 units are employed as trailing units on main line iron ore trains. A number of SD40R units have been fitted out with ATP (Automatic Train Protection) equipment for leading trains if and when required.

Obtained at the same time as the operational fleet was a solitary, former Southern Pacific SD40T-2 'tunnel motor' for use as a spare parts source (which, at the time of writing, remains stored in heavily stripped condition at Nelson Point, Port Hedland). All members of this fleet are of either Union Pacific or Southern Pacific heritage originally.

SD40R

Road #	Original #	Builder's #	Built	Owner	Status
3078	SP 8422	31503 (7861-13)	1966	BHPBIO	In service
Originally SP SD40 8422, then SD40R 7302 rebuilt in 1980, then GATX 6401.					
3079	SP 8461	31542 (7861-52)	1966	BHPBIO	In service
Originally SP SD40 8461, then SD40R 7308 rebuilt in 1980, then GATX 6415.					
3080	SP 8482	33674 (7083-4)	1968	BHPBIO	In service
Originally SP SD40 8482, then SD40R 7377 rebuilt in 1981, then GATX 6407.					

(continued)

Road #	Original #	Builder's #	Built	Owner	Status
3086	SP 8410	31491 (7861-1)	1966	BHPBIO	In service
Originally SP SD40 8410, then SD40R 7354 rebuilt in 1981.					
3087	SP 8438	31519 (7861-29)	1966	BHPBIO	In service
Originally SP SD40 8438, then SD40R 7321 rebuilt in 1980.					
3088	SP 8433	31514 (7861-24)	1966	BHPBIO	In service
Originally SP SD40 8433, then SD40R 7300 rebuilt in 1980.					
3089	SP 8431	31512 (7861-22)	1966	BHPBIO	In service
Originally SP SD40 8431, then SD40R 7331 rebuilt in 1980.					
3090	SP 8488	33680 (7083-10)	1968	BHPBIO	In service
Originally SP SD40 8488, then SD40R 7374 rebuilt in 1981.					
3091	SP 8415	31496 (7861-6)	1966	BHPBIO	In service
Originally SP SD40 8415, then SD40R 7322 rebuilt in 1980.					
3092	SP 8417	31498 (7861-8)	1966	BHPBIO	In service
Originally SP SD40 8417, then SD40R 7334 rebuilt in 1980.					
3093	SP 8487	33679 (7083-9)	1968	BHPBIO	In service
Originally SP SD40 8487, then SD40R 7349 rebuilt in 1981.					
3094	SP 8434	31515 (7861-25)	1966	BHPBIO	In service
Originally SP SD40 8434, then SD40R 7306 rebuilt in 1980.					
3095	SP 8485	33677 (7083-7)	1968	BHPBIO	In service
Originally SP SD40 8485, then SD40R 7327 rebuilt in 1980.					
3096	SP 8429	31510 (7861-20)	1966	BHPBIO	In service
Originally SP SD40 8429, then SD40R 7309 rebuilt in 1980.					
3097	SP 8409	31569 (7875-10)	1966	BHPBIO	In service
Originally SP SD40 8409, then SD40R 7345 rebuilt in 1981.					

Above: SD40R locomotive 3096, operating as a trailing unit behind GE AC6000CW unit 6077, on a loaded iron ore train at Bing on Sunday 22 July 2007. Chris Walters

SD40-2

Road #	Original #	Builder's #	Built	Owner	Status
3081	UP 3573	786170-75	1979	BHPBIO	In service
3082	UP 3639	786263-31	1979	BHPBIO	In service
3083	UP 3500	786170-2	1979	BHPBIO	In service
3084	UP 3643	786263-35	1979	BHPBIO	In service
3085	UP 3523	786170-25	1979	BHPBIO	In service

Above: SD40-2 locomotive 3082 trailing an (out-of-sight) SD70ACe/LC unit and SD40R 3087, while working a loaded iron ore train approaching Boodarie on Sunday 22 July 2007. The five BHP-Billiton Iron Ore SD40-2 locomotives are distinguishable from the SD40R fleet most obviously by their rather plain, grey undercoat finish. Chris Walters

SD40T-2

Road #	Builder's #	Built	Owner	Status
8335	786175.9	1979	BHPBIO	Stored Nelson Point

Ex-Southern Pacific, spare parts unit never used by BHP-Billiton.

2250 Class

Builder:	*Clyde-EMD/QR (Redbank)*	Model:	*GT22C-3M*
Type:	*Co-Co diesel-electric*	Engine:	*EMD 645E3C turbo-charged 2-stroke V12*
Traction power:	*1680 kW (2250 hp)*	Length:	*17.04 m*
Weight:	*110.0 tonnes*	Gauge:	*1067 mm*

Above: 2268 leads 2256 and 2206D on the approach to the Dawson Highway overpass with an empty Moura Line coal, on Thursday 14 June 2007. The rebuilt 2250 Class locomotives can often be found working with the lighter, less powerful 2170 Class units (such as 2206D seen here) on these trains. Steve Munro

Following on from the 1997–2002 program to rebuild members of the 1120 kW 2400 Series into turbo-charged, 1680 kW 2300 Class 'maxi-cab' units (see page 55), QR decided to upgrade and modernise some of the more powerful 1490 kW 2100 Series (see page 65) into '110-tonne' heavy haulers for coal service. Chief among the alterations was the removal of each locomotive's existing roots-blown V16 engine and the installation of a refurbished, turbo-charged V12. Between 2004 and 2007 a total of 18 2250 Class units were obtained from the rebuilding of 1490 kW (16-645E engined) 2130 and 2141 Class units, while even six 1120 kW (12-645E) 1550 Class locomotives were eventually cycled into the program, making for a total of 24 rebuilds.

Unlike the older 2300 Class fleet, which split their service time between mineral and general freight service, the newer 2250 Class were to become dedicated coal units, concentrated mostly on Moura and Collinsville Line services (although a number can be found working Blackwater system trains). Upon completion, the 2250 Class '110-tonne' project rendered 'extinct' both the 1490 kW 2130 and 1120 kW 1550 Classes, while only one 2141 Class unit (2144) escaped the rebuild process.

Road #	Rebuilt	Built	Owner	Status
2251	2142A	2005	QRNational	In service
2252	2136	2005	QRNational	In service
2253	2141A	2005	QRNational	In service
2254	2146F	2005	QRNational	In service
2255	2147F	2005	QRNational	In service
2256	2131F	2005	QRNational	In service
2257	2133F	2005	QRNational	In service
2258	1576H	2005	QRNational	In service
2259	2139	2006	QRNational	In service
2260	1572H	2006	QRNational	In service
2261	2138	2006	QRNational	In service
2262	2140	2006	QRNational	In service
2263	2135	2006	QRNational	In service
2264	1575H	2006	QRNational	In service
2265	1574H	2006	QRNational	In service
2266	2137	2006	QRNational	In service
2267	2134F	2006	QRNational	In service
2268	1571H	2006	QRNational	In service
2269	1573H	2006	QRNational	In service
2270	2130F	2006	QRNational	In service
2271	2132F	2007	QRNational	In service
2272	2148F	2007	QRNational	In service
2273	2145F	2007	QRNational	In service
2274	2143F	2007	QRNational	In service

Above: Class leader 2251 outside the Redbank Locomotive Maintenance Depot on Wednesday 16 February 2005. Michael James

2300 Class

Builder:	*Clyde-EMD/QR (Redbank)*	Model:	*GTL22CU*
Type:	*Co-Co diesel-electric*	Engine:	*EMD 645E3C turbo-charged 2-stroke V12*
Traction power:	*1680 kW (2250 hp)*	Length:	*17.04 m*
Weight:	*94.5 tonnes*	Gauge:	*1067 mm*

Above: 2363 departs Stuart (just west of Townsville) with the southbound *Sunlander* on Friday 14 December 2001. Chris Walters

QR's 2300 Class fleet—consisting of sixty units rebuilt at Redbank Workshops from older locomotives during the period 1997 to 2002—are now the backbone of the QRNational freight haul task in Queensland. Commencing in 2008, a slowly increasing percentage of this fleet now also works in Western Australia for ARG (now a QR subsidiary) as the DFZ Class.

These turbo-charged locomotives were rebuilt from former members of the Clyde 1120 kW 1550, 2400, 2450 and 2470 Classes (Clyde-EMD units that date back to the mid 1970s), and are now used in both general service (in which they support the Goninan/GE 2800 Class) and in selected coal traffic, including services in the south-east, Darling Downs and Moura Line regions. This being the case, the class is fairly common in most areas of the system on a wide range of traffic. As a result of the 2300 Class rebuild project, the former 2450 Class was rendered 'extinct' while the 2400 and 1550 Classes were left with only six un-rebuilt examples each (although the later 2250 Class project—see page 53—eventually consumed the remainder of the 1550 Class fleet). Those 2300s transferred to Western Australia as the DFZ Class are slowly making their presence felt on narrow-gauge south-east mineral haulage and, as of October 2008, were also staring to see increased use based out of Geraldton. As of press time, two were in service, with at least two more being readied for recommissioning.

Road #	Rebuilt	Built	Owner	Status
2301	1564	1997	QRNational	In service
2302	1556	1999	QRNational	In service
2303	1557	1999	QRNational	In service
2304	1558	1998	QRNational	In service
2305	1559	1999	QRNational	In service
2306	1560	2000	QRNational	In service
2307	1561	1998	QRNational	In service
2308	1563	1998	QRNational	In service
2309	1565	1999	QRNational	In service
2310	1550	2000	QRNational	In service
2311	1551	1999	QRNational	In service
2312	1552	1999	QRNational	In service
2313	1553	2000	QRNational	In service
2314	1554	1999	QRNational	In service
2315	1555	1999	QRNational	In service
2320	1570	1998	QRNational	In service
2321	1566	1999	QRNational	In service
2322	1568	1999	QRNational	In service
2323	1569	1999	QRNational	In service
2330	2400	2001	QRNational	In service
2331	2401	1999	QRNational	In service
2332	2402	2001	QRNational	In service
2333	2403	2000	QRNational	In service
2334	2404	2001	QRNational	In service
2335	2405	2001	QRNational	In service
2336	2406	2000	QRNational	In service
2337	2407	2000	QRNational	In service
2338	2408	2001	QRNational	In service
2339	2409	2000	QRNational	In service
2346	2416	2000	QRNational	In service
2347	2417	2001	QRNational	In service
2348	2418	2001	QRNational	In service
2349	2419	2001	QRNational	In service
2350	2420	2000	QRNational	In service
2351	2421	2001	QRNational	In service
2352	2422	2000	QRNational	In service
2353	2423	1999	QRNational	In service
2355	2450	1999	QRNational	In service
2356	2451	2001	ARG	Recommissioning
2357	2452	1999	QRNational	In service
2358	2454	2001	QRNational	In service
2359	2456	2002	QRNational	In service

(continued)

Road #	Rebuilt	Built	Owner	Status
2360	2453	2000	QRNational	In service
2361	2457	2001	QRNational	In service
2362	2458	2001	QRNational	In service
2363	2459	1999	QRNational	In service
2364	2460	2000	QRNational	In service
2365	2461	2002	QRNational	In service
2366	2455	2000	QRNational	In service
2370	2462	2000	ARG	In service as DFZ2404
2371	2464	2002	QRNational	In service
2372	2465	2001	ARG	Recommissioning
2373	2466	2001	ARG	In service as DFZ2406
2374	2463	2001	ARG	Recommissioning
2387	2501	2001	QRNational	In service
2388	2502	2001	QRNational	In service
2389	2503	2002	QRNational	In service
2390	2504	2000	QRNational	In service
2391	2505	2000	QRNational	In service
2392	2506	2001	QRNational	In service

Above: DFZ2404 (ex-2370) stands outside ARG's Forrestfield Workshops on Tuesday 29 July 2008. A number of 2300 Class units are being transferred to ARG (now a QR subsidiary) for service in Western Australia, although DFZ2404 was the first to actually enter service in the west. Chris Miller

N Class

Builder:	*Clyde-EMD (Somerton)*	Model:	*JT22HC-2*
Type:	*Co-Co diesel-electric*	Engine:	*EMD 645E3C turbo-charged 2-stroke V12 N451-N460* *EMD 645E3B turbo-charged 2-stroke V12 N461-N475*
Traction power:	*1840 kW (2480 hp)*	Length:	*18.87 m*
Weight:	*118.0 tonnes*	Gauge:	*1600 mm*

Above: N468 (in one of two variations of the new V/Line livery) leads T320 through Wunghnu on a Seymour Rail Heritage Centre special bound for centenary celebrations at Tocumwal on Saturday 12 July 2008. Ewan McLean

Associated with passenger travel in Victoria since their delivery commencing in 1985, the 25 members of the N Class fleet remain ensconced in such duties almost a quarter of a century later. Although they have been used on freight services during their tenure, record numbers of passengers travelling by train in Victoria will probably ensure they continue to work for V/Line Passenger for quite a while yet, despite the growing fleet of VLocity DMU railcars. The impending conversion of the broad-gauge Seymour to Albury North East Line to standard gauge, will see a number of N Class placed on this gauge for the first time, to work Melbourne–Albury V/Line services. Some of these services may be extended to Wagga Wagga during 2009.

Road #	Builders #	Built	Owner	Status	Name
N451	85-1219	1986	V/Line Passenger	In service	*City of Portland*
N452	85-1220	1986	V/Line Passenger	In service	*Rural City of Wodonga*
N453	85-1221	1986	V/Line Passenger	In service	*City of Albury*

(continued)

Road #	Builders #	Built	Owner	Status	Name
N454	85-1222	1986	V/Line Passenger	In service	*City of Horsham*
N455	85-1223	1986	V/Line Passenger	In service	*City of Swan Hill*
N456	85-1224	1986	V/Line Passenger	In service	*City of Colac*
N457	85-1225	1986	V/Line Passenger	In service	*City of Mildura*
N458	85-1226	1986	V/Line Passenger	In service	*City of Maryborough*
N459	85-1227	1986	V/Line Passenger	In service	*City of Echuca*
N460	85-1228	1986	V/Line Passenger	In service	*City of Castlemaine*
N461	86-1190	1986	V/Line Passenger	In service	*City of Ararat*
N462	86-1191	1986	V/Line Passenger	In service	*City of Shepparton*
N463	86-1192	1986	V/Line Passenger	In service	*City of Bendigo*
N464	86-1193	1986	V/Line Passenger	In service	*City of Geelong*
N465	86-1194	1986	V/Line Passenger	In service	*City of Ballaraat*
N466	86-1195	1986	V/Line Passenger	In service	*City of Warrnambool*
N467	86-1196	1986	V/Line Passenger	In service	*City of Stawell*
N468	86-1197	1986	V/Line Passenger	In service	*City of Bairnsdale*
N469	86-1198	1987	V/Line Passenger	In service	*City of Morwell*
N470	87-1199	1987	V/Line Passenger	In service	*City of Wangaratta*
N471	87-1200	1987	V/Line Passenger	In service	*City of Benalla*
N472	87-1201	1987	V/Line Passenger	In service	*City of Sale*
N473	87-1202	1987	V/Line Passenger	In service	*City of Warragul*
N474	87-1203	1987	V/Line Passenger	In service	*City of Traralgon*
N475	87-1204	1987	V/Line Passenger	In service	*City of Moe*

Above: N473 and N474 (displaying variations of the 1995/96 era maroon, blue and white V/Line Passenger livery) pass Lara as an Up light engine movement on Thursday 23 August 2007. Ewan McLean

A Class

Builder:	*Clyde-EMD (Rosewater)*	Model:	*AAT22C-2R*
Type:	*Co-Co diesel-electric*	Engine:	*EMD 645E3B turbo-charged 2-stroke V12*
Traction power:	*1840 kW (2480 hp)*	Length:	*18.34 m*
Weight:	*118.0 tonnes*	Gauge:	*1600 mm*

Above: A70 southbound at Dysarts Siding on Thursday 21 February 2008. Ewan McLean

The A Class grew out of a mid-1980s effort to modernise the 1952-vintage Clyde-EMD B Class fleet (see page 79) for express passenger working. With the work undertaken by Clyde (Rosewater) the program was cancelled after the eleventh delivery, while V/Line opted instead to invest in additional examples of the N Class design. A remarkable swap has been reported with B60 and B85 being switched in the rebuild cycle due to B60 requiring a greater level of preparation than anticipated.

When V/Line and V/Line Freight were split in 1995 and sold off in 1998, seven members of the A Class were inherited by Freight Australia (and thus, later Pacific National or PN) while the remaining four today are in service with V/Line Passenger. The seven PN A Class units are used exclusively on broad gauge, intrastate Rural and Bulk division freight services within Victoria, while the V/Line foursome work short-haul commuter services, mostly between Melbourne and Seymour. Some of these PN units have been upgraded with Q-Tron traction control, an initiative originally pushed by Freight Australia.

Road #	B Class #	Builders #	Built	Owner	Status	Name
A60	B85	84-1184	1984	V/Line Passenger	In service	*Sir Harold Clapp*
A62	B62	84-1183	1984	V/Line Passenger	In service	-
A66	B66	84-1186	1985	V/Line Passenger	In service	-
A70	B70	84-1187	1985	V/Line Passenger	In service	-
A71	B71	83-1180	1984	Pacific National	In service	*Dick Reynolds*
A73	B73	83-1179	1984	Pacific National	In service	*Bob Skilton*
A77	B77	83-1181	1984	Pacific National	In service	*Ian Stewart*
A78	B78	84-1185	1985	Pacific National	In service	-
A79	B79	84-1188	1985	Pacific National	In service	-
A81	B81	85-1189	1985	Pacific National	In service	-
A85	B60	84-1182	1984	Pacific National	In service	*Haydn Bunton*

DB/DBZ Class

Builder:	*Clyde-EMD (Rosewater)*	Model:	*G26C-2*
Type:	*Co-Co diesel-electric*	Engine:	*EMD 645E 2-stroke V16*
Traction power:	*1490 kW (2000 hp)*	Length:	*18.01 m*
Weight:	*108.0 tonnes*	Gauge:	*1067 mm*

Above: DBZ2304 at Brunswick Junction on Friday 5 September 2008. David Melling

These thirteen locomotives were an update of the 1971/72-vintage D/DA Class units (see pages 62 and 64). Fitted with Dash-2 electronics and a reconfigured cab design (with full-width nose) most of the former Westrail DB Class—as with the DA Class before them—have now been upgraded with ZTR traction control (by new owners, the Australian Railroad Group or ARG), and in this case, reclassified as DBZ. Although the class can appear in southern and eastern regions (encompassing Northam, York and Albany), they are most common on the Kwinana–Bunbury route in mineral haulage. For a time, locomotive 2313 (ex-DB1593) was used on One Steel iron-ore trains out of Whyalla, South Australia (between 2003 and 2006). However, with the ARG split of 2006 (and the Western Australian ARG operation being acquired by QR), its place was taken by former DA Class unit 1907 (now owned by Genesee Wyoming Australia) and the DB was returned 'home'.

Road #	Original #	Builder's #	Built	Owner	Status	Name
DBZ2301	DB1581	81-989	1982	ARG	In service	*City of Bunbury*
DBZ2302	DB1582	81-990	1982	ARG	In service	*Shire of Serpentine-Jarrahdale*
DBZ2303	DB1583	81-991	1982	ARG	In service	*Shire of Murray*
DBZ2304	DB1584	81-992	1982	ARG	In service	*Shire of Waroona*
DBZ2305	DB1585	81-993	1982	ARG	In service	*Shire of Harvey*
DBZ2306	DB1586	81-994	1982	ARG	In service	*Shire of Dardanup*
DBZ2307	DB1587	81-995	1982	ARG	In service	*Shire of Capel*
DBZ2308	DB1588	81-996	1982	ARG	In service	*Shire of Donnybrook/Balingup*
DB2309	DB1589	81-997	1982	ARG	In service	*Shire of Bridgetown-Greenbushes*
DBZ2310	DB1590	81-998	1983	ARG	In service	*Shire of Collie*
DB2311	DB1591	82-1122	1983	ARG	In service	*Shire of Manjimup*
DBZ2312	DB1592	82-1123	1983	ARG	In service	*Shire of Toodyay*
DBZ2313	DB1593	82-1124	1983	ARG	In service	*Shire of Dowerin*

DA/DAZ Class

Builder:	*Clyde-EMD (Clyde)*	Model:	*G26C*
Type:	*Co-Co diesel-electric*	Engine:	*EMD 645E 2-stroke V16*
Traction power:	*1490 kW (2000 hp)*	Length:	*17.20 m*
Weight:	*97.6 tonnes*	Gauge:	*1067 mm*

Above: DAZ1906 and DAZ1903—both in remnants of the former yellow and black Westrail livery—approach Midland on Saturday 28 July 2007. Chris Walters

These 1972-vintage units were originally built as a lighter, non-dynamic-braked version of the D Class (see page 64). Six of these former Westrail DA Class units continued to see service within Western Australia as of late 2008, while final member, 1907 (ex-DA1577), went to Genesee Wyoming Australia (GWA) for service at Whyalla (on South Australia's Eyre Peninsula) as part of the 2006 split up of the former Australian Railroad Group (ARG). Primarily, the ARG six (which are now known as the DAZ Class following their upgrade with ZTR traction control packages during 2006/07), are employed on grain services, while the GWA-owned 1907 continues to operate iron ore trains on OneSteel's narrow-gauge Whyalla system. All seven of the DA Class have been extensively overhauled in recent years, and with traffic in their respective regions remaining strong, this should ensure their presence remains for some time yet.

Road #	Original #	Builder's #	Built	Owner	Status	Notes
DAZ1901	DA1571	72-758	1972	ARG	In service	-
DAZ1902	DA1572	72-759	1972	ARG	In service	-
DAZ1903	DA1573	72-760	1972	ARG	In service	-
DAZ1904	DA1574	72-761	1972	ARG	In service	-
DAZ1905	DA1575	72-762	1972	ARG	In service	-
DAZ1906	DA1576	72-763	1972	ARG	In service	-
1907	DA1577	72-764	1972	GWA	In service	Modified for DOO

Above: The unique, DOO-modified DA Class unit 1907 (formerly DA1577, the last locomotive built in Clyde's original Sydney plant) at Forrestfield on Friday 20 January 2006. This locomotive was subsequently transferred to GWA ownership (the only DA so distributed). Bernie Baker

Below: Rebuilt D Class unit 2020 (see next page) leads English Electric ZR Class locomotive 2101 and DQ unit 2011 on an eastbound freight between Penguin and Ulverstone on Wednesday 31 December 2003. Chris Walters

D Class

Builder:	*Clyde-EMD (Clyde)*	Model:	*G26C*
Type:	*Co-Co diesel-electric*	Engine:	*EMD 645E 2-stroke V16*
Traction power:	*1490 kW (2000 hp)*	Length:	*17.20 m*
Weight:	*111.0 tonnes*	Gauge:	*1067 mm*

Above: D1562 at Kwinana on Friday 20 January 2006. At this stage, and as of going to press, D1562 is the only member of its class still in service in Western Australia. It has been reported that D1561 is under evaluation for recommissioning (it has not operated since 1998), however no news was forthcoming as this book closed for press. Bernie Baker

Although D1562 has been a common sight on the Forrestfield–Kwinana–Bunbury route for many years, D1561 has not turned a wheel in service since withdrawal, from what was then Westrail service, back in 1998. There were originally five D Class built in 1971, but in 1998 D1564 and D1565 were sold for service in Tasmania (rebuilt by Tranz Rail in New Zealand during 2001), and are now operating as 2021 and 2020 respectively. Meanwhile, the fifth (D1563) now operates for FCAB in Chile as locomotive 2000. The Tasmanian pair both received brand new cab sections when rebuilt in New Zealand (based on a now obsolete Tranz Rail DXR Class design dating from 1993) and are common power on Pacific National Tasmania (PNT)-owned DOO freight services between Burnie and Boyer/Hobart. The PNT operation was to be sold by the end of 2008.

Road #	Original #	Builder's #	Built	Owner	Status
D1561	D1561	70-723	1971	ARG	Stored Forrestfield
D1562	D1562	70-724	1971	ARG	In service
(D)2021	D1564	70-726	1971	PNT	In service
(D)2020	D1565	70-727	1971	PNT	In service

2100/2141/2150/2170 Class

Builder:	*Clyde-EMD/Comeng Qld*	Model:	*GL26C/GL26C-2*
Type:	*Co-Co diesel-electric*	Engine:	*EMD 645E 2-stroke V16*
Traction power:	*1490 kW (2000 hp)*	Length:	*17.04 m*
Weight:	*91.5-97.2 tonnes*	Gauge:	*1067 mm*

Above: 2123, final member of the original 2100 Class, shunts at Maryborough on Sunday 18 March 2007. Barry Burton

When the first of what would eventually be 24 members of the 2100 Class arrived in late 1970, this locomotive was in fact be the first of what would ultimately become known as Queensland Rail's 2100 Series. This group would eventually encompass also the 2130 (11 units), 2141 (originally known as the 2200 Class—8 units), 2150 (14 units) and 2170 (45 units) Classes, all based around the same central GL26C design, with only minor variances separating each. Oddly, the last of the group built was 2198, entering service in late February 1984, even though 2214 (which preceded it into traffic by three weeks) was the highest numbered of the class. Most of the fleet were ordered to service a rapidly expanding coal haulage task.

By 2000 most had been modified for DOO (driver-only operation) and shifted to general service after the greater part of the coal network was electrified. Some surplus 2100 Class units were subsequently sold to FCAB in Chile, while in 2004 the first of an eventual 24 older Clydes were rebuilt as the 2250 Class (which followed on from a similar rebuild of 1550/2400 Series units into the 2300 Class previously; see pages 53 and 55). This '110-tonne' project rendered the 2130 Class 'extinct' while only one 2141 Class remained in un-rebuilt form once the production of refurbished units was completed in 2007.

The remaining 2100 Series units continue in regular service, and while the dwindling few 2100 Class themselves are more common in the south of the state, the 2150 and 2170 Classes are reasonably common right up the coast. A number of stored 2100 Class were transferred to the ARG subsidiary operation in WA during 2007 and 2008, and, following an overhaul and a number of modifications (including changes to the cab layout, specifically the relocation of the control stand from right to left) applied en route by Downer-EDI Rail at Port Lincoln (SA), they now operate as the DD Class.

Above: 2213D fresh out of Redbank Workshops, wearing a new coat of QRNational livery on Monday 6 June 2005. Michael James

Road #	Original #	Builder's #	Built	Owner	Status	Name
2100H	2100	70-711	1970	QRN	In service	-
DD2355	2101	70-712	1970	ARG	In service	-
2102H	2102	70-713	1971	QRN	Stored Redbank	-
DD2356	2105	70-716	1971	ARG	In service	-
DD2357	2109	71-720	1971	ARG	In service	-
2110D	2110	71-721	1971	QRN	Stored Redbank	-
2111D	2111	71-722	1971	QRN	In service	-
2115A	2115	72-743	1972	QRN	Stored Redbank	-
2116D	2116	72-744	1972	QRN	In service	-
DD2358	2117	72-745	1972	ARG	In service	-
DD2359	2120	72-748	1972	ARG	In service	-
2121F	2121	72-749	1972	QRN	Stored Redbank	-
2122F	2122	72-750	1972	QRN	In service	-
2123F	2123	72-751	1973	QRN	In service	-

(continued)

Road #	Original #	Builder's #	Built	Owner	Status	Name
2144F	2203	73-774	1973	QRN	In service	-
2150D	2150	79-901	1978	QRN	In service	-
2151D	2151	79-902	1978	QRN	In service	-
2152D	2152	79-903	1979	QRN	In service	-
2153D	2153	79-904	1979	QRN	In service	-
2154D	2154	79-905	1979	QRN	In service	-
2155D	2155	79-906	1979	QRN	In service	-
2156D	2156	79-907	1979	QRN	In service	-
2157D	2157	79-908	1979	QRN	In service	-
2158D	2158	79-909	1979	QRN	Stored Redbank	-
2159D	2159	79-910	1979	QRN	In service	-
2160D	2160	79-911	1979	QRN	In service	-
2161D	2161	79-912	1979	QRN	In service	-
2162D	2162	79-913	1979	QRN	In service	-
2163D	2163	79-914	1979	QRN	In service	-
2170F	2170	82-1100	1982	QRN	In service	-
2171F	2171	82-1101	1982	QRN	In service	-
2172F	2172	82-1102	1982	QRN	In service	-
2173F	2173	82-1103	1982	QRN	In service	-
2174D	2174	82-1104	1982	QRN	In service	-
2176F	2176	82-1106	1982	QRN	In service	-
2177F	2177	82-1107	1982	QRN	In service	-
2178F	2178	82-1108	1982	QRN	In service	-
2179F	2179	82-1109	1982	QRN	In service	-
2180D	2180	82-1125	1982	QRN	In service	-
2181F	2181	83-1146	1983	QRN	In service	*P J Goldston*
2182D	2182	83-1147	1983	QRN	In service	-
2183D	2183	83-1148	1983	QRN	In service	-
2184F	2184	83-1149	1983	QRN	In service	-
2185F	2185	83-1150	1983	QRN	In service	-
2186F	2186	83-1151	1983	QRN	In service	-
2188F	2188	83-1153	1983	QRN	In service	-
2189F	2189	83-1154	1983	QRN	In service	-
2190F	2190	83-1155	1983	QRN	In service	-
2191F	2191	83-1156	1983	QRN	In service	-
2192F	2192	83-1157	1983	QRN	In service	-
2193F	2193	83-1158	1983	QRN	In service	-
2194F	2194	83-1159	1983	QRN	In service	-
2195F	2195	83-1160	1983	QRN	In service	-
2196F	2196	83-1161	1983	QRN	In service	-
2197F	2197	83-1162	1983	QRN	In service	-

(continued)

Road #	Original #	Builder's #	Built	Owner	Status	Name
2198F	2198	84-1218	1984	QRN	In service	-
2199F	2199	83-1163	1983	QRN	In service	-
2200F	2200	83-1164	1983	QRN	In service	-
2201D	2201	83-1165	1983	QRN	In service	-
2202D	2202	83-1166	1983	QRN	In service	-
2203	2203	83-1167	1983	QRN	In service	-
2204D	2204	83-1168	1983	QRN	In service	-
2205	2205	83-1169	1983	QRN	In service	-
2206	2206	83-1170	1983	QRN	In service	-
2207D	2207	83-1171	1983	QRN	In service	-
2208D	2208	83-1172	1983	QRN	In service	-
2209D	2209	83-1173	1983	QRN	In service	-
2210D	2210	83-1174	1983	QRN	In service	-
2211D	2211	83-1175	1983	QRN	In service	-
2212F	2212	83-1176	1983	QRN	In service	-
2213D	2213	83-1177	1984	QRN	In service	-
2214D	2214	83-1178	1984	QRN	In service	-

Above: DD2355 and DBZ2309 haul a loaded Worsley caustic soda train through Burekup (on the Bunbury Line) on Friday 5 September 2008. David Melling

X Class

Builder:	*Clyde-EMD (Clyde and Rosewater)*	Model:	*G26C*
Type:	*Co-Co diesel-electric*	Engine:	*EMD 645E 2-stroke V16*
Traction power:	*1340/1490 kW (1800/2000 hp)*	Length:	*17.37 m*
Weight:	*114.0-115.5 tonnes*	Gauge:	*1435 mm and 1600 mm*

Above: X41 at Dynon on Tuesday 27 December 2005. Bernie Baker

The 24 members of the X Class were delivered in three batches between 1966 and 1976, with the Mk1 (X31–X36) and Mk2 (X37–X44) coming from Clyde in Sydney and the ten, later Mk3 versions (X45–X54) being delivered from the firm's Rosewater plant in suburban Adelaide. Two (X47 and X49) were modified for DOO (driver only operation) during 1998–99 by V/Line Freight, but a more elaborate upgrade ensued when successors Freight Australia rebuilt four Mk1 and two Mk2 units as the XR Class between 2002 and 2005 (see page 33). All are now owned by Pacific National, although class leader X31 is slated for eventual preservation with the Seymour Rail Heritage Centre.

Transferred to CRT/QRN ownership at the same time as the earlier mentioned G516 and G534 (see page 45), Mk3 units X53 and X54 have also become a fixture on the Melbourne–Sydney–Brisbane corridor in recent years. The pair can be found travelling as far north as Brisbane from time to time, while the remainder of the class (not rebuilt into XR units) continue on in Pacific National broad- and standard-gauge service with New South Wales and Victoria, generally hauling intrastate grain, fuel and container services.

Surprisingly, both X31 and X36 are still accredited only as 1800 hp locomotives.

Road #	Builder's #	Built	Owner	Status	Name/Note
X31	66-484	1966	Pacific National	In 1600 mm service	-
X36	66-489	1966	Pacific National	In 1600 mm service	-
X37	70-700	1970	Pacific National	In 1600 mm service	-
X39	70-702	1970	Pacific National	In 1600 mm service	-
X41	70-704	1970	Pacific National	In 1600 mm service	-
X42	70-705	1970	Pacific National	In 1600 mm service	-
X43	70-706	1970	Pacific National	In 1600 mm service	-
X44	70-707	1970	Pacific National	In 1600 mm service	-

(continued)

Road #	Builder's #	Built	Owner	Status	Name/Note
X45	75-792	1975	Pacific National	In 1600 mm service	*Edgar H Brownbill*
X46	75-793	1975	Pacific National	In 1600 mm service	-
X47	75-794	1975	Pacific National	In 1600 mm service	Modified for DOO
X48	75-795	1976	Pacific National	In 1435 mm service	-
X49	75-796	1976	Pacific National	In 1600 mm service	Modified for DOO
X50	75-797	1976	Pacific National	In 1435 mm service	-
X51	75-798	1976	Pacific National	In 1435 mm service	-
X52	75-799	1976	Pacific National	In 1600 mm service	-
X53	75-800	1976	Pacific National	In 1435 mm service	-
X54	75-801	1976	Pacific National	In 1435 mm service	-

Left: X53 (leading G534 at Broadford with a Sydney to Melbourne freight on Saturday 11 August 2007. Travis Simmons

Below: A comparison between driver-only modified Mk3 X49 (left) and rebuilt X38 at South Dynon in 2004. Bernie Baker

422 Class

Builder:	*Clyde-EMD (Clyde)*	Model:	*J26C*
Type:	*Co-Co diesel-electric*	Engine:	*EMD 645E 2-stroke V16*
Traction power:	*1490 kW (2000 hp)*	Length:	*17.17 m*
Weight:	*109.8 tonnes*	Gauge:	*1435 mm*

Above: HL203 and GL107 at Blayney on Wednesday 7 December 2005. Chris Walters

In 2000, what was then Australia Southern Railroad (ASR, later part of the Australian Railroad Group or ARG) obtained sixteen surplus 1969/70-vintage 422 Class locomotives from FreightCorp in NSW. Four were shopped at Port Augusta for refurbishment ahead of railway construction duties on the Alice Springs to Darwin line in 2001 (emerging as the 22 Class), while several others were recommissioned for lease work in South Australia, NSW and Victoria. Eventually most of the remainder were similarly cycled through Port Augusta Workshops for refurbishment, and by the time that ARG was split up in 2006, only 42209 and 42211 remained untreated (although both were still occasionally active in 'unaltered' form). This pair, along with nine of the refurbished 22 Class, were transferred to QR/ARG ownership with the eleven-unit fleet divided fairly evenly between Western Australian and east coast operations. Four of those in the west were eventually reclassified as DC Class units while those not acquired by QR/ARG passed to Genesee Wyoming Australia for continued service in South Australia.

Meanwhile, QR had previously acquired two other 422 Class units during 2002 (42202 and 42206), upon its purchase of Northern Rivers Railroad. Operating under the joint Interail and QRNational banners, these units generally remain with the intermodal side of the QR presence on the east coast, while the 22 Class continue to work ARG (subsidiary) contracts. The final two (42203 and 42220) are now in service with CFCLA's lease fleet (as HL203 and FL220, respectively). 42220 is noteworthy as the original Super Series test unit rebuilt by Clyde back in 1980.

Above: 2214 and 2208 approach Roberston with an ARG flour train from Narrandera on Friday 23 December 2005. Chris Walters

Road #	Original #	Builder's #	Built	Owner	Status	Name
DC2205	42201	69-656	1969	ARG	In service	-
42202	42202	69-657	1969	QRN	In service	*Casino*
HL203	42203	69-658	1969	CFCLA	In service	-
DC2206	42204	69-659	1969	ARG	In service	-
2201	42205	69-660	1969	ARG	In service	*Tennant Creek*
42206	42206	69-661	1969	QRN	In service	-
2207	42207	69-662	1969	GWA	In service	-
2208	42208	69-663	1969	ARG	In service	-
42209	42209	69-664	1969	ARG	Stored Forrestfield	-
2210	42210	69-665	1969	GWA	In service	-
42211	42211	69-666	1969	ARG	In service	-
2212	42212	69-667	1969	GWA	In service	-
2202	42213	69-668	1969	ARG	In service	*Katherine*
2203	42214	69-669	1969	ARG	In service	*Darwin*
DC2213	42215	69-670	1969	ARG	In service	-
2204	42216	69-671	1969	ARG	In service	*Alice*
2214	42217	69-672	1969	GWA	In service	-
DC2215	42218	69-673	1969	ARG	In service	-
2216	42219	69-674	1969	GWA	In service	-
FL220	42220	70-675/80-1000	1970	CFCLA	In service	-

421 Class

Builder:	*Clyde-EMD (Clyde)*	Model:	*AJ16C*
Type:	*Co-Co diesel-electric*	Engine:	*EMD 567C 2-stroke V16*
Traction power:	*1340 kW (1800 hp)*	Length:	*17.63 m*
Weight:	*109.8 tonnes*	Gauge:	*1435 mm*

Above: A view of the No. 2 end of 42107 (with 42109 in the background), as seen at Chullora on Monday 11 August 2008. Bernie Baker

After passing into Northern Rivers Railroad (NRR) ownership during the early part of the 1990s, 42103, 42105, 42107 and 42109 soon found a niche hauling contract freight on the Murwillumbah Line on the far North Coast, as well as high profile spots on the prestige *Ritz Rail* tourist trains. Engine-less 42106 was later acquired for an overhaul that never eventuated while NRR itself was absorbed by QR as its Interail 'arm' during 2002. The end of the *Ritz Rail* and North Coast Line/Murwillumbah traffic saw Interail focus instead on Hunter Valley coal (Duralie and Newstan) before dedicated interstate freight services between Melbourne, Brisbane and Sydney commenced in 2004, in conjunction with the larger QRNational operation. The four operational 421 Class units have since gravitated towards the shorter haul Sydney area trip trains (with 42103 recently receiving a QRNational repaint at Chullora), yard shunting and the occasional Duralie coal train roster. Meanwhile, 42106 remains stored and seemingly forgotten.

Road #	Original #	Builder's #	Built	Owner	Status
42103	42103	66-470	1966	QRNational	In service
42105	42105	66-472	1966	QRNational	In service
42106	42106	66-473	1966	QRNational	Stored Casino
42107	42107	66-474	1966	QRNational	In service
42109	42109	66-476	1966	QRNational	In service

GM12 Class

Builder:	*Clyde-EMD (Clyde)*	Model:	*A16C*
Type:	*Co-Co diesel-electric*	Engine:	*EMD 567C 2-stroke V16*
Traction power:	*GM12–GM21 1300 kW (1750 hp)* *GM22–GM47 1340 kW (1800 hp)*	Length:	*17.88 m*
Weight:	*115.8 tonnes*	Gauge:	*1435 mm*

Above: GM43 at Goobang (Parkes) on Saturday 4 June 2005. Bernie Baker

Following the success of the 1951 GM1 Class (see page 78) and with the introduction of Clyde's three-axle/three-motor bogie (improving on the previous three-axle/four-motor version), the Commonwealth Railways (CR) returned to Clyde for further GM Class orders, which were delivered in groups from 1955 to 1967. These Co-Co units were described as S-type (six motor) by the CR and numbered GM12–GM47. The last batch of the class, GM37–GM47, were fitted with dynamic brakes for Leigh Creek coal haulage, and it is these that have endured most succesfully into the new millenium. Of the 36 built, Genesee Wyoming Australia (GWA) owns the majority of the 17 that remain today (11 units) and these are used mostly on grain in South Australia, New South Wales and Victoria. Meanwhile, long-stored GM30 was transferred to Forrestfield in March 2003 for rebuild into a high-horsepower unit, although at the time of printing it has yet to emerge. In the 2006 split of ARG between GWA and QR, GM30 was the only member of the class to revert to ARG/QR ownership.

In addition to these, CFCLA possesses GM22 and GM27 as part of its extensive lease fleet, RailPower (Goulburn) plans to eventually recommission GM19, and Coote Indutrial retains the derelict pair of GM12 and GM25 in Melbourne. GM28 (renumbered GM22) and GM36 are both preserved (the latter in operational condition), but the rest have been scrapped.

Road #	Builder's #	Built	Owner	Status
GM12	55-70	1955	Coote Industrial	Stored Dynon
GM19	57-148	1957	RailPower	Stored Goulburn
GM22	62-252	1962	CFCLA	In service
GM25	62-255	1962	Coote Industrial	Stored Dynon
GM27	62-267	1963	CFCLA	In service
GM30	64-366	1964	ARG	Stored Forrestfield
GM32	64-368	1965	GWA	Stored Dry Creek
GM34	64-370	1965	GWA	Stored Dry Creek
GM37	66-446	1966	GWA	In service
GM38	66-447	1966	GWA	In service
GM40	66-526	1967	GWA	In service
GM42	67-528	1967	GWA	In service
GM43	67-529	1967	GWA	In service
GM44	67-530	1967	GWA	In service
GM45	67-531	1967	GWA	In service
GM46	67-532	1967	GWA	In service
GM47	67-533	1968	GWA	In service

Above: The semi-rebuilt GM30 (carrying chalked-in 3401 numbers) within Forrestfield Workshops on Wednesday 7 December 2005. Prior to the split up of ARG between QR and GWA in 2006, the previously stored GM30 was to have been a prototype for a potential rebuild program for the remaining GM12 Class units then in ARG ownership; stripped, former Santa Fe SD45-2B locomotive 7507 was even imported from the United States to provide parts. Although the project has since stalled, progress was made beyond that shown here with a new 'CLF/CLP Class' type roof structure subsequently constructed. Bernie Baker

S Class

Builder:	*Clyde-EMD (Clyde)*	Model:	*A16C*
Type:	*Co-Co diesel-electric*	Engine:	*EMD 567C 2-stroke V16*
Traction power:	*1340 kW (1800 hp)*	Length:	*17.88 m*
Weight:	*115.8 tonnes*	Gauge:	*1435 mm or 1600 mm*

Above: S306 and S307 were painted in the standard Pacific National paint scheme following overhaul at Bendigo during 2008. However, a downturn in traffic saw them (and S301) stored at Newport not long after returning to service. During the late 1970s the nose doors were sealed while recent modifications include the Electric Staff exchanger recess being covered over, bifurcation of brake pipe and main reservoir hoses and package bearings replacing the standard roller bearing on the axles. S306 and S307 both still maintain single marker lights and single windscreen wipers, while the original side number plates have been replaced with decals. S306 is seen here in storage at Newport on Tuesday 5 August 2008. Bernie Baker

These former Victorian Railways streamlined units can be regarded as true survivors. CFCLA have recommissioned two (S300 and S311) as part of its lease fleet, while four more are owned by Pacific National (S301, S306, S307 and S310). Unfortunately, periods of traffic downturn usually finds these Pacific National units among the first to be put into storage (as they were at press time), but when in service they are commonly used on broad-gauge grain services. During early 2008, S306 and S307 were given an overhaul and repaint at Bendigo Workshops, however they were stored shortly afterwards as Pacific National wound down many of its Victorian freight services. Steamrail has custody of S301, S306 and S307 at present, and the trio are ostensibly available for heritage and tourist operations. Meanwhile, further examples of the class are in service with El Zorro (S302) and Southern Shorthaul Railroad (S317), while another (S312) was almost ready for recommissioning by emerging lease-firm RailPower, based in Goulburn (NSW), as of press time.

Road #	Builders #	Built	Owner	Status	Name
S300	57-164	1957	CFCLA	In 1435 mm service	-
S301	57-165	1957	PN	Stored (1600 mm)	*Sir Thomas Mitchell*
S302	57-166	1957	El Zorro	In 1600 mm service	*Edward Henty*
S306	57-170	1957	PN	Stored (1600 mm)	-
S307	57-171	1957	PN	Stored (1600 mm)	-
S310	60-227	1960	PN	Stored (1600 mm)	*George Higginbotham*
S311	60-228	1960	CFCLA	In 1600 mm service	-
S312	60-229	1961	RailPower	Restoration (1435 mm)	-
S317	61-240	1961	SSR	In 1435 mm service	-

Above: S311 (and Steamrail's T357) on the then El Zorro-operated freight service at Dennington (just west of Warrnambool) on Wednesday 21 May 2008. Julian Insall
Below: Southern Shorthaul Railroad's S317 leads CFCLA's FL220 on an empty ballast train at Martins Creek on Friday 12 September 2008. Stephen Carr

GM1 Class

Builder:	*Clyde-EMD (Clyde)*	Model:	*ML-1*
Type:	*Co-Co diesel-electric*	Engine:	*EMD 567B/567BC 2-stroke V16*
Traction power:	*1120/1190 kW (1500/1600 hp)*	Length:	*17.88 m*
Weight:	*111.0 tonnes*	Gauge:	*1435 mm*

Designed and built for the then Commonwealth Railways (CR) in 1951, these four motor GM1 units quickly displaced steam on the CR system and were described as F-type (four-motor). GM1 is owned by the Federal Government (see page 256) while in the custodianship of Genesee Wyoming Australia and was fitted with a 16-567C engine, (although down-rated to 1500 hp traction) during its last overhaul. The class also represented the first of EMD's streamline design to be used in Australia. GM10 is the only example of the GM1 Class still in active commercial service (although GM3 is in Downer-EDI Rail ownership), and forms part of CFCLA's lease fleet.

Right: CFCLA's GM10 (leading T387, 2208 and G512) working an ARG Manildra flour train at Unanderra on Saturday 19 July 2008.
Chris Stratton

Road #	Builder's #	Built	Owner	Status	Name
GM3	ML1-3	1951	Downer-EDI Rail	Stored Kelso	*Ray E Purves*
GM10	ML1-10	1952	CFCLA	In service	-

B Class

Builder:	*Clyde-EMD (Clyde)*	Model:	*ML-2*
Type:	*Co-Co diesel-electric*	Engine:	*EMD 567B/567BC 2-stroke V16*
Traction power:	*1120/1190 kW (1500/1600 hp)*	Length:	*18.08 m*
Weight:	*113.2 tonnes*	Gauge:	*1435 mm and 1600 mm*

Above: Auscision-liveried B65 (accompanied by S317) at Forbes on Wednesday 30 July 2008. This is one of four B Class locomotives initially resurrected by West Coast Railway between 1994 and 2001, but which have since passed into CFCLA ownership. B61 and B65 normally work RailCorp and ARTC infrastructure trains while B76 is in the lease pool (and more often than not employed in QRNational service). B80 had just entered CFCLA service as this book went to press. Trish Baker

The introduction of the B Class in 1952 was the beginning of three-axle/three-motor bogie in Australia. Although this was not available at the time, the Victorian Railways (VR) prompted Clyde and EMD to design and manufacture the bogie. The double-ended streamlined locomotive proved successful for the VR and eliminated steam on passenger trains and express freights and, as they did not require turntables, saved turning time on arrival at destinations. Eleven of the units were rebuilt into the A Class during the mid-1980s (see page 60), while others were scrapped or preserved. However, four remain in service as of 2008 (B61, B65, B76 and B80) still earning a dollar hauling freight and trackwork trains as CFCLA-owned lease units.

Road #	Builder's #	Built	Owner	Status
B61	ML2-2	1952	CFCLA	In 1435 mm service
B65	ML2-6	1952	CFCLA	In 1435 mm service
B76	ML2-17	1953	CFCLA	In 1435 mm service
B80	ML2-21	1953	CFCLA	In 1600 mm service

2400/2470 Class

Builder:	*Clyde-EMD (Clyde)*	Model:	*GL22C-2*
Type:	*Co-Co diesel-electric*	Engine:	*EMD 645E 2-stroke V12*
Traction power:	*1120 kW (1500 hp)*	Length:	*17.04 m*
Weight:	*91.5 tonnes*	Gauge:	*1067 mm*

Above: Newly overhauled 2470 Class unit 2473D at Redbank Workshops during an Open Day on Saturday 6 July 2008. Peter Reading

Built more or less concurrently with the 2100 Series (see page 65) was the lighter, less powerful 2400 Series, encompassing the classes of the 1550 (27 units), 2400 (24 units), 2450 (18 units) and 2470 (36 units). Although similar in appearance to the 'coal network' 2100 Series, the similarly large fleet of 2400s were acquired for general service. Interestingly, the fleet 'grew' by one during 1988 when QR purchased the former Townsville Harbour Board unit ST5 (built in 1981), which, due to its similarity to the 2470 Class, was slipped conveniently into the fleet as 2507, although for a long time it was unique among its 'new class' in operating without dynamic braking (it has since been given this modification).

Like the heavier 2100 Series, these units were gradually modified for driver-only operation (DOO) throughout the 1990s, with all but a few left untreated towards the end of that decade. During 1997 a program to upgrade and modernise many of these 1120 kW units was commenced, with the result being the 1680 kW, turbo-charged 2300 Class 'maxi-cab' fleet (see page 55). This program rendered 'extinct' the 2450 Class and left only six each of both the 1550 and 2400 Classes in 'un-rebuilt' form. Meanwhile, the former Townsville unit, 2507, was able to move several numbers 'up the roster' to 2501 after the original 2501–2506 were rebuilt as 2300 Class units.

A follow-up program was commenced in 2004 to similarly refurbish some of the heavier 2100 Series units as the 2250 Class (see page 53), although eventually the remaining 1550 Class, previously skipped by the 2300 Class program, were cycled through the workshops for a 2250 rebuild also.

At around the same time, the remaining non-DOO 2400 Class units were refurbished and these six, along with the remaining 2470 Class units are now used in general service on the QRNational network.

Road #	Original #	Builder's #	Built	Owner	Status
2410D	2410	77-852	1977	QRNational	In service
2411D	2411	71-853	1977	QRNational	In service
2412D	2412	72-854	1977	QRNational	In service
2413D	2413	72-855	1978	QRNational	In service
2414D	2414	72-856	1978	QRNational	In service
2415D	2415	72-857	1978	QRNational	In service
2470D	2470	81-976	1980	QRNational	In service
2471D	2471	81-977	1980	QRNational	In service
2472D	2472	81-978	1980	QRNational	In service
2473D	2473	81-979	1980	QRNational	In service
2474D	2474	81-980	1981	QRNational	In service
2475D	2475	81-981	1981	QRNational	In service
2476D	2476	81-982	1981	QRNational	In service
2477D	2477	81-983	1981	QRNational	In service
2478H	2478	81-984	1981	QRNational	In service
2479D	2479	81-985	1981	QRNational	In service
2480D	2480	81-986	1981	QRNational	In service
2481D	2481	81-987	1981	QRNational	In service
2482D	2482	81-988	1981	QRNational	In service
2483D	2483	81-1006	1981	QRNational	In service
2484H	2484	81-1007	1981	QRNational	In service
2485H	2485	81-1008	1981	QRNational	In service
2486H	2486	81-1009	1981	QRNational	In service
2487H	2487	82-1126	1982	QRNational	In service
2488H	2488	82-1127	1982	QRNational	In service
2489H	2489	82-1128	1982	QRNational	In service
2490H	2490	82-1129	1982	QRNational	In service
2491H	2491	82-1130	1982	QRNational	In service
2492H	2492	82-1131	1982	QRNational	In service
2493H	2493	82-1132	1982	QRNational	In service
2494H	2494	82-1133	1982	QRNational	In service
2495H	2495	82-1134	1982	QRNational	In service
2496H	2496	82-1135	1982	QRNational	In service
2497H	2497	83-1136	1982	QRNational	In service
2498H	2498	83-1137	1982	QRNational	In service
2499D	2499	83-1138	1982	QRNational	In service
2500D	2500	83-1139	1982	QRNational	In service
2501D	ST5	81-999	1982	QRNational	In service

1502/DQ/423/AC/AD Class

Builder:	*Clyde-EMD/Comeng Qld*	Model:	*G22C*
Type:	*Co-Co diesel-electric*	Engine:	*EMD 645E 2-stroke V12*
Traction power:	*1120 kW (1500 hp)*	Length:	*15.04 m*
Weight:	*91.5 tonnes*	Gauge:	*1067 mm and 1435 mm*

Above: Although commonly described as DQ Class locomotives (for that is what they were previously reclassified as in New Zealand) the Tasmanian based units carry no such lettering in actuality. Not long after entering service in Tasmania, 2001 is seen here during shunting movements in Devonport on Thursday 25 February 1999. This particular locomotive was the first DQ Class 'conversion' recommissioned in New Zealand during 1996 (as DQ15215, before being renumbered DQ6007) and as of press time, was still stored in Dynon Workshops (Melbourne) pending completion of a postponed overhaul. Only 2001 and 2002 ever received this bright red livery, the remainder of the Tasmanian DQ Class were painted maroon. Chris Walters

Interestingly, 2008 finds most of the remaining 1502 Class operations happening outside of the class's 'native' Queensland. Six 1502s were converted during 2002–05 into standard-gauge 423 Class units for QRNational/Interail service in New South Wales (generally hauling coal out of Duralie and Newstan—before the latter services finished up in late 2008), while four more form part of the refurbished DQ Class fleet in Tasmania (having been overhauled by Tranz Rail in New Zealand during 1996–1999). Recently, two 1502 Class locomotives formed part of a transfer west of several surplus, formerly Queensland-based Clyde-EMD units, intended to assist in moving booming traffic within Western Australia. AC1520 (ex-1513) was overhauled and refurbished by Downer-EDI Rail in Port Augusta while AC1521 was similarly treated by QR themselves at Redbank, before the pair were delivered separately during late 2007/early 2008. The pair have generally been appearing in a support unit role on the 1067 mm gauge network since recommissioning, with one commonly found on Bunbury Line rosters and the other based at Avon Yard (Northam). AC1520 was recently 'rebadged' as AD1520 , while the remainder of the 1502 Class remain stored at Redbank Workshops.

Above: Former narrow-gauge 1502 Class unit 1526, now running on the NSW standard-gauge as QRNational's 42305, as seen at Broadmeadow on Saturday 16 April 2005. The first two 423 Class conversions (commissioned in 2002) were set up with the driver's control stand located on the right-hand side of the cab (facing forward) as per QR standard. The four subsequent 423 Class units were issued with this reversed, and the control stand located on the left (as per NSW standard). At this point, 42305 (and sister unit 42306) had only been in service a couple of months. Chris Walters

Road #	Original #	Builder's #	Built	Owner	Status
(DQ)2004	1502	67-597	1967	PNT	In 1067 mm service
1503	1503	67-598	1967	QRN	Stored Redbank (1067 mm)
42301	1504	67-599	1967	QRN	In 1435 mm service
1505	1505	67-600	1967	QRN	Stored Redbank (1067 mm)
42302	1507	67-602	1967	QRN	In 1435 mm service
(DQ)2003	1508	67-603	1967	PNT	In 1067 mm service
1509	1509	67-604	1967	QRN	Stored Redbank (1067 mm)
1510	1510	68-605	1968	QRN	Stored Redbank (1067 mm)
1511	1511	68-606	1968	QRN	Stored Redbank (1067 mm)
AD1520	1513	68-608	1968	ARG	In 1067 mm service
AC1521	1514	68-608	1968	ARG	In 1067 mm service
1515	1515	68-610	1968	QRN	Stored Redbank (1067 mm)
1516	1516	68-611	1968	QRN	Stored Redbank (1067 mm)
42303	1518	68-613	1968	QRN	In 1435 mm service
42306	1520	68-615	1968	QRN	In 1435 mm service
(DQ)2001	1521	68-616	1968	PNT	Stored Dynon (1067 mm)
(DQ)2002	1522	68-646	1968	PNT	In 1067 mm service
42304	1524	68-648	1968	QRN	In 1435 mm service
42305	1526	69-650	1969	QRN	In 1435 mm service
1527	1527	69-651	1969	QRN	Stored Redbank (1067 mm)
1528	1528	69-652	1969	QRN	Stored Redbank (1067 mm)
1529	1529	69-653	1969	QRN	Stored Redbank (1067 mm)

Above: Refurbished AD1520 (ex-1513 and recently renumbered from AC1520) at Forrestfield on Friday 19 September 2008. As of press time, sister unit AC1521 (ex-1514) had not yet been given the AD reclassification. Evan Jasper

Below: Decommissioned 1512 at Hamilton Yard on Thursday 14 July 2005. Although 1512 and a number of sister units were on their way to FCAB Chile at this stage, a few 1502 Class units in similar condition remain stored at Redbank Workshops as of late 2008. Michael James

AB Class

Builder:	*Clyde-EMD (Clyde)*	Model:	*G22C*
Type:	*Co-Co diesel-electric*	Engine:	*EMD 645E 2-stroke V12*
Traction power:	*1120 kW (1500 hp)*	Length:	*15.49 m*
Weight:	*94.5 tonnes*	Gauge:	*1067 mm*

Above: AB1501 (formerly AB1531) about to depart Narembeen as a light engine movement on Thursday 24 July 2008. Chris Miller

Originally there were six AB Class locomotives (derivatives of earlier A and AA Class designs), however two were sold to overseas interests during 1998, before Westrail was privatised; AB1532 went to FCAB Chile, while AB1533 was ultimately scrapped after parts salvage in New Zealand. The remaining four have long been associated with grain haulage along lines to the north and east of Perth, however the seasonal nature of this traffic has meant that their recent careers have been somewhat stop-start, and it has not been unusual to see at least one or two stabled for prolonged periods of time at either Forrestfield or Avon Yard (Northam) as a consequence. Two (AB1531 and AB1535) were overhauled, repainted and renumbered (as AB1501 and AB1503 respectively) during 2007, however the second pair remain in rather shabby condition, wearing their original road numbers and faded Westrail livery as this book closed for press. In a move akin to that made when A1202 (ex-A1511, see page 91) was repainted orange a couple of years prior, the two repainted AB units did not get a full ARG 'corporate' livery, and instead their yellow paint job was devoid of the maroon striping typical of other examples of the scheme.

Road #	Original #	Builder's #	Built	Owner	Status
AB1501	AB1531	69-676	1969	ARG	In service
AB1534	AB1534	69-679	1970	ARG	In service
AB1503	AB1535	69-680	1970	ARG	In service
AB1536	AB1536	69-681	1970	ARG	In service

DC Class

Builder:	*EMD Canada/Clyde (Rosewater)*	Model:	*G22AR*
Type:	*A1A-A1A diesel-electric*	Engine:	*EMD 645E 2-stroke V12*
Traction power:	*1120 kW (1500 hp)*	Length:	*14.10 m*
Weight:	*82.0 tonnes*	Gauge:	*1067 mm*

Above: Prior to the commencement of work to convert it for Driver Only Operation (DOO) operation, DC4588 (and QR Class unit 2102) languish in storage at East Tamar Workshops on Wednesday 31 December 2003. Chris Walters

Rebuilt in 1980 by Clyde (Rosewater) from former New Zealand Railways DA Class unit DA1489 (an EMD locomotive built in Canada), DC4588 was destined to become the only one of the 85-member DC Class to return to Australia following the completion of the rebuild program in 1983 (although five of the DCs were actually rebuilt in New Zealand). DC4588 formed part of the shipment of Clyde-EMD locomotives (including also DQ and QR Class units) exported from New Zealand to Tasmania in December 1998, as Tranz Rail and parent company Wisconsin Central sought to populate their then newly acquired ATN Tasrail operation with EMD-type power.

The locomotive was to remain the only DC unit on the system and although it eventually passed to Pacific National Tasmania ownership, had managed only four years of service before catastrophic engine failure saw it stored at East Tamar in 2002. By 2006 an effort to overhaul and modify the unit for continued service had been commenced but was soon postponed as the Pacific National Tasmania business suffered from declining investment. At press time the fate of DC4588 is not known, although dozens of DC Class sister units continue to operate in daily service for KiwiRail in New Zealand.

Road#	Builders #	Built	Owner	Status
DC4588	80-945	1980	PN Tasmania	Stored East Tamar

One of 85 ex-New Zealand Railways DC Class locomotives (only one in Australia). Rebuilt from Canadian-built EMD DA Class unit DA1489 in 1980 by Clyde.

NJ Class

Builder:	*Clyde-EMD (Clyde)*	Model:	*J22C*
Type:	*Co-Co diesel-electric*	Engine:	*EMD 645E 2-stroke V12*
Traction power:	*1120 kW (1500 hp)*	Length:	*13.96 m*
Weight:	*67.0 tonnes*	Gauge:	*1067 mm*

Above: ARG-owned NJ1605 (with NJ1602 out-of-sight at the other end of the rake) leads an empty wood chip train away from Albany on Monday 7 April 2008. The remaining four members of the original six-member NJ Class fleet are owned by Genesee Wyoming Australia and remain on the narrow-gauge Eyre Peninsula system in South Australia. Evan Jasper

Prior to the 2006 split up of the Australian Railroad Group (ARG), two of the six 1971-vintage NJ Class locomotives (NJ2 and NJ5) were transferred from South Australia's Eyre Peninsula (where the class commonly hauled grain and gypsum) to Western Australia to serve as power on Albany wood chip shuttles. With the ARG split, both of these locomotives continue in this role, although are now numbered NJ1602 and NJ1605 respectively. Although permanently based in Albany, the two ARG NJs do occasionally show up in Northam and Perth during periods of maintenance. Meanwhile, the other four—now owned by GWA—continue on in Eyre Peninsula service.

Road #	Original #	Builder's #	Built	Owner	Status	Name
1601	NJ1	70-728	1971	GWA	In service	*Ben Chifley*
NJ1602	NJ2	71-729	1971	ARG	In service	-
1603	NJ3	71-730	1971	GWA	In service	-
1604	NJ4	71-731	1971	GWA	In service	-
NJ1605	NJ5	71-732	1971	ARG	In service	-
1606	NJ6	71-733	1971	GWA	In service	-

EMD

G14M/Rebuilt DE Class

Builder:	*MKA (Whyalla)*	Model:	*G14M*
Type:	*Bo-Bo diesel-electric*	Engine:	*EMD 645E 2-stroke V12*
Traction power:	*1120 kW (1500 hp)*	Length:	*13.57 m*
Weight:	*72.0 tonnes*	Gauge:	*1067 mm*

Above: 1302 and 1301 at Whyalla in 2004. Greg O'Brien

Rebuilt during the short tenure of Morrison Knudsen Australia (MKA) were one G8B and five G12B locomotives for BHP Whyalla during 1992–94. Unlike the concurrent ALF/CLF/CLP MKA rebuilds for Australian National, the BHP project radically altered the appearance of the original Clyde-EMD design. The former BHP operation based at Whyalla ultimately became part of OneSteel, and the rail operations were outsourced to what was then Australia Southern Railroad (ASR, later part of Australian Railroad Group or ARG) during 1999. At that time the former BHP Whyalla fleet (including the six G14M rebuilds) passed to ASR, although DE8 and DE9 were destroyed in a collision two years later, and scrapped. With the split up of ARG in 2006, the former ASR assets at Whyalla passed to Genesee Wyoming Australia, and three of the remaining four G14M locomotives (now numbered in the 1300 Series) continue to be employed in 1067 mm gauge ore haulage (the fourth was recently damaged in a collision).

Road #	Original #	Builder's #	Rebuilt	Owner	Status
1301	DE1	93-BHP-004	1993	GWA	In service
1302	DE3	93-BHP-006	1993	GWA	In service
1303	DE4	93-BHP-005	1993	GWA	In service
1304	DE7	93-BHP-003	1993	GWA	In service

1460/DQ/QR Class

Builder:	*Clyde-EMD/Comeng Qld*	Model:	*G12C 1460/QR Class* *G22C DQ Class*
Type:	*Co-Co diesel-electric*	Engine:	*EMD 567C 2-stroke V12 1460/QR Class* *EMD 645CE 2-stroke V12 DQ Class*
Length:	*15.04 m*	Weight:	*91.6 tonnes*
Traction power:	*980 kW (1310 hp) 1460/QR Class* *1120 kW (1500 hp) DQ Class*	Gauge:	*1067 mm*

Above: DQ Class unit 2005 (leading sister unit 2006) has just arrived in Railton with the coal train from Fingal on Tuesday 4 July 2006. Both 2005 and 2006 were originally 1460 Class locomotives, but were upgraded to match the capability of the four DQ units (2001–2004) converted from the more powerful 1502 Class. Chris Walters

Introduced in 1964, the 1460 Class were a turning point between the EMD export type 1400 and 1450 Class units and the 'Australianised' 1502, 2100 and 2400 Series Clydes that would come to dominate the QR system. By the 1990s the class's usefulness had ended and QR was seeking their disposal. Tranz Rail in New Zealand sensed a cost effective investment in the 1460 and 1502 Class units that QR had put on the market, and so between 1995 and 1997 bought 21 1460s and four 1502s from the Queensland operator. Most of these were eventually refurbished as DQ Class units, however, since the capability of the 567C-engined 1460 could not match that of the four newer 645E powered 1502s (also being converted to DQs), Tranz Rail applied an upgrade to the 1460s in the program, the result of which was a 645CE engine. Six 1460s were also quickly pushed into Tranz Rail service as QR Class 'slave' units, and generally received only a service, repaint and minor modifications, but were not upgraded to the 645CE specification.

Twelve DQs and three QRs (that retained their Tranz Rail numbers) were eventually transferred to ATN Tasrail (with whom Tranz Rail shared a parent company in Wisconsin Central) for service in Tasmania. Although a valuable addition to the Tasmanian fleet, the DQ and QR units have not been without their problems and, as of 2008, two of the QR units have been out of service for some time, while the number of DQ units in service is prone to ebbs and flows (although this is just as much due to a falling level of investment in what has become a Pacific National Tasmania operation, than any problems with the DQ Class themselves). Four 1460-converted DQs remain in service with what is now KiwiRail in New Zealand's South Island, however the remaining QR units (along with a number of former Westrail A Class) were sold to a Brazilian operator in 2004. Two 1460s had been sold to South African company some years prior as well, so the class can be considered 'well travelled'. The table below lists those 1460s still in Australia as of late 2008 (aside from 1461, preserved by QR at The Workshops Museum at Ipswich).

Above: QR Class unit 2102 at Devonport on Thursday 25 February 1999. Unlike the DQ Class units that were given specific liveries for service with ATN Tasrail in Tasmania, the three QR Class retained a simplified version of the Tranz Rail livery with only the lettering being changed form 'Tranz Rail' to 'Tasrail'. As of late 2008, 2102 is in storage at East Tamar, and has been since 2002. Chris Walters

Road#	Original #	Builder's #	Built	Owner	Status
(DQ)2006	1465	64-353	1964	PN Tasmania	In service
(DQ)2010	1466	64-354	1964	PN Tasmania	In service
(DQ)2005	1468	64-356	1964	PN Tasmania	In service
(DQ)2008	1472	64-360	1964	PN Tasmania	In service
(QR)2056	1475	64-363	1964	PN Tasmania	In service
(QR)2062	1477	64-365	1964	PN Tasmania	Stored East Tamar
(DQ)2007	1485	65-451	1965	PN Tasmania	In service
(DQ)2009	1491	66-457	1966	PN Tasmania	In service
(QR)2102	1493	66-459	1966	PN Tasmania	Stored East Tamar
(DQ)2011	1495	66-461	1966	PN Tasmania	In service
(DQ)2012	1497	66-463	1966	PN Tasmania	In service

A Class

Builder:	*Clyde-EMD/Comeng WA*	Model:	*G12C*
Type:	*Co-Co diesel-electric*	Engine:	*EMD 567C 2-stroke V12*
Traction power:	*980 kW (1310 hp)*	Length:	*15.04 m*
Weight:	*67.0 tonnes*	Gauge:	*1067 mm*

Above: 1204 (ex-A1514), 905 (ex-DA6) and 1203 (ex-A1513) at Port Lincoln Saturday 17 November 2007. Greg O'Brien

Once part of a fleet of 14 A Class locomotives (delivered to the Western Australian Government Railways between 1960 and 1965), A1202 (previously A1511) is now the only surviving member in Western Australian service (although class leader A1501 was recently obtained by Rail Heritage Western Australia for preservation). A1202 is a 'general use' 1067 mm-gauge unit, and when not being used as a shunter/transfer unit in the Perth/Kwinana region, can sometimes be found wandering south to Bunbury and east to Northam. It is painted in a variation of the Australian Railroad Group (ARG) orange livery in that it has no black stripes. Meanwhile, two other A Class units, in the form of 1203 and 1204 (formerly A1513 and A1514—originally financed by Western Mining), were acquired by Genesee Wyoming Australia when ARG was split up in 2006. By that time the pair had been transferred to Port Lincoln (South Australia) for grain haulage and have remained there ever since.

Road #	Original #	Builder's #	Built	Owner	Status
A1202	A1511	65-375	1965	ARG	In service
1203	A1513	65-427	1965	GWA	In service
1204	A1514	65-428	1965	GWA	In service

1250 (ex-DE03) Class

Builder:	*Clyde-EMD (Clyde)*	Model:	*G12B*
Type:	*Bo-Bo diesel-electric*	Engine:	*EMD 567C 2-stroke V12*
Traction power:	*980 kW (1310 hp)*	Length:	*13.56 m*
Weight:	*73.8 tonnes*	Gauge:	*1067 mm*

Above: Although 1251 (ex-BHP Whyalla DE05) represents the G12B model and is fitted with a V12 engine, the body design is almost identical to that of the two G8B units delivered to the same customer (interestingly, both exist today albeit in heavily rebuilt form). Here 1251 also shows cab roof modifications and redesigned cab windows, retrofitted by BHP at Whyalla some years after delivery from Clyde Engineering. 1251 is now used as the 1067 mm gauge shunter at the Australian Railroad Group's Forrestfield locomotive facility in Perth. Bernie Baker

The remaining members of the former BHP Whyalla locomotive fleet were acquired by Australia Southern Railroad in 1999, at a time when rail services at this location were being outsourced by new owners OneSteel. It was not long before locomotive DE05, the last remaining member of the seven-unit DE03-type G12B fleet (numbered DE03 to DE09) not rebuilt by Morrison Knudsen Australia as G14M units (see page 88) or scrapped due to collision damage (as was sister unit DE06 only a couple of years earlier), was deemed surplus to requirements at Whyalla by its new owners. As such, the locomotive was transferred to Perth to be used as the narrow-gauge shunter at Forrestfield Workshops. Settled into its new duties, DE05 was soon renumbered 1251, and eventually, and somewhat appropriately, DE1251 (although it does not yet actually display the 'DE' designation). It remains to this day within the workshops precinct as permanent resident, although its use is irregular and essentially 'on demand'.

Road #	Original #	Builder's #	Built	Owner	Status
(DE)1251	DE05	57-136	1957	ARG	In service (Forrestfield)

TL Class

Builder:	*Clyde-EMD (Clyde)*	Model:	*G12B*
Type:	*Bo-Bo diesel-electric*	Engine:	*EMD 567C 2-stroke V12*
Traction power:	*840 kW (1125 hp)*	Length:	*13.56 m*
Weight:	*74.0 tonnes*	Gauge:	*1435 mm*

Above: TL154, the first of the four-unit TL Class recommissioned for service with CFCLA in Australia, at South Dynon on 4 July 2007. Bernie Baker

Originally five Clyde-EMD locomotives were built in Australia for the Kowloon Canton Railway of Hong Kong between 1955 and 1957. This railway connected Hong Kong with mainland China and these locomotives were involved in the movement of both passenger and freight trains along this route (although they were restricted from entering the mainland). Over time a number of newer, more powerful locomotives (including similar G16 and G26 type units) took over frontline duties and some of the G12s found their way into shunting service. Four of the five were purchased by CFCLA and returned to Australia in 2005, and were progressively overhauled at Islington Workshops before entering CFCLA's pool of lease locomotives. Now known as the TL Class, three of the four have entered service, with this group already having seen service in Victoria, South Australia and Western Australia as shunters and transfer units. As of late 2008, TL152 was yet to enter service, while the original class leader (51 *Sir Alexander*) remains in Hong Kong as a museum exhibit.

Road #	Original #	Builder's #	Built	Owner	Status
TL152	52	55-061	1955	CFCLA	Stored
TL153	53	57-143	1957	CFCLA	In service
TL154	54	57-144	1957	CFCLA	In service
TL155	55	57-163	1957	CFCLA	In service

1720 Class

Builder:	*Clyde-EMD/Comeng Qld*	Model:	*GL18C*
Type:	*Co-Co diesel-electric*	Engine:	*EMD 645E 2-stroke V8*
Traction power:	*745 kW (1000 hp)*	Length:	*12.34 m*
Weight:	*62.5 tonnes*	Gauge:	*1067 mm*

Above: The first of the three 1720s upgraded and repainted for Kuranda tourist train duties, 1771D stands at Kuranda, awaiting departure back to Cairns on Sunday 15 September 2002. These trains today usually rate two of the *Buda-ji* 1720 Class locomotives and there are two return trains every day. Chris Walters

The last of QR's 'light lines' fleet, the 1720 Class nonetheless play an important role in the movement of freight and passengers throughout Queensland. From branch line freight (such as the service to/from Dirranbandi) and 'menial' transfer goods and yard shunt jobs, through to support unit roles on the *Sunlander* and heading the famous Kuranda tourist trains out of Cairns, the 1720s are still a valuable force in QRNational's haulage task. However, they are generally less common leading on main line services, even though they can often be sighted trailing larger units up and down the North Coast.

In 2000 1764D was given a thorough refurbishment and 'maxi-cab' overhaul as a prototype for a larger upgrade for the class. This was followed in 2002 by three more units (1734D, 1771D and 1774D) similarly modified, and yet also painted in a special, indigenous-style *Buda-Dji* livery for dedicated service on the Cairns to Kuranda tourist trains. The following year a 'production run' of 1720 Class upgrades then got underway, with 1730D (renumbered simply 1730 following release) the first to re-enter service, with a further eight, similarly overhauled 1720s following over the ensuing year and a half. In 2004 1751D was repainted in the *Buda-Dji* livery to ensure four units in the scheme would be available for the increasingly popular Kuranda trains, although it was not upgraded to the same standard of the other three units at this time.

Road #	Original #	Builder's #	Built	Owner	Status	Name/Note
1720	1720	66-502	1966	QRN	In service	Maxi-cab overhaul
1721D	1721	66-503	1966	QRN	In service	-
1722D	1722	66-504	1966	QRN	Stored Redbank	-
1723D	1723	66-505	1966	QRN	Stored Redbank	-
1724D	1724	66-506	1966	QRN	Stored Redbank	-
1725D	1725	66-507	1966	QRN	In service	-
1727D	1727	66-509	1966	QRN	Stored Redbank	-
1729D	1729	66-511	1966	QRN	In service	-
1730	1730	67-512	1966	QRN	In service	Maxi-cab overhaul
1732D	1732	67-514	1967	QRN	In service	-
1733	1733	67-515	1967	QRN	In service	Maxi-cab overhaul
1734D	1734	67-516	1967	QRN	In service	Maxi-cab overhaul
1735D	1735	67-517	1967	QRN	In service	-
1736	1736	67-518	1967	QRN	In service	Maxi-cab overhaul
1737	1737	67-519	1967	QRN	In service	Maxi-cab overhaul
1738D	1738	67-520	1967	QRN	In service	-
1739D	1739	67-521	1967	QRN	In service	-
1740D	1740	67-522	1967	QRN	In service	-
1741D	1741	67-523	1967	QRN	In service	-
1742D	1742	67-524	1967	QRN	In service	-
1743D	1743	67-525	1967	QRN	In service	-
1744D	1744	67-558	1967	QRN	In service	-
1745D	1745	67-559	1967	QRN	Stored Redbank	-
1746D	1746	67-560	1967	QRN	In service	-
1747D	1747	67-561	1967	QRN	In service	-
1748D	1748	67-562	1967	QRN	In service	-
1749D	1749	67-563	1967	QRN	In service	-
1750D	1750	67-564	1968	QRN	Stored Redbank	-
1751D	1751	67-565	1968	QRN	In service	-
1752D	1752	67-566	1968	QRN	In service	-
1753	1753	67-567	1968	QRN	In service	Maxi-cab overhaul
1754D	1754	68-634	1968	QRN	In service	-
1755D	1755	66-635	1968	QRN	Stored Redbank	-
1756	1756	66-636	1968	QRN	In service	Maxi-cab overhaul
1757D	1757	66-637	1968	QRN	Stored Redbank	-
1758	1758	66-638	1968	QRN	In service	Maxi-cab overhaul
1759D	1759D	66-639	1968	QRN	In service	-

(continued)

Road #	Original #	Builder's #	Built	Owner	Status	Name/Note
1761D	1761D	64-641	1968	QRN	In service	-
1762D	1762D	64-642	1968	QRN	Stored Redbank	-
1763D	1763D	64-643	1968	QRN	In service	-
1764D	1764D	64-644	1968	QRN	In service	Prototype maxi-cab
1766D	1766D	69-683	1969	QRN	Stored Redbank	
1767D	1767	69-684	1969	QRN	Stored Redbank	-
1768D	1768	69-685	1969	QRN	Stored Redbank	-
1769D	1769	69-686	1970	QRN	In service	-
1770D	1770	70-687	1970	QRN	Stored Redbank	Named *James Cook*
1771D	1771	70-688	1970	QRN	In service	Maxi-cab overhaul
1772D	1772	70-689	1970	QRN	In service	-
1773D	1773	70-690	1970	QRN	In service	-
1774D	1774	70-691	1970	QRN	In service	Maxi-cab overhaul
1775D	1775	70-692	1970	QRN	In service	-

Above: A more or less 'stock standard' 1720 Class in the form of 1753D at Portsmith Loco on Saturday 15 December 2001. Portsmith is the central locomotive and maintenance facility for Cairns, and the allotment of 1720s here were used for shunting and, until recently, Arriga sugar-syrup trains which operate during the crushing season (and which are now operated by '90-tonne' Clyde locomotives). Portsmith is also home to the specially painted Kuranda tourist train 1720 Class locomotives 1734D, 1751D, 1771D and 1774D. Chris Walters

P Class

Builder:	*Clyde-EMD (Somerton)*	Model:	*G18HB-R*
Type:	*Bo-Bo diesel-electric*	Engine:	*EMD 645E 2-stroke V8*
Traction power:	*745 kW (1000 hp)*	Length:	*13.96 m*
Weight:	*73.7 tonnes*	Gauge:	*1600 mm*

Above: P18 trails a special push-pull passenger train (led by P15) near Laverton on Saturday 29 September 2007. Bob Grant

As with the A Class (see page 60), that were also a rebuild (including HEP packages) of service-worn locomotives for passenger haulage during the mid-1980s, the 13-member P Class fleet were split when V/Line and V/Line Freight were packaged up in 1995 for eventual sale in 1998. Again like the A Class, this saw the 'freight' allocation of P Class locomotives shifted away from passenger services for which they were acquired. In Freight Australia, and then Pacific National ownership these seven P Class locomotives have been used primarily on broad-gauge intrastate freight services, although they have often been hired back to V/Line Passenger for brief periods. Meanwhile, the eight V/Line units continue to haul shorter commuter services to Sunbury and Bacchus Marsh.

Road #	Rebuilt #	Builders #	Built	Owner	Status
P11	T336	84-1205	1984	V/Line Passenger	In service
P12	T329	84-1206	1984	V/Line Passenger	In service
P13	T340	84-1207	1984	V/Line Passenger	In service
P14	T330	84-1208	1984	V/Line Passenger	In service
P15	T344	84-1209	1984	V/Line Passenger	In service
P16	T332	84-1210	1984	V/Line Passenger	In service
P17	T327	84-1216	1984	V/Line Passenger	In service
P18	T339	84-1211	1985	V/Line Passenger	In service
P19	T331	84-1212	1985	Pacific National	Stored Dynon
P20	T337	84-1213	1985	Pacific National	In service
P21	T338	84-1214	1985	Pacific National	In service
P22	T328	84-1215	1985	Pacific National	In service
P23	T326	84-1217	1985	Pacific National	In service

H Class

Builder:	*Clyde-EMD (Clyde)*	Model:	*G18B*
Type:	*Bo-Bo diesel-electric*	Engine:	*EMD 645E 2-stroke V8*
Traction power:	*745 kW (1000 hp)*	Length:	*12.40 m*
Weight:	*81.2 tonnes*	Gauge:	*1600 mm*

Above: H2, leading XR557 on a Down empty stone train, crosses an Up Shepparton passenger train at Kilmore East, on Monday 3 September 2007. Ewan McLean

The five H Class units (which were briefly numbered T413—T417 upon delivery), ballasted up to be much heavier than their sister T Class units, were initially obtained for Hump Yard shunting in Melbourne, before the closure of these facilities and rural track upgrading eventually allowed them to roam around the Victorian broad-gauge network. Service with Freight Australia, and more recently Pacific National, has seen little change to their employment, although at various times one or two have been made available for standard-gauge use. All five are now on the broad-gauge once more, and employed on shunting, transfer and general freight duties.

Road #	Builder's #	Built	Owner	Status
H1	68-629	1969	Pacific National	In service
H2	68-630	1969	Pacific National	In service
H3	68-631	1969	Pacific National	In service
H4	68-632	1969	Pacific National	In service
H5	68-634	1969	Pacific National	Stored Dynon

T Class

Builder:	*Clyde-EMD (Clyde)*	Model:	*G8B T320–T398*
			G18B T399–T412
Type:	*Bo-Bo diesel-electric*	Engine:	*EMD 567C 2-stroke V8 T320–T346*
			EMD 567CR 2-stroke V8 T347–T398
			EMD 645E 2-stroke V8 T399–T412
Traction	*650 kW (875 hp) T320–T398*	Length:	*13.56 m T320–T346*
power:	*745 kW (1000 hp) T399–T412*		*12.40 m T347–T412*
Weight:	*69.4 tonnes*	Gauge:	*1067 mm, 1435 mm and 1600 mm*

Above: Although many preserved T Class locomotives are available for lease to freight operators, only one 'flat top' T is in regular commercial service; that being SCT's T345, which is based in Adelaide as a yard shunter at Islington. It is seen here in the company of G513 (another former V/Line unit) at Islington on Monday 14 April 2008. Tom Marschall

The first series T Class (T320–T346 and T413) were straight out of EMD's catalogue and are the G8B model. Although they became known as 'flat tops' (due to the cab roof being flush with the hood) the T Class would eventually be delivered in three basic designs. The second series (T347–T366) were designed by Clyde with a raised cab and high short hood, while the third series (T367–T412) possessed a raised cab but lowered short hood. Of the first series only one remains in commercial use, that being SCT's T345 which is employed as a shunter at Islington. CFCLA own the only second series (T363) in commercial use, while the majority of the remaining third series units are owned by Pacific National or CFCLA. Preserved broad gauge T Class units are often hired by private operators for use throughout Victoria, including T413 which was purchased by the Victorian Railways from Australian Portland Cement (APC) in 1969. This was the only T Class fitted with dynamic brakes (although the two BHP Whyalla G8B units were so equipped also—see page 102). Those listed below are nominally available for commercial service, while the preserved members of the class (often leased by commercial operators) are tabulated in the Preserved Locomotives Appendix at the back of the book (see page 264).

Above: T363 and T381 at Moss Vale on Wednesday 27 September 2006. Again, although a number of similar preserved units have seen extensive lease service, T363 is the only representative of its particular T Class design variant (the high cab/high nose type) in regular commercial duties. Although in almost exclusive Southern Shorthaul Railroad contract service, T363 and T381 (and B61, see page 79) are believed to be still financially owned by CFCLA. Chris Walters

Road #	Original #	Builders #	Built	Owner	Status
T345	T345	56-128	1956	SCT	In 1435 mm service—Islington
T363	T363	62-248	1962	CFCLA/SSR	In 1435 mm service
T369	T369	64-324	1964	CFCLA	In 1600 mm service
T371	T371	64-326	1964	Pacific National	In 1435 mm service
T373	T373	64-328	1964	CFCLA	In 1600 mm service
T374	T374	64-329	1964	Pacific National	In 1600 mm service
T376	T376	64-331	1964	CFCLA	In 1600 mm service
T377	T377	64-332	1964	CFCLA	In 1600 mm service
T379	T379	64-334	1964	Pacific National	In 1435 mm service
T381	T381	64-336	1964	CFCLA/SSR	In 1435 mm service
T382	T382	64-337	1964	Victorian DOI	Stored Dynon (1600 mm)
T383	T383	64-338	1964	Coote Industrial	In 1435 mm service
T385	T385	64-340	1964	CFCLA	In 1435 mm service

(continued)

Road #	Original #	Builders #	Built	Owner	Status
T386	T386	64-341	1964	El Zorro	In 1435 mm service
T387	T387	65-417	1965	CFCLA	In 1435 mm service
T388	T388	65-418	1965	Pacific National	In 1435 mm service
T390	T390	65-420	1965	Pacific National	In 1435 mm service
T392	T392	65-422	1965	Pacific National	In 1435 mm service
T396	T396	65-426	1965	Pacific National	In 1600 mm service
T399	T399	66-494	1967	Pacific National	In 1435 mm service
T400	T400	67-495	1967	Pacific National	In 1600 mm service
CK1	T401	67-496	1967	GWA	In 1067 mm service
T402	T402	67-497	1967	Pacific National	In 1600 mm service
T404	T404	67-499	1967	SCT	In 1435 mm service—Laverton
Named *Mick Smith.*					
CK3	T405	67-500	1967	GWA	In 1067 mm service
CK4	T406	67-501	1967	GWA	In 1067 mm service
CK5	T407	68-623	1968	GWA	In 1067 mm service
T408	T408	68-624	1968	Pacific National	In 1435 mm service
T409	T409	68-625	1968	Pacific National	In 1435 mm service

Above: CFCLA's broad-gauge T373 at South Dynon on 8 April 2007. Most of CFCLA's T Class were acquired from the now defunct Great Northern Rail (such as T373 here) or West Coast Railway businesses during 2004. Bernie Baker

DE01 Class

Builder:	*Clyde-EMD (Clyde)*	Model:	*G8B*
Type:	*Bo-Bo diesel-electric*	Engine:	*EMD 567C 2-stroke V8*
Traction power:	*650 kW (875 hp)*	Length:	*13.56 m*
Weight:	*81.3 tonnes*	Gauge:	*1435 mm*

Above: The newly delivered T414 (with G539) in Parkes Yard on Thursday 12 October 2006. This locomotive began life with BHP Whyalla in 1956 as DE02, and was rebuilt for SCT service at Goobang with a new cab patterned on the later-series, low-nose T Class locomotives originally of the Victorian Railways (see page 101). Bernie Baker

This former BHP Whyalla/Coffin Bay G8B unit (once part of a pair numbered DE01 and DE02), after many years of storage, was resurrected during 2005/2006 by RTS and rebuilt for SCT as the Goobang (Parkes) yard shunter. With a new cab and nose design patterned on the low-nose, former Victorian Railways T Class series, DE02, as it was once known, is today T414. Aside from a small number of main line freight runs, T414 is almost exclusively used within the confines of SCT's Goobang freight facility. Its former sister unit (DE01) was rebuilt by Morrison Knudsen Australia as G14M DE1 during 1993 (see page 88) and now operates for Genesee Wyoming Australia.

Road #	Original #	Builder's #	Built	Owner	Status	Name
T414	DE02	56-111	1956	SCT Goobang	In service	*Georgia McKinnon*

49/KL/MM Class

Builder:	*Clyde-EMD (Clyde)*	Model:	*G8C*
Type:	*Co-Co diesel-electric*	Engine:	*EMD 567CR 2-stroke V8*
Traction power:	*650 kW (875 hp)*	Length:	*14.10 m*
Weight:	*81.2 tonnes*	Gauge:	*1435 mm*

Above: Coote Industrial's 4908 (and 603) at Parkes on Monday 11 August 2008. The skirting has been cut down similar to 4913–4918. Bernie Baker

Originally delivered between 1960 and 1965, members of the once 18-strong 49 Class fleet have been gravitating towards private-operator commercial service since the Manildra Group commissioned its pair of MM Class units in 1994/95. Since that time, a number of these former New South Wales Government Railways units have re-entered service, with CFCLA operating three as KL Class lease units, and Patrick PortLink employing two (modified with lowered short hoods, similar to the Manildra pair) for container haulage. More recently former 3801 Limited 'preserved' unit 4908 was recommissioned by Coote Industrial for use on infrastructure train workings during mid-2008.

Road #	Original #	Builder's #	Built	Owner	Status
4903	4903	60-223	1960	Patrick PortLink	In service
KL80	4904	60-224	1960	CFCLA	In service
4906	4906	60-226	1961	Patrick PortLink	In service
MM01	4907	62-257	1962	Manildra Group	In service
4908	4908	62-258	1962	Coote Industrial	In service
KL81	4910	62-260	1962	CFCLA	In service
4911	4911	62-261	1962	Manildra Group	Stored Kelso
MM02	4913	64-342	1964	Manildra Group	In service
KL82	4917	64-346	1964	CFCLA	In service

Above: Seen at Botany on Friday 28 March 2007, 4903 and 4906 were purchased secondhand in 2005 and were subsequently refurbished at Lithgow. Modifications included the cutting-down of the short end nose in a similar fashion to Manildra's MM Class (see below) which includes a large one piece windscreen in the centre. A single illuminated number panel was fitted to the short end and ditch lights added. The Staff exchanger recesses were filled in and aluminium-framed side windows were also fitted. Bernie Baker

Below: By comparison, MM01 (ex-4907) shunting at the Manildra Mill on Wednesday 7 December 2005. Chris Walters

J Class

Builder:	*Clyde-EMD (Clyde)*	Model:	*G6B*
Type:	*Bo-Bo diesel-electric*	Engine:	*EMD 567C 2-stroke V6*
Traction power:	*450 kW (600 hp)*	Length:	*13.03 m*
Weight:	*65.0 tonnes*	Gauge:	*1435 mm*

Above: J103 and J102, both in Southern Shorthaul Railroad livery at Appleton Dock on Sunday 20 March 2005. Bernie Baker

After thirty years of fairly mundane shunting and transfer work for the Western Australian Government Railways and Westrail in Western Australia, the four remaining J Class locomotives (class leader J101 was scrapped in 1993) experienced a meteoric rise in profile when they were shipped to Melbourne in mid-1995 for service with Great Northern Rail in mid-1995. These were the early days of the 'private operators' and the J Class were a novelty. Employed as National Rail shunters, trip train haulers and power for infrastructure trains, perhaps the most noteworthy role for the class was J104 (by then owned by RTS) being used as the *Overland* carriage shunter for a number of years. Like many Victorian-based locomotives of the era, the J Class changed hands a number of times during the ensuing years, and today J102 and J103 are owned by CFCLA while J104 and J105 (now known as FJ104 and FJ105, respectively) are employed by FreightLink as yard shunters at Alice Springs and Darwin.

Road #	Original #	Builder's #	Built	Owner	Status
J102	J102	66-480	1966	CFCLA	In service
J103	J103	66-481	1966	CFCLA	In service
FJ104	J104	66-482	1966	FreightLink	In service
FJ105	J105	66-483	1966	FreightLink	In service

Y Class

Builder:	*Clyde-EMD (Clyde)*		Model:	*G6B*	
Type:	*Bo-Bo diesel-electric*		Engine:	*EMD 567C 2-stroke V6*	*Y101–Y150*
				EMD 645E 2-stroke V6	*Y151–Y175*
Traction power:	*450 kW (600 hp)*	*Y101–Y150*	Length:	*12.19 m*	
	560 kW (750 hp)	*Y151–Y175*			
Weight:	*65.0 tonnes*		Gauge:	*1435 mm and 1600 mm*	

Above: Downer-EDI Rail's 1435 mm-gauge Y134 *Yoda*, at Cardiff Workshops on Wednesday 28 November 2007. Downer-EDI Rail also own Y136, which is a 1600-mm gauge unit employed at Newport Workshops in Melbourne. Chris Walters

The remaining Pacific National-owned Y Class locomotives are used mostly for both broad- and standard-gauge shunting and transfer duties around Melbourne, although a few still operate in rural locations (Y151 was at one point based at Bandiana, near Wodonga, while another is normally allocated to Portland despite the lack of rail traffic to the centre throughout 2008). The recent general traffic downturn in Victoria has perhaps hit this class the hardest, as there are few jobs appropriate to their low power. A number of other Y Class—still owned by the Victorian Department of Infrastructure—are held in Pacific National care at South Dynon Workshops, although most of these have not operated in well over a decade.

Several other examples are also in service, including four used by V/Line Passenger (three at Southern Cross and one at Geelong), one by BlueScope (Long Island), two by Downer-EDI Rail (one at Newport and one at Cardiff) and two by El Zorro.

Above: BlueScope Steel's Y148 undergoing servicing at South Dynon on Tuesday 5 August 2008. This unit is normally based at the Long Island Steelworks at Westernport. Bernie Baker

Road #	Builder's #	Built	Owner	Status	Name/Note
Y102	63-292	1963	Victorian DOI	Stored at Dynon (1600 mm)	-
Y104	63-294	1963	Victorian DOI	Stored at Dynon (1600 mm)	-
Y108	63-298	1963	Victorian DOI	Stored at Dynon (1600 mm)	-
Y109	63-299	1963	El Zorro	In 1600 mm service as Y145	-
Y110	63-300	1963	Victorian DOI	Stored at Dynon (1600 mm)	-
Y113	63-303	1963	Victorian DOI	Stored at Dynon (1600 mm)	-
Y115	63-305	1963	PN	In 1435 mm PN service	-
Y118	63-308	1963	PN	In 1600 mm PN service	-
Y119	63-309	1963	PN	In 1600 mm PN service	-
Y121	63-311	1964	PN	In 1600 mm PN service	-
Y122	63-312	1964	PN	Stored at Dynon (1435 mm)	-
Y124	63-314	1964	PN	In 1435 mm service—Dynon	-
Y125	63-315	1964	Victorian DOI	Stored at Dynon (1600 mm)	-
Y129	65-395	1965	VLP	In 1600 mm service	-
Y130	65-396	1965	Victorian DOI	Stored at Dynon (1600 mm)	-
Y134	65-400	1965	EDI Cardiff	In 1435 mm service	*Yoda*
Y136	65-402	1965	EDI Newport	In 1600 mm service	*James W Ryan*
Y138	65-404	1965	Victorian DOI	Stored at Dynon (1600 mm)	-
Y142	65-408	1965	PN	In 1600 mm service—Dynon	-

(continued)

Road #	Builder's #	Built	Owner	Status	Name/Note
Y143	65-409	1965	Victorian DOI	Stored at Dynon (1600 mm)	-
Y147	65-413	1965	PN	In 1600 mm PN service (Dynon)	-
Y148	65-414	1965	BlueScope	In 1600 mm service (Long Island)	-
Y150	65-416	1965	PN	Stored at Dynon (1600 mm)	-
Y151	67-571	1967	PN	In 1435 mm PN service	-
Y152	67-572	1967	PN	In 1435 mm PN service	DOO
Y156	67-576	1968	VLP	In 1600 mm service	-
Y157	67-577	1968	PN	In 1600 mm service—Dynon	-
Y161	67-581	1968	VLP	In 1600 mm service	-
Y163	67-583	1968	VLP	In 1600 mm service	-
Y165	67-585	1968	PN	In 1600 mm PN service	DOO
Y168	67-588	1968	El Zorro	In 1600 mm EZ service	-
Y169	67-589	1968	PN	In 1435 mm PN service	-
Y171	67-591	1968	PN	In 1600 mm PN service	-
Y174	67-594	1968	PN	In 1600 mm PN service	-

Above: During the 1996–1997 period (immediately prior to the privatisation of V/Line Freight) Y152—eventually followed by Y165—was modified for driver-only operation (DOO). The most obvious element to the modification was the installation of additional windows (although Y152 initially received only one) cut into the face of the cab. This was intended to widen the field of visibility from the point of view of the driver's position. No further Y Class were so treated by either V/Line Freight or Freight Australia, however more recently V/Line Passenger has modified at least one of its four units (Y163) with an additional window, applied in the manner of that initially done to Y152. Here we see Y165, sporting retrofitted full-length handrails along the hood, at South Dynon on Monday 2 January 2006. Bernie Baker

Newly-repainted 80s6 at
RTS Dynon on Tuesday
19 August 2008. Stephen Karas

C636R

Builder:	*Comeng-MLW (Bassendean)*	Model:	*C636R*
Type:	*Co-Co diesel-electric*	Engine:	*ALCo 251F turbo-charged 4-stroke V16*
Traction power:	*2680 kW (3600 hp)*	Length:	*19.71 m*
Weight:	*189.6 tonnes*	Gauge:	*1435 mm*

Above: DR8401 *Jean* (ex-Robe 9426) at East Turner River bridge on a work train involved in the construction of the FMG Line on Sunday 13 July 2008. Peter Clark

These six locomotives represent a larger fleet of Comeng-refurbished 636-type ALCo and MLW units that once dominated the operations of Hamersley Iron, for the decade leading on from the mid-1980s. Four are in fact formerly of Hamersley Iron (via a long period of dismantled storage in Maddington, Perth) while the remaining pair are similar units previously employed by Robe River/Pilbara Iron. The six are owned now by GTSA Engineering (part of Coote Industrial), who provided the initial four for service with the contractors responsible for the construction of the Fortescue Metals Group railway running inland from Port Hedland. Although initially commissioned for railway construction duties the re-entry into service of two additional Maddington units during late 2008 suggests that the extreme demand for Pilbara iron might result in an even bigger C636R comeback.

Road #	Original #	Builder's #	Rebuilt	Owner	Status	Name
DR8401	9426	WA143-01	1986	Coote Industrial	In service	*Jean*
DR8402	3007	WA-135-C-6011-02	1985	Coote Industrial	In service	*Margaret*
DR8403	9427	WA143-02	1986	Coote Industrial	In service	*Rachael*
DR8404	3013	WA-135-C-6040-01	1984	Coote Industrial	In service	*Vera*
DR8405	3011	WA-135-C-6014-04	1984	Coote Industrial	pending	-
DR8406	3008	WA-135-C-6014-01	1984	Coote Industrial	pending	-

N/NA/NB Class

Builder:	*Comeng-MLW (Bassendean)*	Model:	*CE618*
Type:	*Co-Co diesel-electric*	Engine:	*ALCo 251E turbo-charged 4-stroke V12*
Traction power:	*1790 kW (2400 hp)*	Length:	*17.09 m*
Weight:	*103.0 tonnes*	Gauge:	*1435 mm*

Above: 1872 leads 44s1 on No. 4117 Down container train at Two Wells on Wednesday 30 May 2007. Greg O'Brien

Three of the former Westrail N/NA/NB Class locomotives continue on in service well over a decade after the last of the remaining eight were scrapped in their 'native' Western Australia. All three have changed ownership in recent years at least once: NA1874 from Austrac to South Spur Rail (which itself was purchased by Coote Industrial) with the two former NB Class units 1872 and 1873 passing from Austrac to Junee Railway Workshops and then finally to Patrick PortLink, for service in South Australia in 2004. Following a period of service in Western Australia (where it was an ALCo orphan in an otherwise all English Electric South Spur fleet), NA1874 became attached to ballast and infrastructure contract services working east across the Nullarbor. As a consequence the three have become based in South Australia in more recent times: 1872 and 1873 being the primary power for PortLink's container services between Adelaide and Bowmans/Port Pirie, and 1874 (it no longer actually carries the 'NA' classification) on the aforementioned South Spur ballast trains, working under contract to Australian Rail Track Corporation. As an aside, the weight listed in the table above is 'as built' for the Westrail narrow-gauge operation, however 1872 and 1873 were converted to standard-gauge utilising Comeng M636 bogies, and thus would be somewhat heavier than the listed 103.0 tonnes.

Road #	Original #	Builder's #	Built	Owner	Status
1872	N1872	C-6099-02	1977	Patrick PortLink	In service
1873	N1873	C-6099-03	1977	Patrick PortLink	In service
(NA)1874	N1874	C-6099-04	1977	Coote Industrial	In service

80 Class

Builder:	*Comeng-MLW (Granville)*	Model:	*CE615*
Type:	*Co-Co diesel-electric*	Engine:	*ALCo 251CE turbo-charged 4-stroke V12*
Traction power:	*1490 kW (2000 hp)*	Length:	*17.73 m*
Weight:	*120.8 tonnes*	Gauge:	*1435 mm*

Above: 8050 shunts the Mungo Scott Siding at Lewisham (on the Rozelle Line) on Monday 18 February 2008. Jim Bruce

Once frontline power with the State Rail Authority of NSW and then FreightCorp, the 80 Class today plays a reduced role in the transport of freight with the remaining members of the once fifty-member fleet split between Pacific National and Coote Industrial. Of those that have survived, many have been in storage for a number of years, with the remainder used on container, trip freight and fuel trains in NSW with occasional wanderings into Victoria and South Australia on ballast specials. A handful of the Pacific National units are used as shunters as far afield as Adelaide, Perth and Brisbane, proving that while they may not operate in the numbers they once did, nor on the high priority services they once worked, the 80 Class continue to lead an intriguing life.

Road #	Original #	Builder's #	Built	Owner	Status
8003	8003	C-6106-03	1978	Pacific National	In service
8004	8004	C-6106-04	1979	Pacific National	In service
8005	8005	C-6106-05	1979	Pacific National	In service
8006	8006	C-6106-06	1979	Coote Industrial	Stored Werris Creek
8007	8007	C-6106-07	1979	Pacific National	In service

(continued)

Road #	Original #	Builder's #	Built	Owner	Status
8008	8008	C-6106-08	1979	Coote Industrial	Stored Broken Hill
8010	8010	C-6106-10	1979	Coote Industrial	Stored Broken Hill
8011	8011	C-6106-11	1979	Pacific National	Stored Delec
8012	8012	C-6106-12	1979	Pacific National	Stored Werris Creek
8013	8013	C-6106-13	1979	Pacific National	Stored Delec
8014	8014	C-6106-14	1979	Coote Industrial	Stored Werris Creek
8015	8015	C-6106-15	1979	Pacific National	In service
8016	8016	C-6106-16	1979	Coote Industrial	Stored Broken Hill
8017	8017	C-6106-17	1979	Pacific National	Stored Chullora
8018	8018	C-6106-18	1979	Coote Industrial	Stored Broken Hill
8019	8019	C-6106-19	1979	Coote Industrial	Stored Broken Hill
8021	8021	C-6106-21	1979	Coote Industrial	Stored Parkes
8022	8022	C-6106-22	1979	Coote Industrial	Stored Werris Creek
8023	8023	C-6106-23	1980	Coote Industrial	Stored Parkes
8024	8024	C-6106-24	1980	Coote Industrial	Stored Broken Hill
8025	8025	C-6106-25	1980	Pacific National	Stored Delec
80s1	8026	C-6106-26	1980	Coote Industrial	In service
8027	8027	C-6106-27	1980	Pacific National	In service
8028	8028	C-6106-28	1980	Coote Industrial	Stored Werris Creek
8030	8030	C-6106-30	1980	Coote Industrial	Stored Chullora
8031	8031	C-6121-01	1981	Pacific National	Stored Werris Creek
8032	8032	C-6121-02	1981	Pacific National	Stored Enfield
8033	8033	C-6121-03	1981	Pacific National	In service
8034	8034	C-6121-04	1982	Coote Industrial	Stored Werris Creek
8035	8035	C-6121-05	1982	Pacific National	Stored Enfield
8036	8036	C-6121-06	1982	Coote Industrial	Stored Islington
80s4	8037	C-6121-07	1982	Coote Industrial	In service
8038	8038	C-6121-08	1982	Coote Industrial	Stored Parkes
8039	8039	C-6121-09	1982	Pacific National	In service
8040	8040	C-6121-10	1982	Pacific National	In service
8041	8041	C-6121-11	1982	Coote Industrial	Stored Broken Hill
8042	8042	C-6121-12	1982	Pacific National	Stored Werris Creek
8043	8043	C-6121-13	1982	Coote Industrial	Stored Broken Hill
80s2	8044	C-6121-14	1982	Coote Industrial	In service
8045	8045	C-6121-15	1982	Pacific National	In service
8046	8046	C-6121-16	1982	Pacific National	In service
8047	8047	C-6121-17	1983	Pacific National	Stored Enfield
8048	8048	C-6121-18	1982	Coote Industrial	Stored Broken Hill
80s6	8049	C-6121-19	1983	Coote Industrial	In service
8050	8050	C-6121-20	1983	Pacific National	In service

ALCO

700 Class

Builder:	*Goodwin-ALCo (Sydney)*	Model:	*DL500G*
Type:	*Co-Co diesel-electric*	Engine:	*ALCo 251C turbo-charged 4-stroke V12*
Traction power:	*1490 kW (2000 hp)*	Length:	*17.41 m*
Weight:	*112.0 tonnes*	Gauge:	*1435 and 1600 mm*

Above: 704 leads 843 with No. 7E52, the broad-gauge Penrice stone train, at Osborne on Saturday 10 February 2007. Andrew Rosenbauer

Now owned by Genesee Wyoming Australia, the remaining members of the former South Australian Railways/Australian National 700 Class—unlike many similar locomotives around the country—have not strayed far from those regions in which they were common during their 'glory' days. Broad gauge 704 can normally be found working the Penrice stone train (in tandem with one or two of the three remaining broad gauge 830 Class units) while the operational standard gauge units are often used on grain services or shunting duties.

Road #	Original #	Builder's #	Built	Owner	Status
701	701	G-6042-02	1971	GWA	In 1435 mm service
703	703	G-6059-01	1971	GWA	Overhaul (1435 mm)
704	704	G-6059-02	1972	GWA	In 1600 mm service
705	705	G-6059-03	1972	GWA	In 1435 mm service
706	700	G-6042-01	1971	GWA	Stored (1600 mm)

442 Class

Builder:	*Goodwin-ALCo (Sydney)*	Model:	*DL500G*
Type:	*Co-Co diesel-electric*	Engine:	*ALCo 251C turbo-charged 4-stroke V12*
Traction power:	*1490 kW (2000 hp)*	Length:	*17.41 m*
Weight:	*114.8 tonnes*	Gauge:	*1435 mm*

Above: CFCLA's 44204 leads a loaded concrete sleeper train at Inverleigh (west of Geelong) on Thursday 23 August 2007. 44206 (also owned by CFCLA) is in a green and yellow version of this livery (after having—for a very brief time—worn the Freight Australia scheme). Ewan McLean

The remaining members of the once forty-strong 442 Class are now split between CFCLA and Coote Industrial. CFCLA's four (once known as the JL Class, but now 442s once more) are part of the company's lease fleet while the Coote Industrial units divide their time between the operator's own freight services and Australian Rail Track Corporation infrastructure duties, such as ballast and rail set trains. Generally all operate within NSW, however visits to both South Australian and Victoria are not uncommon.

Road #	Original #	Builder's #	Built	Owner	Status
442s4	44202	G-6045-02	1971	Coote Industrial	In service
442s3	44203	G-6045-03	1971	Coote Industrial	In service
44204	44204	G-6045-04	1971	CFCLA	In service
44206	44206	G-6045-06	1971	CFCLA	In service
44208	44208	G-6045-08	1971	CFCLA	In service
44209	44209	G-6045-09	1971	CFCLA	In service
442s2	44217	G-6045-17	1972	Coote Industrial	In service
442s1	44220	G-6045-20	1972	Coote Industrial	In service
442s5	44223	G-6045-23	1972	Coote Industrial	In service
442s6	44226	G-6045-26	1972	Coote Industrial	In service

600 Class

Builder:	*Goodwin-ALCo (Sydney)*	Model:	*DL541*
Type:	*Co-Co diesel-electric*	Engine:	*ALCo 251C turbo-charged 4-stroke V12*
Traction power:	*1340 kW (1800 hp)*	Length:	*16.62 m*
Weight:	*112.9 tonnes*	Gauge:	*1435 mm*

Above: 602 idles away at the head of a works train at Chullora on Saturday 8 July 2006. All three remaining members of the 600 Class still wear faded versions of the old Australian National livery. Bernie Baker

Based upon the NSWGR 45 Class (see next page) originally seven 600 Class locomotives were built for the South Australian Railways (SAR) for standard gauge work between Broken Hill and Port Pirie, and in 1978 they passed into the ownership of Australian National (as did the entire SAR fleet). In 1994 four of the class were rebuilt by Morrison Knudsen Australia as engine-less tractive effort booster units (see page 192) while the remaining trio soldiered on in grain and general freight service. Initially they were retained by Australia Southern Railroad (later part of the Australian Railroad Group or ARG) following the sale in Australian National in 1997, however in early 2005 the units were sold to South Spur and transferred to NSW (although at least one had already been transferred for ARG Manildra work by then). Now in Coote Industrial ownership, the trio juggle container and trip train rosters with infrastructure work, and they spent a great deal of 2008 based on the NSW Main South working sleeper trains as part of Australian Rail Track Corporation upgrading projects. It was surprisingly common to find all three on a single train together during this period.

Road #	Original #	Builder's #	Built	Owner	Status
602	602	G-6015-01	1969	Coote Industrial	In service
603	603	G-6015-02	1969	Coote Industrial	In service
607	600	G-3419-01	1965	Coote Industrial	In service

45 Class

Builder:	*Goodwin-ALCo (Sydney)*	Model:	*DL541*
Type:	*Co-Co diesel-electric*	Engine:	*ALCo 251C turbo-charged 4-stroke V12*
Traction power:	*1340 kW (1800 hp)*	Length:	*16.62 m*
Weight:	*112.9 tonnes*	Gauge:	*1435 mm*

Above: 45s1 at Goulburn on Tuesday 3 July 2007. Phil Martin

This group are survivors of a 1962-vintage, forty-member fleet, most of which were disposed of and scrapped during 1995. The remaining 45 Class units are now split between Patrick Portlink (three units), Coote Industrial (one), JRW (one) and CFCLA (two), although of these only two or three are actually in operation as of late 2008. Two of these are 103 (the modified, former 4537) and 4514, with Coote Industrial's 45s1 sidelined awaiting repairs at press time. Most of the others are stored pending a possible recommissioning, or stripping for parts. 103 is normally based in Adelaide for container train service, while 4514 is based in Sydney for similar duties. JRW retains 3505, which is stored with a 'Pilbara' style cab, but it has never operated in this form (see next page).

Road #	Original #	Builder's #	Built	Owner	Status
4502	4502	84144	1962	CFCLA	Stored Broken Hill
4503	4503	84145	1962	Patrick PortLink	Stored Lithgow
3505	4505	84147	1962	JRW	Stored Junee
4514	4514	84156	1962	Patrick PortLink	In service
4528	4528	84170	1963	CFCLA	Stored Broken Hill
45s1	4532 (3532)	84174	1963	Coote Industrial	Stored Broken Hill
103	4537	84179	1963	Patrick PortLink	In service

Above: For lease service with BHP Port Kembla, Austrac modified 4537 with a lowered short hood prior to despatching the unit (as 103) from Junee in 1995. In 2001 the locomotive was returned from lease, however Austrac collapsed and the assets passed to JRW, who eventually sold 103 and 4503 (see here together at Botany on Monday 5 February 2007) to Patrick PortLink. 4503 is now stored defective at Lithgow and 103 is based in Adelaide. Bernie Baker

Below: Another, more elaborate cab rebuild undertaken by Austrac was that applied to 3505 during 1997. Based on the 'Pilbara' cab first used by Comeng, and then Goninan, the version on 3505 was eventually deemed a failure. 3505 now remains stored at Junee, as seen here on Saturday 3 July 2004. Chris Walters

44 Class

Builder:	*Goodwin-ALCo (Sydney)*	Model:	*DL500B*
Type:	*Co-Co diesel-electric*	Engine:	*ALCo 251B turbo-charged 4-stroke V12*
Traction power:	*1340 kW (1800 hp)*	Length:	*17.02 m*
Weight:	*114.4 tonnes*	Gauge:	*1435 mm*

Above: 4477 leads 607 and Cs4 on No. 1441 Silverton container train at Warnervale on Wednesday 12 April 2006. Stephen Carr

Numbering 100, and delivered to the NSW Government Railways between 1957 and 1968, the 44 Class were once the backbone of NSW main line freight and passenger train operations. Although quite a few remain in preservation (with some of these having operated on long-term lease to freight haulers) CFCLA's four-unit 44 Class fleet represent the only examples of the class owned by a commercial operator. These four have changed hands numerous times: initially all four passed from the State Rail Authority of NSW to Great Northern Rail, however from there 4471 and 4477 were sold to Silverton Rail (as 44s2 and 44s3 respectively) with 4468 and 4483 eventually passing to CFCLA. Ultimately, the four were reunited when 44s2 and 44s3 were acquired by CFCLA also (44s1, aka 961, was also acquired by the lease company at this time—see page 120).

Eventually all four were recommissioned by CFCLA, however both 4468 and 4483 have since fallen by the way side, and are now stored at Lithgow. Meanwhile, both 4471 and 4477 continue on in service, often on hire to QRNatonal or Patrick PortLink.

Road #	Builder's #	Built	Owner	Status	Name
4468	G-3421-08	1966	CFCLA	Stored Lithgow	-
4471	G-3421-11	1966	CFCLA	In CFCLA service	-
4477	G-3421-17	1966	CFCLA	In CFCLA service	*Dave Jones*
4483	G-3421-23	1967	CFCLA	Stored Lithgow	-

930 Class

Builder:	*Goodwin-ALCo (Sydney)*	Model:	*DL500B*
Type:	*Co-Co diesel-electric*	Engine:	*ALCo 251B turbo-charged 4-stroke V12*
Traction power:	*1190 kW (1600 hp)*	Length:	*17.02 m*
Weight:	*105.9 tonnes*	Gauge:	*1435 mm*

Above: 44s1 leads 1872 and 1873 north on No. 7117 Balco container train at Rocky River (near Crystal Brook) on Saturday 16 June 2007. Greg O'Brien

Although a number of others are preserved, 961 is the only surviving member of the once 37-member SAR 930 Class in commercial hands. Class leader 930 appeared in 1955, and it and the ensuing five examples were single-ended variants of the World Series line developed by ALCo (although in this case, built by Goodwin). Subsequent deliveries were equipped with cabs at both ends, and 961 itself was one of the last of the order. Initially all were broad-gauge locomotives, however with the Australian National (AN) era came an increasing sphere of operation, and a number migrated to standard-gauge duties. During 1994, 961 was allotted to AN's short-lived *Explorer* passenger train venture (during which, it gained the unique blue and yellow livery it still wears), however this train operated very rarely. By the time of the AN South Australia Freight sale in 1997, 961 was the only member of the class still active on the roster, and so it passed to Australia Southern Railroad. The new operator retained the locomotive for a time, although used it only infrequently, before it was sold on to Silverton Rail, who renumbered it 44s1 and deployed on Broken Hill ore shunts. As a result of an asset disposal effort in 2004, CFCLA picked up a number of unwanted Silverton Rail locomotives including 44s1 (which CFCLA now records as 961). Intermittent service back in South Australia followed, before the unit was based in Islington Workshops as a local shunter. It remains there today.

Road #	Original #	Builder's #	Built	Owner	Status
44s1	961	G-3388-04	1965	CFCLA	In service (Islington)

830/DA/900 Class

Builder:	*Goodwin-ALCo (Sydney)*	Model:	*DL531*
Type:	*Co-Co diesel-electric*	Engine:	*ALCo 251B turbo-charged 4-stroke 6-cyl*
Traction power:	*670–710 kW (900–950 hp)*	Length:	*13.49 m*
Weight:	*70.0–71.5 tonnes*	Gauge:	*1067 and 1435 mm*

Above: 846 and 847 with an ARG/Manildra contract grain 'feeder' train on the Warren Branch (western NSW) during early 2004. Bernie Baker

Forty-five 830 Class units was the original SAR total, although this 'grew' by one with acquisition of a near-identical Silverton Tramway Company unit (see page 129). By the AN era, the class had been employed already on all three SAR gauges (1067, 1435 and 1600 mm), but with the change of ownership came a change of environment as twenty were gradually transferred to Tasmania, as the former TGR system was now part of the greater AN sphere of operation. These were not a great success and seven eventually returned to the mainland, and the others scrapped. Two of those that returned had been sold to Silverton in 1990, and thus began the era of 830 Class in private ownership. In 1997 most of the class passed to ASR (later part of ARG), however, three were sold on to ATN Access in 2000. The split up of ARG in 2006 saw 852 pass to QR/ARG and the remainder to GWA. By this time, a number had been converted for driver-only operations by AN, and these were known initially as the DA Class, but were later reclassified as the 900 Class under GWA (although two operated for a time with ARG in WA as the T Class). The class is still spread across three gauges, and are most common in South Australia, and yet despite this, keeping track of them is truly a challenge. 830 Class units are known to have operated in all states and territories with the exceptions only of Queensland and the ACT. Unfortunately, GWA unit 844 was recently damaged in a collision at Whyalla.

Road #	Original #	Builder's #	Built	Owner	Status
904	830 (875/DA5)	83721	1959	GWA	In 1067 mm service
831	831	83722	1960	GWA	In 1600 mm service
902	832 (DA2)	83723	1960	GWA	In 1067 mm service
833	833	83724	1960	PN	Stored Cootamundra (1435 mm)
905	836/DA6	83727	1960	GWA	In 1067 mm service
838	838	83729	1960	PN	Stored Junee (1435 mm)
903	839/DA4	83730	1960	GWA	In 1067 mm service
841	841	84139	1962	GWA	In 1600 mm service
842	842	84140	1962	GWA	Stored Port Lincoln (1067 mm)
843	843	84141	1962	GWA	In 1600 mm service
844	844	84142	1962	GWA	Stored (damaged—1067 mm)
845	845	84714	1963	PN	Stored Dynon (1435 mm)
846	846	84715	1963	GWA	In 1067 mm service
847	847	G-6016-01	1969	GWA	In 1067 mm service
848	848	G-6016-02	1969	GWA	In 1435 mm service
901	849/DA1/T02	G-6016-03	1969	GWA	In 1435 mm service
850	850	84136	1962	GWA	Stored Port Lincoln (1067 mm)
851	851	84137	1962	GWA	In 1067 mm service
852	852	84716	1963	ARG	Stored Junee (1435 mm)
48s31	857	84703	1963	Coote Ind	In 1435 mm service as 48s31
859	859	84705	1963	GWA	In 1067 mm service
Named *City of Port Lincoln*.					
863	863	84709	1963	GWA	Stored Port Augusta (1435 mm)
48s30	864	84710	1963	Coote Ind	In 1435 mm service as 48s30
865	865	84711	1963	GWA	Stored Port Lincoln (1067 mm)
869	869	G-6016-05	1970	Coote Ind	In 1435 mm service
871	871	G-3422-01	1966	GWA	Stored Port Lincoln (1067 mm)
872	872	G-3422-02	1966	Coote Ind	In 1435 mm service
873	873	G-3422-03	1966	GWA	In 1067 mm service

Above: 902 leads 831, 904 and 843 through Largs North with the Penrice stone train to Osborne on Thursday 19 October 2007. Bob Grant

48 Class

Builder:	*Goodwin-ALCo (Sydney)*	Model:	*DL531*
Type:	*Co-Co diesel-electric*	Engine:	*ALCo 251B turbo-charged 4-stroke 6-cylinder*
Traction power:	*670–710 kW (900–950 hp)*	Length:	*13.49 m*
Weight:	*73.8–77.8 tonnes*	Gauge:	*1067 and 1435 mm*

Above: 48125 at Delec (Sydney) on Saturday 9 August 2008. Adrian Compton

Once numbering 165 units, and delivered between 1959 and 1970, the 48 Class was once the most numerous class of diesel locomotive in the country. Add in the nearly identical 830 Class and Silverton Tramway DL531 units that followed, and the total clears 200! Although a small number had been withdrawn prior, 1994 was the year in which examples began to be culled from service en masse. Most of those withdrawn were from the Mk1 portion of the class (4801–4845), although after disposal, many of these were recommissioned by private operators. The bulk of the remainder passed to Pacific National (PN) in 2002 (including seven converted to PL Class units 1999–2002 for metropolitan PortLink services), although drought-reduced grain yields subsequently saw many of PN's units placed in storage. While PN's 48 Class fleet is still the largest remnant of the class in traffic, many more are now in the service of operators such as JRW, RailCorp, Coote Industrial and Genesee Wyoming Australia. What might lie ahead for these branch line units is difficult to predict, although one possible outcome is best evidenced by the heavy rebuild being applied to Mk1 unit 4820 by JRW at Junee. With so many of the class now lying in storage, an elaborate rebuild program might well be the way of the future.

Road #	Original #	Builder's #	Built	Owner	Status
4806	4806	83706	1959	Pacific National	Stored Delec
4809	4809	83709	1959	Coote Industrial	Stored Parkes
48s36	4811	83711	1959	Coote Industrial	In service
CAR1	4812	83712	1960	JRW	Stored Junee
906	4813 (DA7)	83713	1960	GWA	In 1067 mm service
4814	4814	83714	1960	JRW	In service

(continued)

Road #	Original #	Builder's #	Built	Owner	Status
48s34	4815	83715	1960	Coote Industrial	In service
4816	4816	83716	1960	JRW	In service
4818	4818	83718	1960	Pacific National	Stored Werris Creek
4819	4819	83719	1960	RailCorp	In service
unknown	4820	83720	1960	JRW	Undergoing remanufacture
48s32	4825	83820	1961	Coote Industrial	In service
4827	4827	83822	1961	RailCorp	In service
4828	4828	83823	1961	Coote Industrial	Stored Broken Hill
48s33	4829	83824	1961	Coote Industrial	In service
4832	4832	84122	1961	CFCLA	Stored Islington
4834	4834	84124	1961	CFCLA	Stored Islington
4836	4836	84126	1961	JRW	In service
4837	4837	84127	1961	Coote Industrial	Stored Broken Hill
48s37	4838	84128	1961	Coote Industrial	In service
4841	4841	84131	1962	Coote Industrial	Stored Parkes
4842	4842	84132	1962	Coote Industrial	Stored Broken Hill
48s35	4843	84133	1962	Coote Industrial	In service
4846	4846	G-3387-01	1964	Pacific National	Stored Port Augusta
PL1	4848	G-3387-03	1964	Pacific National	In service
4849	4849	G-3387-04	1964	Pacific National	Stored Werris Creek
4850	4850	G-3387-05	1964	Pacific National	In service
4851	4851	G-3387-06	1964	Pacific National	In service
4852	4852	G-3387-07	1964	Pacific National	Stored Lithgow
4853	4853	G-3387-08	1964	Pacific National	In service

Above: RailCorp's 4819 and 4837 (towing 8031, 8005 and a ballast plough) at Werai on Thursday 17 August 2000, bound for Goulburn. Chris Walters

(continued)

Road #	Original #	Builder's #	Built	Owner	Status
4854	4854	G-3387-09	1964	Pacific National	In service
4855	4855	G-3387-10	1964	Pacific National	Stored Enfield
PL7	4856	G-3387-11	1964	Pacific National	In service
4859	4859	G-3387-14	1964	Pacific National	Stored Port Augusta
4860	4860	G-3387-15	1964	Pacific National	Stored Werris Creek
4861	4861	G-3387-16	1964	Pacific National	Stored Enfield
4862	4862	G-3387-17	1964	Pacific National	Stored (unknown)
4864	4864	G-3387-19	1964	Pacific National	Stored Port Augusta
4865	4865	G-3387-20	1964	Pacific National	In service
4866	4866	G-3387-21	1965	Pacific National	Stored Werris Creek
PL6	4867	G-3387-22	1965	Pacific National	Stored Enfield
PL4	4868	G-3387-23	1965	Pacific National	Stored Enfield
4869	4869	G-3387-24	1965	Pacific National	In service
PL3	4870	G-3387-25	1965	Pacific National	In service
PL2	4871	G-3387-26	1965	Pacific National	In service
4872	4872	G-3387-27	1965	Pacific National	Stored Port Augusta
4873	4873	G-3387-28	1965	Pacific National	Stored Werris Creek
4874	4874	G-3387-29	1965	Pacific National	Stored Werris Creek
4875	4875	G-3387-30	1965	Pacific National	Stored Werris Creek
4876	4876	G-3387-31	1965	Pacific National	In service
4877	4877	G-3387-32	1965	Pacific National	Stored Werris Creek
4878	4878	G-3387-33	1965	Pacific National	In service
4879	4879	G-3387-34	1965	Pacific National	Stored Enfield
4880	4880	G-3387-35	1965	Pacific National	Stored Enfield
PL5	4881	G-3387-36	1965	Pacific National	In service
4882	4882	G-3387-37	1965	Pacific National	Stored Werris Creek
4883	4883	G-3387-38	1965	Pacific National	Stored Enfield
4884	4884	G-3387-39	1965	Pacific National	Stored Port Augusta
4885	4885	G-3387-40	1965	Pacific National	Stored Werrsis Creek
4886	4886	G-3420-01	1966	Pacific National	In service
4887	4887	G-3420-02	1966	Pacific National	In service
4888	4888	G-3420-03	1966	Pacific National	In service
4889	4889	G-3420-04	1966	Pacific National	In service
4890	4890	G-3420-05	1966	Pacific National	In service
4891	4891	G-3420-06	1966	Pacific National	In service
4892	4892	G-3420-07	1966	Pacific National	In service
4893	4893	G-3420-08	1966	Pacific National	In service
4894	4894	G-3420-09	1966	Pacific National	In service
4896	4896	G-3420-11	1966	Pacific National	In service
4897	4897	G-3420-12	1966	Pacific National	In service
4898	4898	G-3420-13	1966	Pacific National	In service

Above: JRW's 4836 at Narrandera on Monday 5 March 2007. This scheme was originally conceived by Austrac in 1996. Ewan McLean

(continued)

Road #	Original #	Builder's #	Built	Owner	Status
4899	4899	G-3420-14	1966	Pacific National	In service
48100	48100	G-3420-15	1967	Pacific National	In service
48101	48101	G-3420-16	1967	Pacific National	In service
48102	48102	G-3420-17	1967	Pacific National	In service
48103	48103	G-3420-18	1967	Pacific National	In service
48104	48104	G-3420-19	1967	Pacific National	In service
48105	48105	G-3420-20	1967	Pacific National	In service
48106	48106	G-3420-21	1967	Pacific National	Stored Lithgow
48107	48107	G-3420-22	1967	Pacific National	Stored Chullora
48108	48108	G-3420-23	1967	Pacific National	In service
48109	48109	G-3420-24	1967	Pacific National	Stored Lithgow
48110	48110	G-3420-25	1967	Pacific National	In service
48111	48111	G-3420-26	1967	Pacific National	In service
48112	48112	G-3420-27	1967	Pacific National	Stored Chullora
48113	48113	G-3420-28	1967	Pacific National	In service
48114	48114	G-3420-29	1967	Pacific National	In service
48115	48115	G-3420-30	1967	Pacific National	In service
48116	48116	G-3420-31	1967	Pacific National	In service
48117	48117	G-3420-32	1967	Pacific National	In service
48118	48118	G-3420-33	1967	Pacific National	In service
48119	48119	G-3420-34	1967	Pacific National	In service
48120	48120	G-3420-35	1967	Pacific National	In service

(continued)

Road #	Original #	Builder's #	Built	Owner	Status
48121	48121	G-3420-36	1967	Pacific National	In service
48122	48122	G-3420-37	1968	Pacific National	In service
48123	48123	G-3420-38	1968	Pacific National	In service
48124	48124	G-3420-39	1968	Pacific National	In service
48125	48125	G-3420-40	1968	Pacific National	In service
48127	48127	G-6013-02	1969	Pacific National	In service
48128	48128	G-6013-03	1969	Pacific National	In service
48129	48129	G-6013-04	1969	Pacific National	In service
48130	48130	G-6013-05	1969	Pacific National	In service
48132	48132	G-6013-07	1969	Pacific National	In service
48134	48134	G-6013-09	1969	Pacific National	In service
48135	48135	G-6013-10	1969	Pacific National	In service
48136	48136	G-6013-11	1969	Pacific National	In service
48137	48137	G-6013-12	1969	Pacific National	In service
48138	48138	G-6013-13	1969	Pacific National	In service
48139	48139	G-6013-14	1969	Pacific National	In service
48140	48140	G-6013-15	1969	Pacific National	In service
48142	48142	G-6013-17	1969	Pacific National	In service
48143	48143	G-6013-18	1969	Pacific National	In service
48144	48144	G-6013-19	1969	Pacific National	In service
48145	48145	G-6013-20	1970	Pacific National	In service
48146	48146	G-6013-21	1970	Pacific National	In service
48147	48147	G-6013-22	1970	Pacific National	Stored Cardiff
48148	48148	G-6013-23	1970	Pacific National	In service
48149	48149	G-6013-24	1970	Pacific National	In service
48150	48150	G-6013-25	1970	Pacific National	In service
48151	48151	G-6013-26	1970	Pacific National	In service
48152	48152	G-6013-27	1970	Pacific National	In service
48153	48153	G-6013-28	1970	Pacific National	In service
48154	48154	G-6013-29	1970	Pacific National	In service
48155	48155	G-6013-30	1970	Pacific National	Stored Lithgow
48156	48156	G-6013-31	1970	Pacific National	In service
48157	48157	G-6013-32	1970	Pacific National	In service
48158	48158	G-6013-33	1970	Pacific National	In service
48159	48159	G-6013-34	1970	Pacific National	In service
48160	48160	G-6013-35	1970	Pacific National	In service
48161	48161	G-6013-36	1970	Pacific National	In service
48162	48162	G-6013-37	1970	Pacific National	In service
48163	48163	G-6013-38	1970	Pacific National	In service
48164	48164	G-6013-39	1970	Pacific National	In service
48165	48165	G-6013-40	1970	Pacific National	In service

Above: Modified PL5 (ex-4881) and 8234 shunt through Port Waratah on Sunday 17 July 2005. Chris Walters

Below: Coote Industrial's 48s33 (ex-Silverton, and before that, FreightCorp 4829) and JRW's 4816 (on hire) lead T461, an empty Pelton coal train, through Kearsley on Sunday 4 May 2008. Stephen Carr

Above: 48s35 (and 48s28) at Broken Hill in the early hours of Sunday 24 August 2008. Coote Industrial is presently repainting its locomotive fleet in the green and yellow livery displayed here. Bernie Baker

Below: En route from Cargill Australia at Kooragang Island, to new owners JRW at Junee, CAR1 (ex-4812) lays over at Botany on Thursday 19 April 2007. Bernie Baker

Silverton Tramway DL531

Builder:	*Goodwin-ALCo (Sydney)*	Model:	*DL531*
Type:	*Co-Co diesel-electric*	Engine:	*ALCo 251B turbo-charged 4-stroke 6-cylinder*
Traction power:	*670 kW (900 hp)*	Length:	*13.49 m*
Weight:	*73.8 tonnes*	Gauge:	*1435 mm*

Above: 907 (formerly STC 27 and later SAR/AN 874) leads CLF7 through Unanderra with an empty ARG grain train during May 2004. Chris Walters

Following on from the 830 and 48 Class was a small order for three similar units, filed with Goodwin by the Silverton Tramway Company based in western NSW. With a cross-border narrow-gauge line that linked Broken Hill with Cockburn, the company used the three units to dieselise its all-steam operation by 1961. The opening of the through standard-gauge line in 1970 rendered the Silverton link redundant and the company then focussed on standard-gauge shunting services within Broken Hill. This only required two units, and so 27 was sold to the SAR as 874. While 28 and 29 continued on in day-to-day service in Broken Hill, 874 eventually became part of the AN fleet in 1978, and with the sale of AN in 1997, it went into ASR/ARG ownership. In 2001 ARG chose to transfer the unit to WA, where it was given a DA Class-style rebuild and put into service with DA Class prototype DA1, with the pair based in Albany to haul woodchip shuttles as T01 and T02 respectively. They were not a success in this role, and so were sent back east (with T01 being renumbered 907) and were based in Whyalla as of mid-2008. Meanwhile, 28 and 29 passed into Coote Industrial ownership during 2007, while a derailment in early 2008 saw 48s28 (as it was by then known) leave Broken Hill for the first time, for repairs and a repaint in Adelaide's Islington Workshops.

Road #	Original #	Builder's #	Built	Owner	Status
907	27	83826	1960	GWA	In 1435 mm service
48s28	28	83827	1961	Coote Industrial	In 1435 mm service
48s29	29	83828	1961	Coote Industrial	In 1435 mm service

General
Electric

AC6000CW

Builder:	*GE USA*	Model:	*AC6000CW*
Type:	*Co-Co diesel-electric*	Engine:	*GE 7HDL turbo-charged 4-stroke V16*
Traction power:	*4470 kW (6000 hp)*	Length:	*23.17 m*
Weight:	*199.6 tonnes*	Gauge:	*1435 mm*

Above: 6077 at Bing on Sunday 22 July 2007. Chris Walters

This small fleet of eight locomotives represent the most powerful locomotives to ever run in Australia. Delivered during 1999, these eight 6000 hp locomotives were soon incorporated into BHP Iron Ore's mostly-General Electric fleet, used here and there in publicity runs to establish a number of world records. Since the arrival of secondhand EMD SD40R and SD40-2 locomotives during 2004, the AC6000CW units have been commonly paired with these older units, while the entire fleet has more recently been overhauled and re-engined with GEVO engines (similar to the previous HDL units) for continued service.

Road #	Builder's #	Built	Owner	Status	Name
6070	51062	1998	BHP-Billiton Iron Ore	In service	*Port Hedland*
6071	51063	1999	BHP-Billiton Iron Ore	In service	*Chichester*
6072	51064	1999	BHP-Billiton Iron Ore	In service	*Hesta*
6073	51065	1999	BHP-Billiton Iron Ore	In service	*Fortescue*
6074	51066	1999	BHP-Billiton Iron Ore	In service	*Kalgan*
6075	51067	1999	BHP-Billiton Iron Ore	In service	*Newman*
6076	51068	1999	BHP-Billiton Iron Ore	In service	*Mt Goldsworthy*
6077	51069	1999	BHP-Billiton Iron Ore	In service	*Nimingarra*

ES44DCi

Builder:	*GE USA*	Model:	*C44-9W*
Type:	*Co-Co diesel-electric*	Engine:	*GE 7FDL turbo-charged 4-stroke V16*
Traction power:	*3270 kW (4380 hp)*	Length:	*22.30 m*
Weight:	*196.9 tonnes*	Gauge:	*1435 mm*

Above: 8100 at Cape Lambert on Wednesday 2 April 2008. Stephen Karas

Rio Tinto's new ES44DCi GEVO locomotives are a response to soaring iron ore demand and a need to continually modernise the rail operation designed to move those tonnages. Initially ten were ordered with these being delivered in a single shipment during early 2008, however an additional thirty were already on General Electric's books at that time, and these were delivered before the end of 2008. In service, the ES44DCi units will operate side by side with the older C44-9W locomotives.

Road #	Builder's #	Built	Owner	Status
8100	57996	2007	Rio Tinto	In service
8101	57997	2007	Rio Tinto	In service
8102	57998	2007	Rio Tinto	In service
8103	57999	2007	Rio Tinto	In service
8104	58000	2007	Rio Tinto	In service
8105	58001	2007	Rio Tinto	In service
8106	58002	2007	Rio Tinto	In service

(continued)

Road #	Builder's #	Built	Owner	Status
8107	58003	2007	Rio Tinto	In service
8108	58004	2007	Rio Tinto	In service
8109	58005	2007	Rio Tinto	In service
8110	59102	2008	Rio Tinto	In service
8111	59103	2008	Rio Tinto	In service
8112	59104	2008	Rio Tinto	In service
8113	59105	2008	Rio Tinto	In service
8114	59106	2008	Rio Tinto	In service
8115	59107	2008	Rio Tinto	In service
8116	59108	2008	Rio Tinto	In service
8117	59109	2008	Rio Tinto	In service
8118	59110	2008	Rio Tinto	In service
8119	59111	2008	Rio Tinto	In service
8120	59112	2008	Rio Tinto	In service
8121	59113	2008	Rio Tinto	In service
8122	59114	2008	Rio Tinto	In service
8123	59115	2008	Rio Tinto	In service
8124	59116	2008	Rio Tinto	In service
8125	59117	2008	Rio Tinto	In service
8126	59118	2008	Rio Tinto	In service
8127	59119	2008	Rio Tinto	In service
8128	59120	2008	Rio Tinto	In service
8129	59121	2008	Rio Tinto	In service
8130	59122	2008	Rio Tinto	In service
8131	59123	2008	Rio Tinto	In service
8132	59124	2008	Rio Tinto	In service
8133	59125	2008	Rio Tinto	In service
8134	59126	2008	Rio Tinto	In service
8135	59127	2008	Rio Tinto	In service
8136	59128	2008	Rio Tinto	In service
8137	59129	2008	Rio Tinto	In service
8138	59130	2008	Rio Tinto	In service
8139	59131	2008	Rio Tinto	In service

Rio Tinto Dash 9-44CW

Builder:	*GE USA*	Model:	*Dash 9-44CW*
Type:	*Co-Co diesel-electric*	Engine:	*GE 7FDL turbo-charged 4-stroke V16*
Traction power:	*3270 kW (4380 hp)*	Length:	*22.30 m*
Weight:	*196.9 tonnes*	Gauge:	*1435 mm*

Above: 7046 and 7090 pass the Karratha Roadhouse with an inbound loaded iron ore train on Wednesday 25 July 2007. Chris Walters

Beginning in 1995 with 29 units of a single order for Hamersley Iron, through additional orders placed for Robe River, and the merged operations of first Pilbara Rail and then Pilbara Iron, the now-combined fleet of Rio Tinto Dash 9-44CW General Electric units are the most numerous locomotive type in the Pilbara iron ore industry with a total of 72 in service on both former Hamersley and Robe River systems. Although new ES44DCi GEVO units are now entering service (see page 133), the Dash-9s dominate iron ore trains between the mines and Cape Lambert (the Robe River export facility) and Seven Mile Yard (where loads are shuttled on to Dampier by older, less powerful C36-7M and CM40-8M locomotives).

Road #	Builder's #	Built	Owner	Status	Notes
7043	57094	2006	Rio Tinto	In service	-
7044	57095	2006	Rio Tinto	In service	-
7045	57096	2006	Rio Tinto	In service	-
7046	57097	2006	Rio Tinto	In service	-
7047	57098	2006	Rio Tinto	In service	-
7048	57099	2006	Rio Tinto	In service	-
7049	57100	2006	Rio Tinto	In service	-
7050	57101	2006	Rio Tinto	In service	-
7053	56154	2006	Rio Tinto	In service	-
7054	56155	2006	Rio Tinto	In service	-

(continued)

Road #	Builder's #	Built	Owner	Status	Notes
7055	55880	2005	Rio Tinto	In service	-
7056	55881	2005	Rio Tinto	In service	-
7057	55882	2005	Rio Tinto	In service	-
7058	55883	2005	Rio Tinto	In service	-
7059	55884	2005	Rio Tinto	In service	-
7060	55885	2005	Rio Tinto	In service	-
7061	54768	2004	Rio Tinto	In service	-
7062	54769	2004	Rio Tinto	In service	-
7063	54243	2003	Rio Tinto	In service	-
7064	54244	2003	Rio Tinto	In service	-
7065	47744	1994	Rio Tinto	In service	-
7066	47745	1994	Rio Tinto	In service	-
7067	47746	1994	Rio Tinto	In service	-
7068	47747	1994	Rio Tinto	In service	-
7069	47748	1994	Rio Tinto	In service	-
7070	47749	1994	Rio Tinto	In service	-
7071	47750	1994	Rio Tinto	In service	-
7072	47751	1994	Rio Tinto	In service	-
7073	47752	1994	Rio Tinto	In service	-
7074	47753	1994	Rio Tinto	In service	-
7075	47754	1994	Rio Tinto	In service	-
7076	47755	1994	Rio Tinto	In service	-
7077	47756	1994	Rio Tinto	In service	-
7078	47757	1994	Rio Tinto	In service	-
7079	47758	1994	Rio Tinto	In service	-
7080	47759	1994	Rio Tinto	In service	-
7081	47760	1994	Rio Tinto	In service	-
7082	47761	1994	Rio Tinto	In service	-
7083	47762	1994	Rio Tinto	In service	-
7084	47763	1994	Rio Tinto	In service	-
7085	47764	1994	Rio Tinto	In service	-
7086	47765	1994	Rio Tinto	In service	-
7087	47766	1994	Rio Tinto	In service	-
7088	47767	1994	Rio Tinto	In service	-
7089	47768	1994	Rio Tinto	In service	-
7090	47769	1994	Rio Tinto	In service	-
7091	47770	1994	Rio Tinto	In service	-
7092	47771	1994	Rio Tinto	In service	-
7093	47772	1994	Rio Tinto	In service	-
7094	52841	2001	Rio Tinto	In service	-

(continued)

Road #	Builder's #	Built	Owner	Status	Notes
7095	52842	2001	Rio Tinto	In service	-
7096	52843	2001	Rio Tinto	In service	-
7097	54160	2003	Rio Tinto	In service	Named *Ken Onley*.
7098	54161	2003	Rio Tinto	In service	-
9401	53455	2002	Rio Tinto	In service	Originally numbered 9470.
9402	53456	2002	Rio Tinto	In service	Originally numbered 9471.
9403	53457	2002	Rio Tinto	In service	Originally numbered 9472.
9404	54154	2003	Rio Tinto	In service	-
9405	54155	2003	Rio Tinto	In service	-
9406	54156	2003	Rio Tinto	In service	-
9407	54157	2003	Rio Tinto	In service	-
9408	54158	2003	Rio Tinto	In service	-
9409	54159	2003	Rio Tinto	In service	-
9428	54187	2003	Rio Tinto	In service	-
9429	54188	2003	Rio Tinto	In service	-
9430	54189	2003	Rio Tinto	In service	-
9431	54241	2003	Rio Tinto	In service	-
9432	54242	2003	Rio Tinto	In service	-
9433	54766	2004	Rio Tinto	In service	-
9434	54767	2004	Rio Tinto	In service	-
9435	57102	2006	Rio Tinto	In service	-
9436	57103	2006	Rio Tinto	In service	-

Above: 7047 and 7053 leave Seven Mile Yard behind with an empty iron ore train late in the afternoon of Wednesday 25 July 2007. Chris Walters

Fortescue Dash 9-44CW

Builder:	*GE USA*	Model:	*Dash 9-44CW*
Type:	*Co-Co diesel-electric*	Engine:	*GE 7FDL turbo-charged 4-stroke V16*
Traction power:	*3270 kW (4380 hp)*	Length:	*22.30 m*
Weight:	*196.9 tonnes*	Gauge:	*1435 mm*

Above: Fortescue's 010 at Boodarie on Wednesday 9 July 2008. Peter Clark

Following on from the Dash-9 fleet established by Hamersley Iron and Robe River (now merged as Rio Tinto) between 1995 and 2007 (see page 135), Pilbara newcomer, Fortescue Metals Group (FMG), were suitably impressed enough to also invest in the design. The 15 units actually ordered by FMG are believed to have been among the last production Dash-9 units constructed by General Electric in the US, and were delivered in late 2007 as one shipment. Initial operations were fairly low key due to the incomplete nature of FMG's railway, although front-end loaded ore trains began to run in early 2008.

Road #	Builder's #	Built	Owner	Status
001	58178	2007	Fortescue Metal Groups	In service
002	58179	2007	Fortescue Metal Groups	In service
003	58180	2007	Fortescue Metal Groups	In service
004	58181	2007	Fortescue Metal Groups	In service
005	58182	2007	Fortescue Metal Groups	In service
006	58183	2007	Fortescue Metal Groups	In service
007	58184	2007	Fortescue Metal Groups	In service
008	58185	2007	Fortescue Metal Groups	In service
009	58186	2007	Fortescue Metal Groups	In service
010	58187	2007	Fortescue Metal Groups	In service
011	58188	2007	Fortescue Metal Groups	In service
012	58189	2007	Fortescue Metal Groups	In service
013	58190	2007	Fortescue Metal Groups	In service
014	58191	2007	Fortescue Metal Groups	In service
015	58192	2007	Fortescue Metal Groups	In service

92 Class

Builder:	*UGR/GE (Broadmeadow)*	Model:	*C40aci*
Type:	*Co-Co diesel-electric*	Engine:	*GE 7FDL turbo-charged 4-stroke V16*
Traction power:	*3000 kW (4020 hp)*	Length:	*22.00 m*
Weight:	*176.0 tonnes*	Gauge:	*1435 mm*

Above: 9203 at UGR Broadmeadow on Friday 19 September 2008. Robert Rouse

Although designed for both fast intermodal freight and hauling heavy coal loads, Pacific National's new UGR/General Electric 92 Class locomotives appear more likely to work Hunter Valley coal trains as their primary task. The first main line tests for the class began on 24 August 2008 when 9201 made a number of load trials between Willow Tree and Ardglen, and within weeks of this, the class began to appear on coal services. A number of other operators, including CFCLA, have subsequently ordered very similar locomotives.

Road #	Builder's #	Built	Owner	Status
9201	unknown	2008	Pacific National	In service
9202	unknown	2008	Pacific National	In service
9203	unknown	2008	Pacific National	In service
9204	unknown	2008	Pacific National	In service
9205	unknown	2008	Pacific National	In service
9206	unknown	2008	Pacific National	In service
9207	unknown	2008	Pacific National	In service
9208	unknown	2008	Pacific National	In service
9209	unknown	2008	Pacific National	In service
9210	unknown	2008	Pacific National	In service
9211	unknown	2008	Pacific National	In service
9212	unknown	2008	Pacific National	In service
9213	unknown	2008	Pacific National	pending
9214	unknown	2008	Pacific National	pending
9215	unknown	2008	Pacific National	pending

5000 Class

Builder:	*UG/GE (Broadmeadow)*	Model:	*C40aci*
Type:	*Co-Co diesel-electric*	Engine:	*GE 7FDL turbo-charged 4-stroke V16*
Traction power:	*3000 kW (4020 hp)*	Length:	*22.00 m*
Weight:	*176.0 tonnes*	Gauge:	*1435 mm*

Above: 5002 and 5001 at Lochinvar on Sunday 17 July 2005. Chris Walters

These 12 AC-traction, United Goninan/General Electric locomotives (ordered in two batches of nine and three respectively) are the heaviest and most powerful locomotives employed on the Australian main line network (outside of the isolated Pilbara iron ore industry of Western Australia). Obtained as part of a QRNational push into the NSW Hunter Valley coal market, the first nine entered service from June 2005 hauling a fleet of new QHAH coal hoppers delivered only months earlier. Initially the QRNational coal trains served only the Mount Arthur coal loader, but other contracts soon emerged and eventually the 5000 Class could be seen as far away as Ulan. Such was the demand that three additional units were acquired during the first half of 2007.

Road #	Builder's #	Built	Owner	Status
5001	24000-06/05-345	2005	QRNational	In service
5002	24000-06/05-346	2005	QRNational	In service
5003	24000-06/05-347	2005	QRNational	In service
5004	24000-06/05-348	2005	QRNational	In service
5005	24000-06/05-349	2005	QRNational	In service
5006	24000-06/05-350	2005	QRNational	In service
5007	24000-08/05-351	2005	QRNational	In service
5008	24000-08/05-352	2005	QRNational	In service
5009	24000-08/05-353	2005	QRNational	In service
5010	25000-02/07-354	2007	QRNational	In service
5011	25000-02/07-355	2007	QRNational	In service
5012	25000-02/07-356	2007	QRNational	In service

NR Class

Builder:	*Goninan/GE (Broadmeadow) NR1–NR60* *Goninan/GE (Bassendean) NR61–NR120*	Model:	*Cv40-9i*
Type:	*Co-Co diesel-electric*	Engine:	*GE 7FDL turbo-charged 4-stroke V16*
Traction power:	*3000 kW (4020 hp)*	Length:	*22.00 m*
Weight:	*132.0 tonnes*	Gauge:	*1435 mm*

Above: NR84 *Southern Cross* in new *Southern Spirit* livery at Goulburn on Saturday 11 October 2008. NR85 is also in this scheme (both for working luxury passenger 'cruise' trains), while NR25, NR26, NR27 and NR28 are in a dark blue *Indian Pacific* livery (for the famous Sydney–Perth service) and NR74, NR75 and NR109 are in a red and silver colours, designed to promote *The Ghan* passenger train that operates between Adelaide and Alice Springs/Darwin. All of these listed services are operated by Pacific National client, Great Southern Rail. Leon Oberg

A truly interstate locomotive, the NR Class became National Rail's front line power following their introduction in late 1996/early 1997, with all 120 of these 1435 mm-gauge locomotives delivered by mid-1998. Although now part of the Pacific National fleet, their haulage task has changed little over the years with a particular emphasis on interstate intermodal freight services and steel trains. However, around the country NR Class are involved in a number of intrastate services while the class is also regular power on Great Southern Rails' *Indian Pacific*, *Overland*, *Ghan* and *Southern Spirit* passenger trains (with a number of units specially painted to work some of these services). Although the class has been unlucky enough to be involved in a number of collisions and derailments, only NR33 (involved in the Lismore, Victoria, level crossing collision of 25 May 2006) has been scrapped. NR3 was involved in a fatal accident near Robertson on 19 May 1998 and subsequently rebuilt as NR121.

Road #	Builder's #	Built	Owner	Status	Name
NR1	7250-10/96-203	1996	PN	In service	*City of Melbourne*
NR2	7250-11/96-204	1996	PN	In service	*Rawlinna*
NR4	7250-11/96-206	1996	PN	In service	*Hobson's Bay*
NR5	7250-12/96-207	1996	PN	In service	*Shire of Junee*
NR6	7250-12/96-208	1996	PN	In service	*City of Newcastle*
NR7	7250-12/96-209	1996	PN	In service	*City of Brisbane*
NR8	7250-01/97-210	1997	PN	In service	*City of Goulburn*
NR9	7250-01/97-211	1997	PN	In service	-
NR10	7250-01/97-212	1997	PN	In service	-
NR11	7250-02/97-213	1997	PN	In service	-
NR12	7250-02/97-214	1997	PN	In service	*Footscray*
NR13	7250-02/97-215	1997	PN	In service	-
NR14	7250-02/97-216	1997	PN	In service	-
NR15	7250-03/97-217	1997	PN	In service	*Meningie*
NR16	7250-03/97-218	1997	PN	In service	*Forrest*
NR17	7250-03/97-219	1997	PN	In service	*Bathurst*
NR18	7250-03/97-220	1997	PN	In service	-
NR19	7250-03/97-221	1997	PN	In service	*Maitland*
NR20	7250-04/97-222	1997	PN	In service	-
NR21	7250-04/97-223	1997	PN	In service	-
NR22	7250-04/97-224	1997	PN	In service	*Kalgoorlie*
NR23	7250-04/97-225	1997	PN	In service	-
NR24	7250-04/97-226	1997	PN	In service	*City of Wollongong*
NR25	7250-05/97-227	1997	PN	In service	-
NR26	7250-05/97-228	1997	PN	In service	*Named Hindmarsh*
NR27	7250-05/97-229	1997	PN	In service	-
NR28	7250-05/97-230	1997	PN	In service	*City of Port Augusta*
NR29	7250-05/97-231	1997	PN	In service	*Kwinana*
NR30	7250-05/97-232	1997	PN	In service	*Warmi*
NR31	7250-05/97-233	1997	PN	In service	-
NR32	7250-06/97-234	1997	PN	In service	-
NR34	7250-06/97-236	1997	PN	In service	*Boulder*
NR35	7250-06/97-237	1997	PN	In service	-
NR36	7250-06/97-238	1997	PN	In service	*City of Sydney*
NR37	7250-06/97-239	1997	PN	In service	*Impardna*
NR38	7250-07/97-240	1997	PN	In service	*Greater Geelong*
NR39	7250-07/97-241	1997	PN	In service	*Gladstone*
NR40	7250-07/97-242	1997	PN	In service	*City of Broken Hill*
NR41	7250-07/97-243	1997	PN	In service	*Tintinara*
NR42	7250-07/97-244	1997	PN	In service	-
NR43	7250-07/97-245	1997	PN	In service	-

(continued)

Road #	Builder's #	Built	Owner	Status	Name
NR44	7250-07/97-246	1997	PN	In service	-
NR45	7250-07/97-247	1997	PN	In service	-
NR46	7250-08/97-248	1997	PN	In service	-
NR47	7250-08/97-249	1997	PN	In service	*Fremantle*
NR48	7250-08/97-250	1997	PN	In service	*Northam*
NR49	7250-08/97-251	1997	PN	In service	*Coffs Harbour*
NR50	7250-08/97-252	1997	PN	In service	-
NR51	7250-08/97-253	1997	PN	In service	-
NR52	7250-09/97-254	1997	PN	In service	-
NR53	7250-09/97-255	1997	PN	In service	-
NR54	7250-09/97-256	1997	PN	In service	-
NR55	7250-09/97-257	1997	PN	In service	-
NR56	7250-09/97-258	1997	PN	In service	*Port Botany*
NR57	7250-09/97-259	1997	PN	In service	-
NR58	7250-09/97-260	1997	PN	In service	*City of Whyalla*
NR59	7250-09/97-261	1997	PN	In service	-
NR60	7250-10/97-262	1997	PN	In service	-
NR61	7250-11/96-263	1996	PN	In service	*La Trobe*
NR62	7250-11/96-264	1996	PN	In service	*Tarcoola*
NR63	7250-11/96-265	1996	PN	In service	-
NR64	7250-11/96-266	1996	PN	In service	*Zanthus*
NR65	7250-11/96-267	1996	PN	In service	*Horsham*
NR66	7250-12/96-268	1996	PN	In service	*Marrickville*
NR67	7250-12/96-269	1996	PN	In service	*Mulwala*
NR68	7250-12/96-270	1996	PN	In service	*Cook*
NR69	7250-12/96-271	1996	PN	In service	*Acacia Ridge*
NR70	7250-01/97-272	1996	PN	In service	-
NR71	7250-01/97-273	1996	PN	In service	*Barton*
NR72	7250-01/97-274	1996	PN	In service	-
NR73	7250-01/97-275	1996	PN	In service	*Maribyrnong*
NR74	7250-02/97-276	1997	PN	In service	*Port Pirie*
NR75	7250-02/97-277	1997	PN	In service	*Steve Irwin*
NR76	7250-02/97-278	1997	PN	In service	-
NR77	7250-02/97-279	1997	PN	In service	-
NR78	7250-02/97-280	1997	PN	In service	-
NR79	7250-03/97-281	1997	PN	In service	*Bassendean*
NR80	7250-03/97-282	1997	PN	In service	*City of Perth*
NR81	7250-03/97-283	1997	PN	In service	-
NR82	7250-03/97-284	1997	PN	In service	-

(continued)

Road #	Builder's #	Built	Owner	Status	Name
NR83	7250-03/97-285	1997	PN	In service	*Merredin*
NR84	7250-04/97-286	1997	PN	In service	*Southern Cross*
NR85	7250-04/97-287	1997	PN	In service	-
NR86	7250-04/97-288	1997	PN	In service	*Mount Barker*
NR87	7250-04/97-289	1997	PN	In service	*Loongana*
NR88	7250-05/97-290	1997	PN	In service	*Dimboola*
NR89	7250-05/97-292	1997	PN	In service	*Port Adelaide*
NR90	7250-05/97-293	1997	PN	In service	*Spotswood*
NR91	7250-05/97-294	1997	PN	In service	*Chullora*
NR92	7250-05/97-291	1997	PN	In service	*City of Bankstown*
NR93	7250-06/97-295	1997	PN	In service	-
NR94	7250-07/97-300	1997	PN	In service	*Belair*
NR95	7250-06/97-296	1997	PN	In service	-
NR96	7250-06/97-297	1997	PN	In service	-
NR97	7250-06/97-298	1997	PN	In service	*City of Parramatta*
NR98	7250-06/97-299	1997	PN	In service	-
NR99	7250-07/97-305	1997	PN	In service	-
NR100	7250-07/97-304	1997	PN	In service	-
NR101	7250-07/97-303	1997	PN	In service	*Crystal Book/Redhill*
NR102	7250-07/97-302	1997	PN	In service	*Wyndham*
NR103	7250-07/97-301	1997	PN	In service	*Pimba*
NR104	7250-08/97-309	1997	PN	In service	*Murray Bridge*
NR105	7250-08/97-310	1997	PN	In service	*Port Wakefield*
NR106	7250-08/97-308	1997	PN	In service	*Casino*
NR107	7250-08/97-307	1997	PN	In service	*Peterborough*
NR108	7250-08/97-306	1997	PN	In service	*Town of Alice*
NR109	7250-09/97-315	1997	PN	In service	*Sandfly II*
NR110	7250-10/97-316	1997	PN	In service	-
NR111	7250-09/97-314	1997	PN	In service	-
NR112	7250-09/97-313	1997	PN	In service	-
NR113	7250-09/97-312	1997	PN	In service	-
NR114	7250-09/97-311	1997	PN	In service	*Kulgera*
NR115	7250-11/97-322	1997	PN	In service	-
NR116	7250-11/97-321	1997	PN	In service	-
NR117	7250-10/97-320	1997	PN	In service	-
NR118	7250-10/97-319	1997	PN	In service	*Parkes*
NR119	7250-10/97-318	1997	PN	In service	*City of Belmont*
NR120	7250-10/97-317	1997	PN	In service	*Taree*
NR121	7250-11/96-205	2000	PN	In service	-

Rebuilt and renumbered from NR3 following May 1998 Robertson derailment.

Robe River CM40-8M

Builder:	*Goninan/GE (Bassendean)*	Model:	*CM40-8M*
Type:	*Co-Co diesel-electric*	Engine:	*GE 7FDL turbo-charged 4-stroke V16*
Traction power:	*2980 kW (4000 hp)*	Length:	*19.71–19.83 m*
Weight:	*195.0 tonnes*	Gauge:	*1435 mm*

Above: 9417 and 9425 climb upgrade off the causeway with a loaded iron ore train from Seven Mile bound for Dampier on Tuesday 24 July 2007. Chris Walters

These units (constructed using the frames of assorted Robe and second-hand ALCo 630 and 636 Series locomotives) were front line power on Robe River's iron ore trains until the merger of operations with Hamersley Iron as Pilbara Rail (running today as Rio Tinto Iron Ore) eventually saw this small fleet replaced by newer Dash 9-44CW units from General Electric in the United States (see page 135). As of late 2008 the CM40-8M units were used for shuttling loaded trains between Seven Mile Yard and the port facilities near Dampier.

Road #	630/636 #	Builder's #	Rebuilt	Owner	Status
9410	BHPIO 5500	2160-03/96-202	1996	Rio Tinto	In service
9411	9411	8206-02/92-125	1992	Rio Tinto	In service
9414	9414	8206-11/91-124	1991	Rio Tinto	In service
9417	BN 4366	6266-05/89-083	1989	Rio Tinto	In service
9418	9418	8109-12/90-118	1990	Rio Tinto	In service
9419	9419	8109-10/90-117	1990	Rio Tinto	In service
9420	9420	8109-03/91-119	1991	Rio Tinto	In service
9421	9421	8297-02/93-137	1993	Rio Tinto	In service
9422	9422	8297-03/93-138	1993	Rio Tinto	In service
9423	9423	8206-04/92-126	1992	Rio Tinto	In service
9424	9424	6266-07/89-084	1989	Rio Tinto	In service
9425	9425	6266-08/89-085	1989	Rio Tinto	In service

BHP-Billiton CM40-8

Builder:	*Goninan/GE (Bassendean)*	Model:	*CM40-8*
Type:	*Co-Co diesel-electric*	Engine:	*GE 7FDL turbo-charged 4-stroke V16*
Traction power:	*2980 kW (4000 hp)*	Length:	*20.20 m*
Weight:	*196.0 tonnes*	Gauge:	*1435 mm*

Above: 5631 heads a loaded ore train on an arrival road at Port Hedland's extensive Nelson Point facility on Sunday 22 July 2007. Chris Walters

The Dash-8 era began in the Pilbara with Mount Newman Mining's four General Electric CM39-8 units, acquired from licensee A Goninan & Company in 1988. During 1991 Mount Newman Mining merged with Goldsworthy Mining Limited and two things then occurred; the first was that the new BHP Iron Ore operation commenced an extensive program to cycle its aging ALCo and MLW 636 fleet through A Goninan's Bassendean plant for use in the construction of a fleet of similar CM40-8M units (see next page). The other was that an order for locomotives destined for the Goldsworthy Line service was adjusted to a pair of new CM40-8 units (5646 and 5647) based on the ongoing CM40-8M locomotives. Eventually the four ex-Mount Newman Mining CM39-8 locomotives were upgraded to CM40-8 capability, although for all intents and purpose the six 'new builds' were pooled with the far more numerous CM40-8M units. For a time, the ride of these six 'new build' units was suited more to the poorer track of the former Goldsworthy Line than the 'main' Newman system, however the number of services on this route have since been reduced.

Road #	Builder's #	Built	Owner	Status	Name
5630	5831-09/88-079	1988	BHP-Billiton Iron Ore	In service	*Zeus*
5631	5831-10/88-080	1988	BHP-Billiton Iron Ore	In service	*Apollo*
5632	5831-11/88-081	1988	BHP-Billiton Iron Ore	In service	*Poseidon*
5633	5831-12/88-082	1989	BHP-Billiton Iron Ore	In service	*Hephaestus*
5646	8244-11/92-135	1992	BHP-Billiton Iron Ore	In service	*White Springs*
5647	8244-12/92-136	1992	BHP-Billiton Iron Ore	In service	*Abydos*

Robe River CM40-8M

Builder:	*Goninan/GE (Bassendean)*	Model:	*CM40-8M*
Type:	*Co-Co diesel-electric*	Engine:	*GE 7FDL turbo-charged 4-stroke V16*
Traction power:	*2980 kW (4000 hp)*	Length:	*19.71–19.83 m*
Weight:	*195.0 tonnes*	Gauge:	*1435 mm*

Above: 5662 at Goldsworthy Junction, Thursday 26 July 2007. Chris Walters

In one of the most elaborate schemes, yet seen in Australia, to employ an aging locomotive fleet in replacing itself, dozens of former Mount Newman Mining C636 and M636 locomotives were stripped, dismantled and used in the construction of a series of new CM40-8M units for BHP Iron Ore between 1991 and 1995. These new General Electrics (along with six 'new build' CM40-8 units, see previous page) then formed the backbone of the fleet for the next decade. The Dash-8 fleet is now approaching the end of its frontline role in BHP-Billiton's iron ore haulage task, although the soaring demand for tonnages is unlikely to see them withdrawn altogether, despite the growing number of EMD SD70ACe/LC and SD70ACe locomotives acquired since 2005.

Road #	636 #	Builder's #	Built	Owner	Status	Name
5634	5457	8151-07/91-120	1991	BHP-Billiton Iron Ore	In service	*Boodarie*
5635	5460	8151-09/91-121	1991	BHP-Billiton Iron Ore	In service	*Pippingarra*
5636	5462	8151-11/91-122	1991	BHP-Billiton Iron Ore	In service	*Munda*
5637	5456	8151-01/92-123	1992	BHP-Billiton Iron Ore	In service	*De Grey*
5638	5464	8281-02/92-127	1992	BHP-Billiton Iron Ore	In service	*Mallina*
5639	5459	8281-03/92-128	1992	BHP-Billiton Iron Ore	In service	*Corrunna Downs*
5640	5479	8281-05/92-129	1992	BHP-Billiton Iron Ore	In service	*Ethel Creek*
5641	5454	8281-06/92-130	1992	BHP-Billiton Iron Ore	In service	*Indee*
5642	5467	8281-07/92-131	1992	BHP-Billiton Iron Ore	In service	*Wallareenya*
5643	5470	8281-08/92-132	1992	BHP-Billiton Iron Ore	In service	*Mt Whaleback*
5644	5471	8281-09/92-133	1992	BHP-Billiton Iron Ore	In service	*Kangan*

(continued)

Road #	636 #	Builder's #	Built	Owner	Status	Name
5645	5475	8281-11/92-134	1992	BHP-Billiton Iron Ore	In service	*Sherlock*
5648	5477	8412-06/93-139	1993	BHP-Billiton Iron Ore	In service	*Kwangyang Bay*
5649	5473	8412-07/93-140	1993	BHP-Billiton Iron Ore	In service	*Pohang*
5650	5481	8412-07/93-141	1993	BHP-Billiton Iron Ore	In service	*Yawata*
5651	5472	8412-08/93-142	1993	BHP-Billiton Iron Ore	In service	*Tobata*
5652	5482	8412-09/93-143	1993	BHP-Billiton Iron Ore	In service	*Villanueva*
5653	5484	8412-10/93-144	1993	BHP-Billiton Iron Ore	In service	*Chiba*
5654	5493	8412-11/93-145	1993	BHP-Billiton Iron Ore	In service	*Kashima*
5655	5474	8412-12/93-146	1993	BHP-Billiton Iron Ore	In service	*Wakayama*
5656	5494	8412-01/94-147	1994	BHP-Billiton Iron Ore	In service	*Keihan*
5657	5492	8412-02/94-148	1994	BHP-Billiton Iron Ore	In service	*Fukuyama*
5658	5480	8412-03/94-149	1994	BHP-Billiton Iron Ore	In service	*Kakogawa*
5659	5483	8412-04/94-150	1994	BHP-Billiton Iron Ore	In service	*Kobe*
5660	5478	8412-05/94-151	1994	BHP-Billiton Iron Ore	In service	*Hure*
5661	5488	8412-06/94-152	1994	BHP-Billiton Iron Ore	In service	*Funamachi*
5662	5490	8412-07/94-153	1994	BHP-Billiton Iron Ore	In service	*Port Kembla*
5663	5476	8412-08/94-154	1994	BHP-Billiton Iron Ore	In service	*Newcastle*
5664	5469	8412-09/94-155	1994	BHP-Billiton Iron Ore	In service	*Kaohsiung*
5665	5491	8412-10/94-156	1994	BHP-Billiton Iron Ore	In service	*Rotterdam*
5666	5487	8412-11/94-157	1995	BHP-Billiton Iron Ore	In service	*Taranto*
5667	5485	8412-12/94-158	1995	BHP-Billiton Iron Ore	In service	*Recar*
5668	5489	8412-01/95-159	1995	BHP-Billiton Iron Ore	In service	*Dunkirk*
5669	5486	8412-02/95-160	1995	BHP-Billiton Iron Ore	In service	*Beilun*

Above: 5638 (and 5630) Port Hedland on Monday 23 July 2007. Chris Walters

C36-7M

Builder:	*Goninan/GE (Bassendean)*	Model:	*C36-7M*
Type:	*Co-Co diesel-electric*	Engine:	*GE 7FDL turbo-charged 4-stroke V16*
Traction power:	*2685 kW (3600 hp)*	Length:	*19.71 m*
Weight:	*190.0 tonnes*	Gauge:	*1435 mm*

Above: 5052 (and 5051) near Seven Mile, Wednesday 25 July 2007. Chris Walters

Originally part of a fleet of eight locomotives, built using the frames of ALCo C636 units during 1987 for Mount Newman Mining, the C36-7M rebuilds were the first of what would become a fleet of over forty General Electrics working for BHP and BHP-Billiton Iron Ore. The eight C36-7M locomotives were rendered surplus upon the delivery and commissioning of eight AC6000CW units from General Electric in 1999 (see page 132) the United States, and were eventually sold off. Four ended up with GTSA Maddington and were progressively dismantled, while the remainder were acquired by Goninan (which later became United Group Rail). Two of these Goninan units were overhauled and leased to Pilbara Rail (known today as Rio Tinto Iron Ore) and are now used for shuttling loaded ore trains between Seven Mile Yard and the port facilities at Dampier. Another was later dispatched to NSW in 'cut down' form to become an engine test-bed at the firm's Lansdowne (Taree) plant while the final unit, 5513 was stored partially stripped at the Rail Heritage Western Australia (ARHS WA Division) museum adjacent to the United Group Rail factory at Bassendean (although it may have recently been cut up).

Road #	Original #	636 #	Builder's #	Built	Owner	Status
5051	5507	5461	4839-03/87-072	1987	UGR/Rio Tinto	In service
5052	5508	5466	4839-04/87-073	1987	UGR/Rio Tinto	In service
-	5509	5453	4839-05/87-074	1987	UGR Landsowne	Engine test bed
5513	5513	5453	4839-02/88-078	1987	UGR Bassendean	Stored

2800 Class

Builder:	*Goninan/GE (Bohle)*	Model:	*CM30-8*
Type:	*Co-Co diesel-electric*	Engine:	*GE 7FDL turbo-charged 4-stroke V12*
Traction power:	*2380 kW (3190 hp)*	Length:	*21.42 m*
Weight:	*116.7 tonnes*	Gauge:	*1067 mm and 1435 mm*

Above: 2846 at Acacia Ridge on Monday 4 August 2008. Peter Reading

Following the Goninan/GE 2600 Class in 1983 (see page 156) came the 2800 Class, of shared heritage in 1995. Obtained for freight and passenger working, the 2800 Class soon came to dominate both the North Coast and Mount Isa Lines. In recent years, the reduction in electric locomotive usage on services south of Rockhampton has increased the 2800 Class sphere of influence, however the biggest 'leap' came in 2006, when 2819 was converted to standard-gauge (thus increasing its weight to 118 tonnes) and despatched to work QRNational's Brisbane–Sydney–Melbourne freight services. However, the unit encountered a number of bureaucratic and logistical problems working in NSW and so was shifted in 2007, becoming a more regular fixture on the Melbourne–Adelaide corridor. The remaining 49 2800 Class continue in service as before in Queensland.

Road #	Builder's #	Built	Owner	Status
2801	6030-05/95-162	1995	QRN	In 1067 mm service
2802	6030-07/95-163	1995	QRN	In 1067 mm service
2803	6030-07/95-164	1995	QRN	In 1067 mm service
2804	6030-07/95-165	1995	QRN	In 1067 mm service
2805	6030-08/95-166	1995	QRN	In 1067 mm service
2806	6030-09/95-167	1995	QRN	In 1067 mm service
2807	6030-10/95-168	1995	QRN	In 1067 mm service
2808	6030-11/95-169	1995	QRN	In 1067 mm service
2809	6030-11/95-170	1995	QRN	In 1067 mm service
2810	6030-12/95-171	1995	QRN	In 1067 mm service

(continued)

Road #	Builder's #	Built	Owner	Status
2811	6030-12/95-172	1995	QRN	In 1067 mm service
2812	6030-12/95-173	1996	QRN	In 1067 mm service
2813	6030-12/95-174	1996	QRN	In 1067 mm service
2814	6030-12/95-175	1996	QRN	In 1067 mm service
2815	6030-01/96-176	1996	QRN	In 1067 mm service
2816	6030-01/96-177	1996	QRN	In 1067 mm service
2817	6030-02/96-178	1996	QRN	In 1067 mm service
2818	6030-03/96-179	1996	QRN	In 1067 mm service
2819	6030-03/96-180	1996	QRN	In 1435 mm service
2820	6030-03/96-181	1996	QRN	In 1067 mm service
2821	6030-04/96-182	1996	QRN	In 1067 mm service
2822	6030-04/96-183	1996	QRN	In 1067 mm service
2823	6030-05/96-184	1996	QRN	In 1067 mm service
2824	6030-05/96-185	1996	QRN	In 1067 mm service
2825	6030-06/96-186	1996	QRN	In 1067 mm service
2826	6030-06/96-187	1996	QRN	In 1067 mm service
2827	6030-06/96-188	1996	QRN	In 1067 mm service
2828	6030-06/96-189	1996	QRN	In 1067 mm service
2829	6030-07/96-190	1996	QRN	In 1067 mm service
2830	6030-07/96-191	1996	QRN	In 1067 mm service
2831	6030-08/96-192	1996	QRN	In 1067 mm service
2832	6030-08/96-193	1996	QRN	In 1067 mm service
2833	6030-08/96-194	1996	QRN	In 1067 mm service
2834	6030-09/96-195	1996	QRN	In 1067 mm service
2835	6030-09/96-196	1996	QRN	In 1067 mm service
2836	6030-10/96-197	1996	QRN	In 1067 mm service
2837	6030-11/96-198	1996	QRN	In 1067 mm service
2838	6030-11/96-199	1996	QRN	In 1067 mm service
2839	6030-12/96-200	1997	QRN	In 1067 mm service
2840	6030-12/96-201	1997	QRN	In 1067 mm service
2841	6030-02/98-323	1998	QRN	In 1067 mm service
2842	6030-02/98-324	1998	QRN	In 1067 mm service
2843	6030-04/98-325	1998	QRN	In 1067 mm service
2844	6030-04/98-326	1998	QRN	In 1067 mm service
2845	6030-05/98-327	1998	QRN	In 1067 mm service
2846	6030-05/98-328	1998	QRN	In 1067 mm service
2847	6030-05/98-329	1998	QRN	In 1067 mm service
2848	6030-05/98-330	1998	QRN	In 1067 mm service
2849	6030-05/98-331	1998	QRN	In 1067 mm service
2850	6030-05/98-332	1998	QRN	In 1067 mm service

** Builders plates on 2841–2850 show 202 to 211 (in error) instead of 323 to 332.*

EL Class

Builder:	*Goninan/GE (Broadmeadow)*	Model:	*CM30-8*
Type:	*Co-Co diesel-electric*	Engine:	*GE 7FDL turbo-charged 4-stroke V12*
Traction power:	*2380 kW (3190 hp)*	Length:	*19.60 m*
Weight:	*113.6 tonnes*	Gauge:	*1435 mm*

Above: EL52 leads SRHC heritage units GM36 and C501 on MQ5 El Zorro empty grain train, working into Parkes from the south on Thursday 31 July 2008. Trish Baker

These former Australian National locomotives today form the core of CFCLA's lease fleet, and as such have been involved in a myriad of operations (and operators) across most states. Despite their age (they were delivered during 1990 and 1991) they continue to perform reliably and are common in QRNational, El Zorro and Patrick Portlink service throughout New South Wales, Victoria and South Australia.

Road #	Builder's #	Built	Owner	Status	Name
EL51	8013-07/90-103	1990	CFCLA	In service	*Might & Power*
EL52	8013-09/90-104	1990	CFCLA	In service	*Light Fingers*
EL53	8013-09/90-105	1990	CFCLA	In service	*Northerly*
EL54	8013-10/90-106	1990	CFCLA	In service	*Bonecrusher*
EL55	8013-11/90-107	1990	CFCLA	In service	*Kensei*
EL56	8013-12/90-108	1990	CFCLA	In service	*Doremus*
EL57	8013-02/91-109	1991	CFCLA	In service	*Gunsynd*
EL58	8013-03/91-110	1991	CFCLA	In service	*Kingston Rule 3:16.3*
EL60	8013-06/91-112	1991	CFCLA	In service	*Octagonal*
EL61	8013-07/91-113	1991	CFCLA	In service	*Ethereal*
EL62	8013-08/91-114	1991	CFCLA	In service	*Archer*
EL63	8013-08/91-115	1991	CFCLA	In service	*Saintly*
EL64	8013-10/91-116	1991	CFCLA	In service	*Super Impose*

GL Class

Builder:	*Goninan/GE (Broadmeadow)*	Model:	*C30-MMi*
Type:	*Co-Co diesel-electric*	Engine:	*GE 7FDL turbo-charged 4-stroke V12*
Traction power:	*2380 kW (3190 hp)*	Length:	*17.40 m*
Weight:	*132.0 tonnes*	Gauge:	*1435 mm*

Above: GL108 at South Dynon on Wednesday 27 December 2006. Bernie Baker

Constructed using the frames, fuel tanks and bogies of dismantled 442 Class Goodwin/ALCo units (see page 115) during 2002–04, the CFCLA GL Class is now a vital part of the operator's growing lease fleet. Unlike the similar EL Class units, the GL Class have proven far more regular on slower intrastate coal, grain and container services, and as of 2008 are common in both Pacific National and Patrick Portlink service, primarily in New South Wales but on occasions in both Victoria and South Australia also.

Road #	442 #	Builder's #	Built	Owner	Status	Name
GL101	44207	84040-02/03-333	2003	CFCLA	In service	*Think Big*
GL102	44216	84040-04/03-334	2003	CFCLA	In service	*Sunline*
GL103	44228	84040-06/03-335	2003	CFCLA	In service	*Brew*
GL104	44230	84040-07/03-336	2003	CFCLA	In service	*Jezabeel*
GL105	44201	84040-08/03-337	2003	CFCLA	In service	*Let's Elope*
GL106	44218	84040-09/03-338	2003	CFCLA	In service	*Sub Zero*
GL107	44233	84040-10/03-339	2003	CFCLA	In service	*Rogan Josh*
GL108	44222	84040-10/03-340	2003	CFCLA	In service	*Rain Lover*
GL109	44229	84040-11/03-341	2004	CFCLA	In service	*Just a Dash*
GL110	44215	84040-12/03-342	2004	CFCLA	In service	*Tawriffic*
GL111	44232	84040-12/03-343	2004	CFCLA	In service	*Galilee*
GL112	44212	84040-01/04-344	2004	CFCLA	In service	*Jeune*

P Class

Builder:	*Goninan/GE (Bassendean)*	Model:	*CM25-8*
Type:	*Co-Co diesel-electric*	Engine:	*GE 7FDL turbo-charged 4-stroke V12*
Traction power:	*1830 kW (2450 hp)*	Length:	*18.90 m*
Weight:	*100.5 tonnes*	Gauge:	*1067 mm*

Above: P2508 stabled at Forrestfield on Wednesday 19 December 2007. After a number of livery variations applied during the Australia Western Railroad/Australian Railroad Group (ARG) and then QR/ARG eras, this scheme of predominantly yellow with maroon and black lettering has been settled on as the scheme of choice for the Australian Railroad Group operation in Western Australia. Evan Jasper

Although the P Class were something of a development of the older 2600 Class built for QR some years before (see page 156), these 17 locomotives marked the true beginning of General Electric developing into a force to be reckoned within the Australian locomotive market. Although the class were initially used quite extensively in mineral haulage, in more recent years they've been devoted also to grain traffic. Iron ore developments in the Geraldton region have seen many of the class gravitate north, and this shift of the P Class away from southern traffics has formed one of the key reasons behind a number of former Queensland locomotives being transferred to Western Australia (see the AC/AD, DD and DFZ classes) to fill the void. The P Class is currently undergoing a major overhaul program, and one by one they are being cycled through the United Group Rail works at Bassendean (where they were built in 1989–91), although a rash of collisions and derailments over the years has seen the class returned to the workshops far more frequently than their owners would prefer.

Road #	Original #	Builder's #	Built	Owner	Status	Name
P2501	P2001	6320-12/89-086	1989	ARG	In service	*Shire of Mingenew*
P2502	P2002	6320-01/90-087	1990	ARG	In service	*Shire of Moora*
P2503	P2003	6320-02/90-088	1990	ARG	In service	*Shire of Victoria Plains*
P2504	P2004	6320-03/90-089	1990	ARG	In service	*Shire of Dalwallinu*
P2505	P2005	6320-04/90-090	1990	ARG	In service	*Shire of Lake Grace*
P2506	P2006	6320-05/90-091	1990	ARG	In service	*Shire of Quairading*
P2507	P2007	6320-06/90-092	1990	ARG	In service	*Shire of Perenjori*
P2508	P2008	6320-07/90-093	1990	ARG	In service	*Shire of Carnamah*
P2509	P2009	6320-07/90-094	1990	ARG	In service	*Shire of Three Springs*
P2510	P2010	6320-08/90-095	1990	ARG	In service	*Shire of Corrigin*
P2511	P2011	6320-09/90-096	1990	ARG	In service	*Shire of Narembeen*
P2512	P2012	6320-10/90-097	1990	ARG	In service	*Shire of Mullewa*
P2513	P2013	6320-11/90-098	1990	ARG	In service	*Shire of Morawa*
P2514	P2014	6320-12/90-099	1990	ARG	In service	*Shire of Wongan/Ballidu*
P2515	P2015	6320-01/91-100	1991	ARG	In service	*Shire of Kulin*
P2516	P2016	6320-03/91-101	1991	ARG	In service	*Shire of Coorow*
P2517	P2017	6320-04/91-102	1991	ARG	In service	*City of Geraldton*

Above: P2509 outside Forrestfield Workshops on the evening of Friday 23 March 2008. This all-over orange livery was an interim livery applied between the QR take over of the former Western Australian ARG operation in 2006, and the application of the final yellow scheme now being applied to the fleet. Evan Jasper

2600 Class

Builder:	*Goninan/GE (Bohle)*	Model:	*C22-MMi (rebuilt)*
Type:	*Co-Co diesel-electric*	Engine:	*GE 7FDL turbo-charged 4-stroke V12*
Traction power:	*1640 kW (2200 hp)*	Length:	*18.89 m*
Weight:	*112.3 tonnes*	Gauge:	*1067 mm*

Above: Not long out of rebuild, 2607 is stabled at Stuart locomotive depot (near Townsville) on Friday 14 December 2001. Chris Walters

After literally hundreds of Clyde-EMD deliveries throughout the 1970s and 1980s, the notion that QR might suddenly change tack and invest in a small fleet of GE locomotives was something of a surprise. Thirteen were ordered in all, and eventually these model U22C units came to dominate the somewhat isolated Collinsville (Newlands) branch running south from Pring (near Bowen). With the commissioning of the EDI/EMD 4000 Class units in 2000, the class were cycled through their 'birth place' at Bohle (Townsville) and rebuilt by Goninan as model C22-MMi complete with a new QR-style 'maxi-cab'. Following this the class was transferred to Mount Isa Line mineral and freight haulage for a number of years, before eventually returning to Pring to work Newlands coal trains again by 2007.

Road #	Builder's #	Built	Owner	Status
2600	2500-12/83-58	1983	QRNational	In service
2601	2500-12/83-59	1983	QRNational	In service
2602	2500-01/84-60	1984	QRNational	In service
2603	2500-02/84-61	1984	QRNational	In service
2604	2500-03/84-62	1984	QRNational	In service
2605	2500-04/84-63	1984	QRNational	In service
2606	2500-05/84-64	1984	QRNational	In service
2607	2500-06/84-65	1984	QRNational	In service
2608	2500-07/84-66	1984	QRNational	In service
2609	2500-08/84-67	1984	QRNational	In service
2610	2500-09/84-68	1984	QRNational	In service
2611	2500-10/84-69	1984	QRNational	In service
2612	2500-11/84-70	1984	QRNational	In service

UM20C Class

Builder:	*PT GE Lokindo (Indonesia)*	Model:	*UM20C*
Type:	*Co-Co diesel-electric*	Engine:	*GE 7FDL turbo-charged 4-stroke V8*
Traction power:	*1490 kW (2000 hp)*	Length:	*?*
Weight:	*?*	Gauge:	*1067 mm*

Above: The former International Container Terminal Services Incorporated General Electric locomotive, imported recently from the Philippines, in the Flashbutt Siding compound near Midland on Tuesday 29 July 2008. At this stage the locomotive had not yet been renumbered, or entered Coote Industrial service. Chris Miller

Purchased second hand from the International Container Terminal Services Incorporated (ICTSI) operation in Manila, capital of the Philippines, South Spur Rail Services shipped this 1067mm-gauge General Electric to Perth where it was serviced at GTSA Engineering's Maddington compound. During this time it was repainted from the ICTSI red and silver livery—that it had arrived in—to South Spur's two-tone blue livery. However, this all occurred during a time when South Spur was acquired by Coote Industrial, and by the time the General Electric unit was transferred over to the company's Flashbutt locomotive compound near Midland, it had again been repainted, this time into Coote Industrial's green and yellow; three liveries without having turned a wheel in Australian service by August 2008.

Road #	Builder's #	Built	Owner	Status	Notes
ICTSI 1	?	1996	Coote Industrial	In service	Ex-ICTSI Philippines

GE L80T 'centre cab'

Builder:	*Goninan/GE (Broadmeadow)*	Model:	*80-tonne*
Type:	*Bo-Bo diesel-electric*	Weight:	*78.2 tonnes*
Gauge:	*1435 mm*	Length:	*10.33 m*

Engine	*2 x Rolls Royce C6TFL-6 turbo-charged 4-stroke 6-cylinder*	*49, 50, MM03 and MM04*
	2 x Cummins NT855-L2 turbo-charged 4 stroke 6 cylinders	*55*
	2 x Cummins NT855-L4 turbo-charged 4 stroke 6 cylinders	*57 and HBL58*

Traction	*340 kW (460 hp)*	*49, 50, MM03 and MM04*
power:	*410 kW (470 hp)*	*55, 57 and HBL58*

Above: MM03 stabled at Manildra on Sunday 18 May 2008. Chris Walters

With the exception of the very similar D2 (formerly of Blue Circle Southern Cement, Berrima and now working for the Manildra Group a Bomaderry), this group of General Electric 'industrial' shunters were once part of a larger fleet belonging to BHP Newcastle. The steelworks closure in 1999 rendered the group surplus, and over time they have slowly passed into other hands and a variety of new service roles. However, the need for specialised shunters across the rail industry is fairly low, and in most cases these units are held on standby or are used fairly intermittently, with the Loongana Lime pair and the former Blue Circle unit at Bomaderry probably receiving the most regular use.

Road #	Orig #	Builder's #	Built	Owner	Status	Note
MM04	48	4970-09/61-012	1961	Manildra Group	In service—Gunnedah	-
49	49	4970-09/61-013	1961	Loongana Lime	In service—Parkeston	-
50	50	4970-10/61-014	1961	Loongana Lime	In service—Rawlinna	-
MM03	51	4970-11/61-015	1961	Manildra Group	In service—Manildra	-
55	55	3275-09/77-051	1977	JRW Junee	In service—Junee	Named *Folly*

(continued)

Road #	Orig #	Builder's #	Built	Owner	Status	Note
57	57	6606-01/82-056	1982	JRW Junee	In service—Junee	-
HBL58	58	6606-01/82-057	1982	Heggies	In service—Pt Kembla	-
D2	D2	6626-06/67-024	1967	Manildra Group	In service—Bomaderry	Ex-Blue Circle

Above: ***Folly*** **(ex-BHP 55) at Junee on Saturday 23 October 2004.** Chris Walters

Above: HBL58 at Port Kembla in December 1999. Phil Martin

Goninan/GE Bo

Builder:	*Goninan/GE (Broadmeadow)*	Model:	*35T*
Type:	*Bo diesel-electric*	Engine:	*Cummins NHS-6-BH 4-stoke 6-cyliner (originally)* *Cummins NS743-B 4-stroke 6-cylinder*
Traction power:	*210 kW (280 hp)*	Length:	*?*
Weight:	*32.5 tonnes*	Gauge:	*1435 mm*

GE

Above: The Comsteel Goninan/GE Bo locomotive outside the Waratah works on Saturday 26 September 1998. Ed Tonks

This four-wheeled General Electric diesel-electric is perhaps the smallest locomotive to have ever been built by Goninan in Australia. Effectively the little unit is 'half' a 80-tonne centre-cab locomotive (see page 158), and as such possesses only one engine. Designed and built for shunting at the former Commonwealth Steel Company (Comsteel) sidings at Waratah (a western suburb of Newcastle), the locomotive replaced two steam engines in this role (although one, *Juno*, was retained as a back-up before passing into preservation by 1977). Rail despatch from the works finished on 13 September 2002 (with the rail connection to the adjacent government-owned Coal Roads subsequently severed), by which time the locomotive (and factory) had passed to Smorgon Steel. During 2003, the little unit was transferred by road to the Acacia Ridge plant in suburban Brisbane, where it continues in service today. Subsequent to the transfer, Smorgon merged with and became part of OneSteel.

Road #	Builder's #	Built	Owner	Status
-	4740-07/72-030	1972	OneSteel/Smorgon	In service—Acacia Ridge

Originally used at Comsteel, Waratah

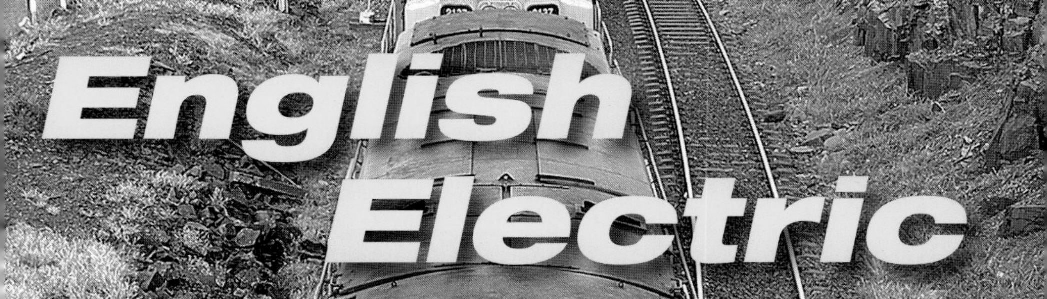

English Electric

MKA unit 2138 in Hobart on Saturday 8 July 2006.
Chris Walters

ZP/ZR Class

Builder:	*English Electric (Rocklea)/AN*	Model:	*n/a*
Type:	*Co-Co diesel-electric*	Engine:	*EE CSVT MkIII turbo-charged 4-stroke V12*
Traction power:	*1340 kW (1800 hp)*	Length:	*15.85 m*
Weight:	*97.5 tonnes*	Gauge:	*1067 mm*

Left: ZP unit 2100 and its ZR Class sister, 2101, head a very light train 31 (with no loading on the 39-wagon consist) past Burnie Station on Tuesday 16 March 1999.

Left: 2101 and MKA unit 2137 lead No. 336 Freight across Hopkinson Street, South Burnie, on Wednesday 13 September 2006.

Both photos Damien Smith

EE

Rebuilt from ZB Class units (see next page), 'modernised' English Electrics 2100 and 2101 represent a 'what might have been', had Australian National's (AN) Tasrail division not been sold off in 1997, or had successors ATN Tasrail not nurtured a significant EMD bias. The former was rebuilt by AN at its Port Augusta Workshops in 1996 (initially as ZR1, later renumbered as ZP1) while the latter was rebuilt at East Tamar and issued to traffic in 1997 as ZR2. Subsequent modifications to their control and braking systems allowed them to operate with the ATN Tasrail EMD D/DC/DQ/QR fleet, and despite the changes of ownership since that time, both units continue in service, working with the EMD fleet (and subsequent English Electric MKA Class—see page 170) on all manner of services throughout Tasmania.

Road #	Original #	Rebuilt	Built	Owner	Status
(ZP)2100	ZR1/ZP1	ZB9	1996	PN Tasmania	In service
(ZR)2101	ZR2	ZB6	1997	PN Tasmania	In service

ZB/2350/2370 Class

Builder:	*English Electric (Rocklea)*	Model:	*n/a*
Type:	*Co-Co diesel-electric*	Engine:	*EE CSVT MkIII turbo-charged 4-stroke V12*
Traction power:	*1340 kW (1800 hp)*	Length:	*15.85 m*
Weight:	*91.5 tonnes*	Gauge:	*1067 mm*

Above: ZB2129 and ZB2125 at Midland on Thursday 26 June 2008. Evan Jasper

EE

One of the more travelled classes of locomotive in Australia—without having ever switched gauges—the remaining 2350/2370 Class units are today known as the ZB, and have been since sale by QR to AN Tasrail in 1987. In fact, the group now has a more enduring association with their post-Tasmania classification and career than their previous QR tenure. Like the similar ZA Class units built for the Tasmanian Government Railways (see page 164), the 2350/2370 Class was de-rated from 1750 to 1340 kW to conserve engine life. Three of the class are now part of Coote Industrial's Western Australian fleet (following their purchase by South Spur in 2002), while seven remain in Tasmania as part of the Pacific National Tasmania operation. Of these latter units, only four remain in service and they are used on shunting and transfer duties at Boyer and East Tamar, in addition to appearances between Western Junction and Bell Bay.

Road #	ZB #	2350/70 #	Builders #	Built	Owner	Status
ZB2120	ZB1	2350	A.253	1973	Coote Industrial	In service
(ZB)2121	ZB2	2351	A.254	1973	PN Tasmania	In service
(ZB)2122	ZB3	2352	A.255	1973	PN Tasmania	In service
ZB4	ZB4	2353	A.256	1973	PN Tasmania	Stored East Tamar
(ZB)2123	ZB5	2354	A.257	1973	PN Tasmania	In service
ZB2125	ZB10	2359	A.266	1973	Coote Industrial	In service
(ZB)2126	ZB12	2361	A.268	1974	PN Tasmania	Stored East Tamar
(ZB)2127	ZB13	2370	A.274	1975	PN Tasmania	Stored East Tamar
(ZB)2128	ZB14	2371	A.275	1975	PN Tasmania	In service
ZB2129	ZB15	2372	A.276	1975	Coote Industrial	In service

ZA Class

Builder:	*English Electric (Rocklea)*	Model:	*n/a*
Type:	*Co-Co diesel-electric*	Engine:	*EE CSVT MkIII turbo-charged 4-stroke V12*
Traction power:	*1340 kW (1800 hp)*	Length:	*16.10 m*
Weight:	*97.5 tonnes*	Gauge:	*1067 mm*

Above: ZA Class unit 2114 at Burnie on Friday 26 February 1999. Chris Walters

A development of the design that peaked with the earlier Z Class, the 1973-vintage ZA Class were also similar to the QR 2350/2370 units, which ultimately joined them in Tasmania when purchased by AN Tasrail in 1987 (see page 163). All three types represent the most powerful locomotives built in Australia by English Electric, and were among the last deliveries made by the company before Rocklea closed its doors. Unlike the Z Class, the ZA units did not receive DOO (driver-only operation) modification subsequent to the takeover of the system by ATN Tasrail in 1997, and as such their role in Tasmania has diminished such, that at best, only two or three have normally been available for service in more recent years. These were commonly used as trailing units behind DOO Z Class units, but with a shift of Z Class units away from DOO rosters and a downturn in traffic across the state as Pacific National Tasmania has reduced investment in the business, the remaining ZA Class units rarely stray from the Western Junction—East Tamar–Bell Bay corridor.

Road #	Original #	Builders #	Built	Owner	Status
(ZA)2114	ZA1	A.259	1973	PN Tasmania	In service
(ZA)2115	ZA2	A.260	1973	PN Tasmania	Stored East Tamar
(ZA)2116	ZA3	A.261	1973	PN Tasmania	In service
ZA4	ZA4	A.262	1973	PN Tasmania	Stored East Tamar
(ZA)2117	ZA5	A.278	1976	PN Tasmania	Stored East Tamar
(ZA)2118	ZA6	A.279	1976	PN Tasmania	Stored East Tamar

Z Class

Builder:	*English Electric (Rocklea)*	Model:	*n/a*
Type:	*Co-Co diesel-electric*	Engine:	*EE CSVT turbo-charged 4-stroke V12*
Traction power:	*1340 kW (1800 hp)*	Length:	*15.85 m*
Weight:	*97.4 tonnes*	Gauge:	*1067 mm*

Above: Z Class units 2111 and 2113 lead a load of coal from Fingal near Cleveland Wednesday 5 March 2008. Ewan McLean

Potentially one of the most successful English Electric designs in Australia, and certainly one of the longest serving and hardest working, the four Z Class units continue to soldier on in Tasmania while more recent locomotives have declined in use, and in some cases fallen by the wayside. Although converted for DOO (driver only operation) service between 1998 and 2000 by previous owners ATN Tasrail, the class is no longer common on DOO services (and thus, in the south of the state) and instead are focussed on Bell Bay and Fingal Line coal trains. The impending change of ownership of the Tasmanian rail operation is likely to change little in regards to the Z Class, and they are likely to remain a fixture on the Apple Isle for some time yet.

Road#	Original #	Builders #	Built	Owner	Status	Name
(Z)2110	Z1	A.249	1972	PN Tasmania	In service	*Northern Progress*
(Z)2111	Z2	A.250	1972	PN Tasmania	In service	*Bell Bay Pioneer*
(Z)2112	Z3	A.251	1972	PN Tasmania	In service	-
(Z)2113	Z4	A.252	1972	PN Tasmania	In service	-

K Class

Builder:	*English Electric (Rocklea)*	Model:	*n/a*
Type:	*Co-Co diesel-electric*	Engine:	*EE 12CSVT turbo-charged 4-stroke V12*
Traction power:	*1340 kW (1800 hp)*	Length:	*16.76 m*
Weight:	*109.8–120.0 tonnes*	Gauge:	*1435 mm*

Above: SCT's K208 at Forrestfield on Sunday 29 July 2007. Chris Walters

Designed and built for both the Western Australian Government Railways and Goldsworthy Mining Limited, sales, mergers and transfers have seen the surviving members of this group of 1960s English Electrics cross the country numerous times and operate for a number of companies in a variety of tasks. As of 2008 the class is split between SCT and Coote Industrial, although all operational examples are now based in Perth with a further three stored in Melbourne. Australian Rail Track Corporation duties have sometimes carried the former South Spur units east into South Australia, however these workings seem now the domain of Coote Industrial's Comeng/MLW NA and 80 and Clyde/EMD C Class locomotives.

Road #	Original #	Builder's #	Built	Owner	Status	Name
K201	K201	A.109	1966	SCT Melbourne	Stored Dynon	-
D51	K203	A.111	1966	Coote Industrial	In service	-
K205	K205	A.135	1966	Coote Industrial	In service	-
K206	K206	A.133	1966	Coote Industrial	In service	-
K207	K207	A.136	1966	SCT Melbourne	Stored Laverton	-
K208	K208	A.137	1966	SCT Perth	In service	*Thomas Smith*
K209	K209	A.142	1967	SCT Melbourne	Stored Dynon	-
K210	K210	A.186	1969	Coote Industrial	In service	-
D47	GML5	A.146	1967	Coote Industrial	In service	-
D48	GML7	A.242	1972	Coote Industrial	In service	-
D49	GML8	A.243	1972	Coote Industrial	In service	-

KA Class

Builder:	*English Electric (Rocklea)*	Model:	*n/a*
Type:	*Co-Co diesel-electric*	Engine:	*EE CSVT turbo-charged 4-stroke V12*
Traction power:	*1340 kW (1800 hp)*	Length:	*15.85 m*
Weight:	*99.2 tonnes*	Gauge:	*1435 mm*

Above: While awaiting engine repair, KA212 sits within the Flashbutt compound near Midland on Saturday 28 July 2007. This unit was repainted in Coote Industrial's green and yellow livery during the second half of 2008. Chris Walters

Originally there were three KA Class units, sourced from converting three 1067 mm gauge RA Class locomotives to 1435 mm to cover a standard-gauge motive power shortage during 1974 (a move that foreshadowed the similar redeployment of two narrow-gauge NA Class units twenty years later). Oddly enough, all three examples remain (where none of the other RA units have survived), although KA213 was eventually returned to the narrower gauge and is today preserved as RA1918 (the only member of either class so 'saved'). Coote Industrial employ KA212 as part of their Western Australian allocation, while the cab and frame of KA211 are now almost unrecognisable as an engine test bed located within the compound of United Group Rail's Bassendean plant. As of late 2008, there were reports emerging from Western Australia that Coote Industrial were giving consideration to the notion of returning KA212 to the narrow gauge, and renumbering it back to RA1917. As of going to press, no confirmation of this had been forthcoming.

Road #	Original #	Builder's #	Built	Owner	Status
KA211	RA1914	A.220	1971	UGR Bassendean	Engine test bed
KA212	RA1917	A.244	1972	Coote Industrial	In service

R Class

Builder:	*English Electric (Rocklea)*	Model:	*n/a*
Type:	*Co-Co diesel-electric*	Engine:	*EE CSVT turbo-charged 4-stroke V12*
Traction power:	*1340 kW (1800 hp)*	Length:	*15.24 m*
Weight:	*97.4 tonnes*	Gauge:	*1067 mm*

Above: R1902 works No. 2S17 concrete sleeper train as it propels into Calcine bauxite siding near an ALCOA refinery. Evan Jasper

Another of those interesting cases of a once preserved locomotive returning to commercial service (much like both F40 and 4908, also owned by Coote Industrial) R1902 is also special, for it is the only survivor of its class. Originally numbering five, the remainder of the 1968-vintage English Electric R Class were all scrapped during 1991, while R1902 itself was held as an attraction within Cohuna Wildlife Park (Kelmscott) between 1992 and 2000. Recommissioned initially by South Spur, the locomotive is today part of Coote Industrial's narrow-gauge fleet, being commonly used for ballast trains and rail set transfers, having visited many corners of the Transperth network (new and old) in these tasks.

Road #	Builder's #	Built	Owner	Status
R1902	A.167	1968	Coote Industrial	In service

1300/ZC/MKA Class

Builder:	*English Electric (Rocklea)*	Model:	*n/a*
Type:	*Co-Co diesel-electric*	Engine:	*EE CSVT turbo-charged 4-stroke V12*
Traction power:	*1340 kW (1800 hp)*	Length:	*14.63 m*
Weight:	*89.5 tonnes*	Gauge:	*1067 mm*

Above: 2141 shunts loading for that evening's Burnie to Hobart container freight in Devonport on Thursday 8 January 2004. This was one of the last duties (along with the declining North East Line freight services) for the remaining ZC Class units before they were withdrawn later that year. 2141 and the remaining 'standard' ZC units are now all stored at East Tamar. Chris Walters

Built originally for QR between 1967 and 1972, all 45 members of the 1300 Class were sold to Australian National (Tasrail Division) as the ZC Class in 1988 (although only 33 operated in Tasmania). The ensuing years have seen the fleet whittled down and mostly sold off, and those ZC units remaining in Tasmania are now all stored, with the exception of six (2131, 2132, 2133, 2134, 2137 and 2138), which have now returned following rebuild (and in some cases, service elsewhere) as the MKA Class. These units possess radically new cab designs and have been rewired to allow multiple-unit operation with EMD (and other) type locomotives; something not possible previously. Bogies from ZC units 2140, 2141 and 2145 were used under the first batch of returning MKA rebuilds (2134, 2137 and 2138) when they arrived in Tasmania during late 2004/early 2005, and with ZC locomotive 2146 stored with parts missing, 2144 is in theory the only 'standard' ZC in Tasmania in nominally complete condition. Originally eight MKA Class rebuilds were undertaken by Morrison Knudsen Australia (when the project was commenced in 1994), however the other two were sold to an operator in Senegal some years ago.

Road #	MKA #	ZC #	1300 #	Builders #	Built	Owner	Status
(MKA)2131	MKA1	ZC21	1320	A.208	1969	PN Tasmania	In service
(MKA)2132	MKA2	-	1329	A.217	1970	PN Tasmania	In service
(MKA)2133	MKA3	ZC22	1321	A.209	1969	PN Tasmania	In service
(MKA)2134	MKA4	ZC27	1326	A.214	1970	PN Tasmania	In service
(MKA)2137	MKA7	ZC31	1330	A.223	1971	PN Tasmania	In service
(MKA)2138	MKA8	ZC41	1340	A.234	1971	PN Tasmania	In service
(ZC)2140		ZC9	1308	A.176	1968	PN Tasmania	Stored East Tamar
(ZC)2141		ZC11	1310	A.181	1968	PN Tasmania	Stored East Tamar
(ZC)2144		ZC19	1318	A.201	1969	PN Tasmania	Stored East Tamar
(ZC)2145		ZC20	1319	A.200	1969	PN Tasmania	Stored East Tamar
ZC32		ZC32	1331	A.224	1971	PN Tasmania	Stored East Tamar
(ZC)2146		ZC42	1341	A.235	1971	PN Tasmania	Stored East Tamar

** The eight MKA Class units were alloted the Morrison Knudsen Australia builder's numbers of 95-MKA-001 to 95-MKA-008 in numerical order (ie. MKA1–MKA8), despite MKA8 not being completed until 2005 by NREC.*

Above: MKA units 2137 and 2138 wait at a pre-dawn South Burnie with the overnight freight service from Hobart and Western Junction, on the morning of Thursday 6 July 2006. Following the arrival of the eastbound Paper Train from the opposite direction, the MKA pair continued on into Burnie. The first three MKA Class locomotives were delivered to Tasmania in 2004/05, but underwent an intensive period of modification and testing prior to the either eventual commissioning in late 2005/early 2006. The remaining three MKA units were eventually shipped to Tasmania by early 2007, following workshops attention at Dynon, in Melbourne. Although a 'stop gap' motive power solution, the six refurbished English Electrics have proven fairly reliable. Phil Martin

D34 Class

Builder:	*English Electric (Rocklea)*	Model:	*n/a*
Type:	*Co-Co diesel-electric*	Engine:	*EE CSVT turbo-charged 4-stroke V12*
Traction power:	*1340 kW (1800 hp)*	Length:	*16.50 m*
Weight:	*139.0 tonnes*	Gauge:	*1435 mm*

Above: Back when it was still used in coal service (and when K Class units, such as D47 seen here, were still employed on site), D34 passes through Cringila with an empty Kemira-bound coal train during May 2001. Since this photo was taken, the elaborate muffler system atop the hood behind the cab has been removed. Chris Walters

Built in 1969, D34 has always been the heaviest locomotive on the Australian Iron & Steel (later BHP, now BlueScope) Port Kembla Steelworks railway system. Purchased specifically to haul coal trains, the increasing use of 81 Class units to fulfil these duties during more recent times has pushed this unique locomotive into internal steelworks service. However, the outsourcing of rail operations within the Port Kembla plant, surprisingly, saw D34 overlooked for sale on to Pacific National in 2007, with the result that it is believed to be the only operational locomotive owned by BlueScope at Port Kembla. Being the heaviest 2000 hp-range locomotive in the country by a significant margin reduces the potential use of this specialised unit beyond the steelworks, and so its future is somewhat cloudy.

Road #	Builders #	Built	Owner	Status
D34	A.197	1969	BlueScope Steel, Port Kembla	In service

1000 Class

Builder:	*English Electric (Rocklea)*	Model:	*n/a*
Type:	*Bo-Bo diesel-electric*	Engine:	*EE CSRKT turbo-charged 4-stroke 6-cylinder*
Traction power:	*690 kW (930 hp)*	Length:	*12.80 m*
Weight:	*89.5 tonnes*	Gauge:	*1435 mm*

Above: D36 shunting at Unanderra on Thursday 11 September 2008. A number of 850 and 1000-type units were upgraded by United Group Rail at Steelhaven between 2003 and 2005, including D19, D28, D36, D38 and D40. Chris Stratton

This group of nine locomotives (originally 11, before D35 and D37 were destroyed in a 1993 head-on collision at Cordeaux Heights) form the backbone of current Port Kembla Steelworks rail operation, and were one of the last models delivered by English Electric (known as GEC during that last year or so) before the company closed down their Australian business in 1976. All nine are now owned by Pacific National (although two are currently stored out of service), who manage the steelworks rail operation, although the 1000s still leave the works to run to Unanderra and occasionally to slag dump sites west of the plant. One or two 1000s are also regularly used at the Springhill (former Lysaghts) works across the RailCorp Port Kembla branch from the main steelworks, while another common roster is the shunt to Commonwealth Rolling Mills near Port Kembla Station.

Road #	Builders #	Built	Owner	Status
D36	A.237	1971	Pacific National, Port Kembla	In service
D38	A.239	1971	Pacific National, Port Kembla	In service
D39	A.240	1972	Pacific National, Port Kembla	Stored
D40	A.241	1972	Pacific National, Port Kembla	In service
D41	A.269	1972	Pacific National, Port Kembla	In service
D42	A.270	1972	Pacific National, Port Kembla	In service
D43	A.271	1974	Pacific National, Port Kembla	In service
D44	A.272	1975	Pacific National, Port Kembla	Stored
D45	A.273	1975	Pacific National, Port Kembla	In service

850 Class

Builder:	*English Electric (Rocklea)*	Model:	*n/a*
Type:	*Bo-Bo diesel-electric*	Engine:	*EE SRKT turbo-charged 4-stroke 8-cylinder*
Traction power:	*590 kW (790 hp)*	Length:	*12.50 m*
Weight:	*89.8–93.4 tonnes*	Gauge:	*1435 mm*

Above: D33 at Cringila on Tuesday 12 April 2005. Chris Walters

Based on the original 1950-vintage 750-type (delivered from English Electric in the UK, but assembled by Comeng—see page 174) the 850-type were delivered in batches between 1959 and 1964, and acquired by what was then Australian Iron & Steel (AIS) for both coal haulage and steelworks traffic. Throughout the AIS and BHP eras, these duties changed little, although over time newer locomotives assumed the coal haulage task, and more and more the 850s were confined to Port Kembla. Although a number were overhauled and modernised by BlueScope between 2003 and 2005, the number of 850s in traffic has fallen to just over half their original number. Only D18 has been scrapped (during 1994), while a number lie in storage near the Steelhaven workshops in varying states of disrepair.

Road #	Builders #	Built	Owner	Status
D16	A.030	1959	Pacific National, Port Kembla	Stored
D17	A.031	1960	Pacific National, Port Kembla	Stored
D19	A.033	1960	Pacific National, Port Kembla	In service
D26	A.039	1960	Pacific National, Port Kembla	Stored
D27	A.040	1960	Pacific National, Port Kembla	In service
D28	A.053	1960	Pacific National, Port Kembla	In service
D29	A.054	1960	Pacific National, Port Kembla	In service
D30	A.083	1964	Pacific National, Port Kembla	In service
D31	A.084	1964	Pacific National, Port Kembla	Stored
D32	A.088	1964	Pacific National, Port Kembla	Stored
D33	A.089	1964	Pacific National, Port Kembla	In service

750 Class

Builder:	*English Electric UK/Comeng*	Model:	*n/a*
Type:	*Bo-Bo diesel-electric*	Engine:	*EE SRKT turbo-charged 4-stroke 8-cylinder*
Traction power:	*450 kW (600 hp)*	Length:	*12.50 m*
Weight:	*86.3 tonnes*	Gauge:	*1435 mm*

Above: Running along behind a special train hauled by steam locomotive *Bronzewing*, D6 hauls a 'support' train for the day's running, along Warehouses 1 and 2 on its way from the Steelhaven Workshops to Waters Siding on Sunday 14 April 1997. The tour program that day provided for passenger shuttles between the Waters Siding and Kemira Colliery. Chris Walters

Built by English Electric in the United Kingdom (although designed and assembled in Australia by Comeng) these locomotives were the first main line diesel locomotives in the country. Initially used on coal haulage, they eventually gravitated more into dedicated steelworks traffic. From Australian Iron & Steel, through BHP, they endured until a steel industry decline in the early 1980s saw many stored. Many of these were never recommissioned and were eventually scrapped in 1990, while two (D1 and D7) were disposed of into preservation. This left only D6, which was maintained by BHP, and then BlueScope, as a quasi-heritage unit and diesel shop shunter at Steelhaven before it was finally stored with defective batteries around 2001. It remains stored near the Steelhaven workshops, although is likely to outlast the newer 850-types abandoned nearby due to its value as a heritage unit.

Road #	Built	Owner	Status
D6	1951	BlueScope Steel	Stored Port Kembla

Y Class

Builder:	*EE/TGR (Launceston)*	Model:	*n/a*
Type:	*Bo-Bo diesel-electric*	Engine:	*EE SRKT turbo-charged 4-stroke 6-cylinder*
Traction power:	*600 kW (800 hp)*	Length:	*12.65 m*
Weight:	*59.0 tonnes*	Gauge:	*1067 mm*

Left: Y1, now known as 2150, at Burnie on Friday 25 February 1999. Chris Walters

Left: The rebuilt DV1 (ex-Y7) at Devonport on Wednesday 31 December 2003. Chris Walters

The pride of the Tasmanian Government Railways when they first appeared in 1961, the Y Class today are one of Tasmania's great survivors. Y1 and Y5 are today 2150 and 2151, and are based in Burnie for yard and wharf shunting (for which their light weight makes them ideal), while Y7 is now DV1, an unpowered 'cab unit' employed on the Railton Cement train, and used to remotely control the DQ Class locomotive at the opposite end of the rake (in order to eliminate the need for extra shunting or additional locomotives).

Road #	Original #	Built	Owner	Status	Name
(Y)2150	Y1	1961	PN Tasmania	In service	-
(Y)2151	Y5	1964	PN Tasmania	In service	*Sir Charles Gairdner*
DV1	Y7	1971	PN Tasmania	In service (unpowered)	-

H Class

Builder:	*English Electric (Rocklea)*	Model:	*n/a*
Type:	*Bo-Bo diesel-electric*	Engine:	*EE CSRKT turbo-charged 4-stroke 6-cylinder*
Traction power:	*640 kW (860 hp)*	Length:	*12.95 m*
Weight:	*72.4 tonnes*	Gauge:	*1435 mm*

Above: SCT's H5 shunting at Forrestfield on 8 December 2005. Bernie Baker

The H Class were originally purchased by the Western Australian Government Railways during 1965 to assist in the completion of the new Kwinana–Perth–Kalgoorlie standard-gauge route. Once this was completed, the class were assigned to shunting and transfer duties. The five-member fleet was down to four (H4 was scrapped in 1992) by the time they were withdrawn by Westrail in 1994, and these were sold to SCT for continued service as yard shunters in 1998. In time these remaining four became dispersed across the country, with all but H5 now gone from their 'native' Perth. As of 2008, this unit is based at Forrestfield and shares shunting duties with the larger K208, while H2 and H3 are based in Adelaide for shunting in Islington (where they work alongside Clyde-EMD unit T345). Meanwhile, H1 has remained stored in Melbourne since 2000, although it was moved from Dynon to SCT's Laverton property at some point (and may have even been cut up during the last year or so, although this is unconfirmed).

Road #	Builder's #	Built	Owner	Status
H1	A.081	1965	SCT Melbourne	Stored Laverton
H2	A.082	1965	SCT Adelaide	In service (Islington)
H3	A.085	1965	SCT Adelaide	In service (Islington)
H5	A.087	1965	SCT Perth	In service (Forrestfield)

F Class

Builder:	*English Electric (Rocklea)*	Model:	*n/a*
Type:	*A1A-A1A diesel-electric*	Engine:	*EE SRKT turbo-charged 4-stroke 6-cylinder*
Traction power:	*510 kW (685 hp)*	Length:	*12.80 m*
Weight:	*64.8 tonnes*	Gauge:	*1067 mm*

Above: F40 at Coote Industrial's Flashbutt Siding compound, near Midland on Saturday 21 June 2008. John Bollans

This original Midland Railway Company English Electric unit dates back to 1958. As such, it is Coote Industrial's oldest locomotive, and for a time was a heritage unit and privately owned. Following purchase from Westrail in 1989, it spent time in the service of the Hotham Valley Tourist Railway (based at Pinjarra), for whom it operated main line tours, and for a period was also an exhibit within the Boyanup Transport Museum before it was acquired by South Spur in 2004. Today it is in Coote Industrial service and is usually employed on 1067 mm rail set transfers and other odd tasks. It is worth noting that both F41 and F43 are preserved, while F44 was for some years employed by ALCOA as a stationary generator at a number of sites in the south-west of the state.

Road #	Builder's #	Built	Owner	Status
F40	A.018	1958	Coote Industrial	In service

500 Class

Builder:	*EE/SAR (Islington)*	Model:	*n/a*
Type:	*Bo-Bo diesel-electric*	Engine:	*EE SRKT turbo-charged 4-stroke 4-cylinder*
Traction power:	*370 kW (500 hp)*	Length:	*11.73 m*
Weight:	*56.9 tonnes*	Gauge:	*1435 and 1600 mm*

Above: 527 at Forrestfield on Sunday 19 March 2006. Bernie Baker

Once numbering 34 units, the 1964-vintage 500 Class could be found right around the former South Australian Railways system as standard power for shunting, transfer and light duties on both the broad and standard gauge networks. Time has proven less kind to low-power locomotives than larger and more powerful designs, although examples of the 500 Class have endured due to their rugged reliability. Of those that now remain, 508, 527 and 53 (ex-533) are workshops shunters (at Port Augusta, Forrestfield and Islington, respectively) while 517 is commonly hired to Penrice Soda for shunting within the cement plant at Osborne. The remaining pair (518 and 532) are reportedly operational, although have no fixed duties. It is worth noting that both 508 and 527 served as shunters at Tennant Creek and Katherine during the construction of the Alice Springs to Darwin line during 2002–2003.

Road #	Original #	Builder's #	Built	Owner	Status
508	508	113	1965	GWA	In 1435 mm service (Port Augusta)
517	517	122	1967	GWA	In 1600 mm service (Penrice Soda)
518	518	123	1967	Coote Industrial	Stored Islington (1435 mm)
527	527	132	1969	ARG	In 1435 mm service (Forrestfield)
532	532	137	1969	GWA	Stored Whyalla (1435 mm)
53	533	138	1969	NREC	In 1435 mm service (Islington)

Walkers Limited

7340 (being towed on an ARG freight) near Illabo, during its transfer to Narrandera on Saturday 3 July 2004. Chris Walters

3500/3600/3551/3900 Class

Builder:	*Clyde/ASEA/Walkers (Maryborough)*		
Type:	*Bo-Bo-Bo electric*	Traction motors/line voltage:	*25 kV*
Continuous power:	*2900 kW (3890 hp)*	Length:	*20.02 m*
Weight:	*108.0 tonnes*	Gauge:	*1067 mm*

Above: 3508 and 3536 (in original condition) at Westwood (between Rockhampton and Emerald) on Sunday 24 June 2007. Stephen Miller

Built more or less concurrently with the Comeng/Hitachi 3100/3200 Class fleet were the 50 3500/3600 Class 'command' and 'slave' electric locomotives, that made their debut in late 1986 purely for use on the newly electrified Queensland Rail (QR) coal network. When the time came to extend the locomotive orders, in addition to procuring further 'coal network' locomotives (as had been done with the 3100/3200 Classes), QR also asked the Clyde/ASEA/Walkers consortium for a 'general service' version of the 3500/3600, resulting in 30 3900 Class locomotives for use on the North Coast Line between Brisbane and Rockhampton (although they would also appear on the Emerald Line, west from Rockhampton). The 3900 Class were delivered between 1988 and 1989.

Just as the 3100/3200 fleet had come to dominate the Goonyella network, the 3500/3600 Class locomotives eventually settled in to call Blackwater system home, and thus were based at Callemondah in Gladstone. By 2002, QR had begun diverting some of the 3900 Class off the North Coast Line and into Blackwater coal traffic. However the 3900 Class had been built primarily for speed and as such could not quite match the 3500/3600 Class low-speed haulage capacity. In order to better outfit the 3900s for coal service, they began to be shopped at Rockhampton for rebuild in order to upgrade their specifications. The resulting 3551 Class was deemed a success, and eventually 19 of the 3900 Class were so refurbished (although no 3552 will ever materialise due to the year 2000 scrapping of 3902, following severe collision damage sustained some years prior).

Ten 3900 Class were initially left unaltered, although even these were eventually cycled through a 3551-type program. This project stopped short of a full rebuild, as the bogie/traction motor changes of the full 3551 Class specification were skipped. These locomotives were released still carrying their 3900 Class road numbers and could, in theory, switch between coal and general service if required. At around this time the 3500 and 3600 Classes were also being put through the workshops for a 3551-type upgrade. The updated Locotrol equipment used by the coal trains (in order to remotely control mid-train, distributed-power locomotives), had become sufficiently compact enough to install inside locomotive cabs (rather than on separate Locotrol wagons), and this became a factor capable of wiping out the need for dedicated command and slave units. As such, all 3600 Class units passing through the program emerged as 3500 Class locomotives. By 2010 the modernisation of the entire Clyde/ASEA/Walkers fleet should be completed, with the result that many more years of service will lie ahead of them.

Right: Refurbished 3529 and 3522 lead an eastbound, loaded coal train at Stanwell on Monday 11 August 2008. Stephen Miller

Below: Overhauled locomotive 3926 at the Downer-EDI Rail plant in Maryborough, on Thursday 6 April 2006. Arthur Shale

Walkers

Road #	Original #	Builder's #	Built	Owner	Status
3501	3501	807	1986	QRNational	In service
3502	3502	808	1986	QRNational	In service
3503	3503	809	1986	QRNational	In service
3504	3504	810	1986	QRNational	In service
Named *D V Mendoza*.					
3505	3605	811	1986	QRNational	In service
3606	3606	812	1986	QRNational	In service
3507	3607	813	1986	QRNational	In service
3508	3508	814	1987	QRNational	In service
3609	3609	815	1987	QRNational	In service
3510	3610	816	1987	QRNational	In service
3611	3611	817	1987	QRNational	In service
3512	3512	818	1987	QRNational	In service
3513	3613	819	1987	QRNational	In service
3614	3614	820	1987	QRNational	In service
3615	3615	821	1987	QRNational	In service
3516	3516	822	1987	QRNational	In service
3617	3617	823	1987	QRNational	In service
3518	3618	824	1987	QRNational	In service
3619	3619	825	1987	QRNational	In service
3520	3520	826	1987	QRNational	In service
3621	3621	827	1987	QRNational	In service
3522	3622	828	1987	QRNational	In service
3523	3623	829	1987	QRNational	In service
3524	3524	830	1987	QRNational	In service
3525	3625	831	1987	QRNational	In service
3626	3626	832	1987	QRNational	In service
3627	3627	833	1987	QRNational	In service
3528	3528	834	1987	QRNational	In service
3529	3629	835	1987	QRNational	In service
3530	3630	836	1987	QRNational	In service
3631	3631	837	1987	QRNational	In service
3532	3532	838	1987	QRNational	In service
3533	3633	839	1987	QRNational	In service
3634	3634	840	1987	QRNational	In service
3635	3635	841	1987	QRNational	In service
3536	3536	842	1988	QRNational	In service
3537	3637	843	1988	QRNational	In service
3538	3638	844	1988	QRNational	In service
3539	3639	845	1988	QRNational	In service
3540	3540	846	1988	QRNational	In service
3541	3641	847	1988	QRNational	In service

(continued)

Road #	Original #	Builder's #	Built	Owner	Status
3642	3642	848	1988	QRNational	In service
3543	3643	849	1988	QRNational	In service
3544	3544	850	1988	QRNational	In service
3545	3645	851	1988	QRNational	In service
3546	3546	852	1988	QRNational	In service
3547	3547	853	1988	QRNational	In service
3548	3548	854	1988	QRNational	In service
Named *City of Gladstone*.					
3549	3549	855	1988	QRNational	In service
3550	3550	856	1988	QRNational	In service
3551 †	3901	857	1988 (2003)	QRNational	In service
3553 †	3903	859	1988 (2003)	QRNational	In service
3554 †	3904	860	1988 (2003)	QRNational	In service
3555 †	3905	861	1988 (2003)	QRNational	In service
3556 †	3906	862	1988 (2003)	QRNational	In service
3557 †	3907	863	1988 (2003)	QRNational	In service
3558 †	3908	864	1988 (2003)	QRNational	In service
3559 †	3909	865	1988 (2004)	QRNational	In service
3560 †	3910	866	1988 (2004)	QRNational	In service
3561 †	3911	867	1988 (2004)	QRNational	In service
3562 †	3912	868	1988 (2005)	QRNational	In service
3563 †	3913	869	1989 (2005)	QRNational	In service
3564 †	3914	870	1989 (2005)	QRNational	In service
3565 †	3915	871	1989 (2003)	QRNational	In service
3566 †	3916	872	1989 (2004)	QRNational	In service
3567 †	3917	873	1989 (2004)	QRNational	In service
3569 †	3919	875	1989 (2004)	QRNational	In service
3573 †	3923	879	1989 (2004)	QRNational	In service
3918 ‡	3918	874	1989	QRNational	In service
3920 ‡	3920	876	1989	QRNational	In service
3921 ‡	3921	877	1989	QRNational	In service
3922 ‡	3922	878	1989	QRNational	In service
3924 ‡	3924	880	1989	QRNational	In service
3925 ‡	3925	881	1989	QRNational	In service
3926 ‡	3926	882	1989	QRNational	In service
3927 ‡	3927	883	1989	QRNational	In service
3928 ‡	3928	884	1989	QRNational	In service
3929 ‡	3929	885	1990	QRNational	In service
3930 ‡	3930	886	1990	QRNational	In service

† Denotes 3551 Class (build date in bracket reflects time of converison from 3900 Class)

‡ Denotes 3900 Class

DTD Class (Cairns Tilt Train)

Builder:	*EDI/Hitachi (Maryborough)*	Model:	*n/a*
Type:	*B-B diesel-hydraulic*	Engine:	*2 x MTU 12V396*
Traction power:	*2700 kW (3620 hp)—less HEP*	Length:	*20.05 m*
Weight:	*60.0 tonnes*	Gauge:	*1067 mm*

Above: DTD5403 (with DTD5404 trailing) leads the southbound Cairns Tilt Train at White Rock (just south of Cairns) on Friday 6 July 2007. Chris Stratton

Following on from the commissioning of a new electric tilt train passenger service between Brisbane and Rockhampton during 1998, QR decided to extend the concept—literally—with a diesel version operating through to Cairns. As with the electric fleet, the new train was actually two identical train sets (although, controversially, no overnight sleeping accommodation was incorporated into the concept). Each of these two train sets have a locomotive, or power car, at each end, to provide both propulsion and the onboard power supply. Testing of the new diesel-hydraulic DTD locomotives (built by EDI in partnership with Hitachi) began in 2002, ahead of the official launch of the new service on 15 June 2003. Unfortunately a serious derailment north of Bundaberg on 15 November 2004 resulted in one of the trains being out of service for around 18 months, while the remaining tilt services were limited to 100 km/h until mid-2007.

Road #	Built	Owner	Status
DTD5401	2002	QR Traveltrain	In service
DTD5402	2002	QR Traveltrain	In service
DTD5403	2002	QR Traveltrain	In service
DTD5404	2002	QR Traveltrain	In service

11 Class

Builder:	*Walkers (Maryborough)*	Model:	*GH1000V*
Type:	*B-B diesel-hydraulic*	Engine:	*Caterpillar D398 series B V12*
Traction power:	*530 kW (710 hp)*	Length:	*10.97 m*
Weight:	*54.9 tonnes*	Gauge:	*1067 mm*

Above: 1104, 1101, 1002 and 1106 are about to depart Burnie for the Hellyer mine in the early hours of Monday 1 March 1999. Chris Walters

The 11 Class was part of an investment to improve the former Emu Bay Railway (EBR) system, although the operation was sold to ATN Tasrail in 1998. The vacuum-braked EBR services soon came under heavy scrutiny, and the last vacuum-braked, 11 Class-hauled services occurred when 1106, 1105, 1102 and 1104 operated to Melba Flats on 22 March 2002. Soon after 1101 and 1105 were quickly purchased by Queensland-based tourist operators with the former going to the Cairns Kuranda Steam Train Group and the latter to Beaudesert Rail (which proved a short-lived operation, and in fact 1105 was eventually sold to join 1101). 1101 and 1105 were made available for hire with 1101 (at least) being employed, for a time, by Pacific National Queensland for shunting in Mackay. Eventually the remaining five also left Tasmania, with 1102 also going to Cairns and the remaining four to Townsville-based engineering group, Curtain Bros, for proposed railway construction work. By mid-2008 all seven of the class had been shipped to Queensland.

Road #	Builder's #	Built	Owner	Status
1103	640	1969	Curtain Bros, Townsville	Stored
1104	641	1969	Curtain Bros, Townsville	Stored
1106	658	1971	Curtain Bros, Townsville	Stored
1107	659	1971	Curtain Bros, Townsville	Stored

73 Class

Builder:	*Walkers (Maryborough)*	Model:	*GH700V*
Type:	*B-B diesel-hydraulic*	Engine:	*Caterpillar D379 Series B 4-stroke turbo-charged V12*
Traction power:	*485 kW (650 hp)*	Length:	*10.97 m*
Weight:	*49.8 tonnes*	Gauge:	*1435 mm*

Above: 7340 at Manildra on Wednesday 14 April 1995. This unit was transferred to Narrandera in July 2004. Chris Stratton

The 73 Class were delivered to the NSW Government Railways in two batches (20 and 30) from 1970. They were intended, as were most of the Walkers B-B diesel-hydraulics, to dieselise that last bastion of steam: yard shunting. The 1980s and 1990s saw their usefulness decline, however, and slowly, but steadily quite a number were withdrawn and sold off. Many of these were acquired for rebuild, conversion to 610 mm-gauge and a new career within the Queensland sugar industry (see page 242), however several more were disposed of into preservation or simply scrapped. Those that remain in commercial service cling to service life, although none are involved in anything that could be described as intensive use. Five are currently in service (in addition to those now working in the sugar industry), while a number of others are stored for potential recommissioning, however this seems unlikely any time soon.

Road #	Builder's #	Built	Owner	Status
7301	660	1970	CountryLink	Stored Chullora
7307	666	1971	Patrick PortLink	In service
7321	683	1972	Patrick PortLink	In service
7322	684	1972	QRN Yennora	Stored Yennora
7333	695	1972	QRN Yennora	In service
7334	696	1972	Wimmera Container Lines	In service
7340	702	1972	Manildra Corp	In service

MA Class

Builder:	*Walkers (Maryborough)*	Model:	*GH700*
Type:	*B-B diesel-hydraulic*	Engine:	*Caterpillar D379 series B turbo-charged 4-stroke V8*
Traction power:	*485 kW (650 hp)*	Length:	*10.97 m*
Weight:	*44.6 tonnes*	Gauge:	*1067 mm*

Above: MA1862 at Claisebrook on Sunday 29 July 2007. Chris Walters

The Western Australian Government Railways also invested in the popular Walkers diesel-hydraulic, although its interest eventuated in two separate classes: the M and MA. The two M Class units (1851 and 1852) arrived in 1972, and were followed a year later by the three MA Class locomotives (1861, 1862 and 1863). The differences between the two could be summarised as both weight (the M Class were slightly heavier, for hump yard shunting) and power: the M Class possessed Cummins engines, while the MAs were powered by a Caterpillar unit, similar to many of the other Walkers types. During 1994, four of these five shunting units were sold to CSR for potential 610 mm-gauge service in Queensland, with M1851 and M1852 now operating for Victoria Mill, near Ingham (see page 242) and MA1861 and MA1863 stored (untouched) at Plane Creek Mill (near Sarina) pending future use. This left only MA1862 in Western Australia, and for more than a decade this locomotive has been attached to the Transperth EMU depot at Claisebrook, where it is employed as a shunter, 'rescue' unit and power for EMU transfers to the wheel lathe at Forrestfield.

Road #	Builder's #	Built	Owner	Status
MA1862	714	1973	Transperth Claisebrook	In service

DH Class

Builder:	*Walkers (Maryborough)*	Model:	*GH500*
Type:	*B-B diesel-hydraulic*	Engine:	*Caterpillar D353 Series-E 6-cylinder*
Traction power:	*350 kW (465 hp)*	Length:	*10.06 m*
Weight:	*36.6 tonnes*	Gauge:	*1067 mm*

Above: DH73 at Jilalan on Sunday 22 September 2002. Chris Walters

In 1966 Walkers Limited delivered to Queensland Railways a demonstrator unit, simply numbered W1. A development of the three 10 Class locomotives built for the Emu Bay Railway three years earlier, the success of W1 (later known as DH1) resulted in a further 72 'production' DH Class units, which by 1974 came to dominate the system's marshalling yards, transfer duties and even some lightly-laid branch lines. As with dedicated shunting designs right around the country, their value began to lessen as a move was made to fewer, longer unit-type trains and the DH Class ranks were decimated throughout the 1980s and 1990s. Many DH Class units were subsequently acquired by members of the Australian sugar industry for rebuild and conversion to 610 mm gauge for cane train haulage (see page 242), however as of 2008, only five remained in QR ownership. Two are attached to QR's infrastructure division to aid in track work and related duties, and three are with QRN. Of those, one is the depot shunter at Jilalan, another similarly employed at Callemondah, while the third is stored defective at Rockhampton.

Road #	Original #	Builder's #	Built	Owner	Status
MMY37	DH37	619	1969	QR	In service
MMY45	DH45	627	1969	QR	In service
DH71	DH71	716	1973	QRN Rockhampton	Stored
DH72	DH72	717	1974	QRN Callemondah	In service
DH73	DH73	718	1974	QRN Jilalan	In service

DL Class

Builder:	*Walkers Limited (Maryborough)*	Model:	*n/a*
Type:	*2-6-0 diesel-mechanical*	Engine:	*Gardner 6L3, 6 cylinders*
Traction power:	*115 kW (150 hp)*	Length:	*6.25 m*
Weight:	*17.8 tonnes*	Gauge:	*1067 mm*

Above: DL4 at Normanton for *Gulflander* duties on Monday 8 July 1996.
Harry Wright (ARHS/nsw Rail Resource Centre)

Class leader DL1 was the first diesel locomotive in government service in Australia when it entered service in 1939. At 150 hp it was a small start, but the QR-built unit was just the beginning. Oddly enough, three more DL Class locomotives were eventually delivered, although the second, DL2 (built in the UK by Stephenson & Hawthorn) did not follow until 1954, while DL3 and DL4 were built locally by Walkers and commissioned in 1961. DL1 and its sisters were devoted to the Etheridge Line through the Atherton Tablelands west of Cairns. Rebuilding of the regions lines to allow the use of heavier locomotives by 1968 saw the four relegated to shunting work. Although its sister units were withdrawn and preserved, during 1988 DL4 was transferred to Normanton in 1988 to be held on standby to the vintage rail motor employed on the *Gulflander* services run on the isolated section of line to Croydon.

Road #	Builders #	Built	Owner	Status	Name
DL4	572	1961	QR	In service	*Almaden*

Goninan
Comeng
Clyde
NSWGR
Tulloch
Siemens
MKA

UGR/Siemens rebuilds 3702 and 3706 at Wandoo, near Nebo, on Friday 15 August 2008. Stephen Miller

47 Class

Builder:	*Goninan/Hitachi (Broadmeadow)*	Model:	*n/a*
Type:	*Co-Co diesel-electric*	Engine:	*Caterpillar D399TA turbo-charged 4-stroke V16*
Traction power:	*745 kW (1000 hp)*	Length:	*14.00 m*
Weight:	*85.3 tonnes*	Gauge:	*1435 mm*

Left: 4717 leads train WL81, a westbound run of the AK track-inspection cars, into Molong on Monday 19 May 2008.
Greg Pringle

Other

Delivered to the NSWGR at the tail-end of the steam era, the 47 Class originally tallied 20 members, although a number of reliability issues ensured their governmental career was not as long as the other branch line classes (the 48 and 49). A number of Lachlan Valley Railway (LVR) members of the class are common in lease service, however Independent Rail's 4717 is the only remaining member of the class owned by a commercial operator (although it commonly works with LVR's 4703 and 4708). It (and the LVR lease units) can be found on all manner of Independent Rail rosters, whether it be rural freight services in tandem with the MZ units, Minto trip trains or even RailCorp contracts.

Road #	Builder's #	Built	Owner	Status
4717	047	1973	Independent Rail	In service

BU Class

Builder:	*MKA/Goodwin*	Model:	*n/a*
Type:	*A1A-A1A booster unit*	Engine:	*n/a*
Traction power:	*n/a*	Length:	*11.74 m*
Weight:	*56.9 tonnes*	Gauge:	*1435 mm*

Above: BU2 in storage at Dry Creek on Saturday 7 June 1997. Chris Walters

In 1994 Morrison Knudsen Australia (MKA) rebuilt four service-worn Australian National (AN) 600 Class locomotives (see page 116) as engine-less 'slugs', or perhaps more accurately—tractive effort booster units. Using the basis of the shortened description of 'booster unit', the four were reclassed as the BU Class, and leased back to AN for exclusive use with the ALF Class locomotives MKA delivered earlier that same year.

The logic was that power 'wasted' between the engine and railhead on a standard locomotive, could be channelled through the traction motors of a coupled booster unit to better utilise the potential tractive effort, although such potential only really existed in certain circumstances. With that in mind, the units were tested, and then commissioned in slow, comparatively heavy traffics such as the Leigh Creek coal train, and both grain and ore services. The units were eventually deemed a failure due to reliability issues, and within a year were all in storage at Dry Creek. They remained there until moved back to Whyalla in 1997. This was just prior to the sale of AN to Australia Southern Railroad (ASR), and in a surprise move, ASR chose to trial BU1 for a period during 2000. The unit was used on grain services, but did not last long in traffic, before being withdrawn again. The assets of MKA eventually came under NREC ownership and were eventually moved to Islington Workshops, where they remain today.

Road #	Rebuilt	Builder's #	Built	Owner	Status
BU1	605	94-AN-029	1994	NREC	Stored Islington
BU2	601	94-AN-027	1994	NREC	Stored Islington
BU3	604	94-AN-028	1994	NREC	Stored Islington
BU4	606	94-AN-026	1994	NREC	Stored Islington

3100/3200/3700/3800 Class

Builder:	*3100/3200:*	*Comeng/Hitachi (Eagle Farm)*			
	3700:	*United Group Rail/Siemens (Bohle and Broadmeadow)*			
	3800:	*Siemens (Munich, Germany)*			
Type:	*Bo-Bo-Bo electric*		Line voltage:	*25 kV*	
Continuous power:	*3100/3200:*	*2900 kW (3890 hp)*	Length:	*3100/3200/3700:*	*19.38 m*
	3700/3800:	*4000 kW (5360 hp)*		*3800:*	*20.40 m*
Weight:	*3100/3200:*	*108.0 tonnes*	Gauge:	*1067 mm*	
	3700:	*126.0 tonnes*			
	3800:	*132.0 tonnes*			

Above: 3108, 3208 and 3407 lead a Goonyella System loaded coal train between Balook and Bolingbroke on Thursday 10 July 2008. John Hoyle

A total of 86 3100 (command) and 3200 (slave) class Bo-Bo-Bo electric locomotives were acquired from a Comeng/Hitachi consortium between 1986 and 1988 for service on the then newly electrified QR coal network. Electrification eventually came to cover both the Goonyella and Blackwater systems in Central Queensland, and while the Clyde/ASEA/Walkers-built 3500/3600 Classes came to dominate the latter, the 3100/3200 Class fleet gravitated towards Jilalan (Sarina) and the Goonyella System, servicing the export facilities at Hay Point and Dalrymple Bay just south of Mackay. Unfortunately, 3267 and 3282 were scrapped following a derailment at Black Mountain (west of Sarina) on 17 November 1994.

After nearly twenty years of intensive coal haulage service, 3226 (in need of repair following a derailment at Waitara) was shopped at the Bohle (Townsville) works of the United Rail Group (formerly Goninan) for rebuild using new and more advanced Siemens equipment. Sister units 3213 and 3217 soon followed, and these three were prototypes for a proposed remanufacture of the whole 3100/3200 Class fleet.

Even before the release of these three prototypes, it had been announced that Siemens/UGR had won a $250 million contract to similarly upgrade and rebuild sixty members of the 3100/3200 Class fleet as the 4000 kW, AC-traction 3700 Class.

The first prototype, 3701 (ex-3226), arrived in Jilalan on 21 December 2005, with main line trials following thereafter. The intention of the 3700 Class project being to replace five 3100/3200 Class locomotives in traffic with three 3700 Class units.

Among the changes wrought by this rebuild was the deletion of one of the two crew cabs (which was no longer required), although the outline of the former cab profile is still obvious at the No. 2 end of the 3700 Class. Unlike the three prototypes, most of the subsequent rebuilds have been undertaken at UGR's Broadmeadow plant in Broadmeadow (Newcastle, NSW), necessitating a complex series of road transfers of locomotives between Acacia Ridge and Newcastle.

At around the same time as the announcement of the 3700 Class project, QR also made public its decision to order 20 new 3800 Class AC-traction locomotives, which, although very similar in appearance to the rebuilt locomotives, are actually six tonnes heavier. These new locomotives are being built by Siemens in Munich, Germany rather than by UGR in Australia (as with the 3700 Class). This order was subsequently increased to 45, with the first two examples arriving in Brisbane during late June 2008. The most obviously difference between these and the 3700 Class rebuilds—visually, at least—is a completely flat No. 2 end. The new and rebuilt units will allow a two for three replacement on Goonyella coal trains, thus requiring fewer locomotives for each load or allowing an increased number of trains to be hauled. Pacific National is believed to have placed an order for units based on the 3800 Class, to be known as the 71 Class.

3100/3200 Class

Road #	Built	Owner	Status	Name
3101	1986	QRNational	In service	*Sir Joh Bjelke Peterson*
3102	1986	QRNational	In service	-
3103	1986	QRNational	In service	*John Jeffcoat*
3104	1986	QRNational	In service	-
3207	1987	QRNational	In service	-
3108	1987	QRNational	In service	-
3209	1987	QRNational	In service	-
3211	1987	QRNational	In service	-
3112	1987	QRNational	In service	-
3214	1987	QRNational	In service	-
3116	1987	QRNational	In service	-
3218	1987	QRNational	In service	-
3219	1987	QRNational	In service	-
3120	1987	QRNational	In service	-
3221	1987	QRNational	In service	-
3222	1987	QRNational	In service	-
3124	1987	QRNational	In service	-
3227	1987	QRNational	In service	-

(continued)

Road #	Built	Owner	Status	Name
3128	1987	QRNational	In service	-
3229	1987	QRNational	In service	-
3230	1987	QRNational	In service	-
3132	1988	QRNational	In service	-
3136	1988	QRNational	In service	-
3237	1988	QRNational	In service	-
3239	1988	QRNational	In service	-
3140	1988	QRNational	In service	-
3241	1988	QRNational	In service	-
3243	1988	QRNational	In service	-
3144	1988	QRNational	In service	-
3247	1988	QRNational	In service	-
3148	1988	QRNational	In service	-
3251	1988	QRNational	In service	-
3152	1988	QRNational	In service	-
3253	1988	QRNational	In service	-
3254	1988	QRNational	In service	-
3156	1988	QRNational	In service	-
3258	1988	QRNational	In service	-
3160	1988	QRNational	In service	-
3261	1988	QRNational	In service	-
3263	1988	QRNational	In service	-
3164	1988	QRNational	In service	-
3168	1988	QRNational	In service	-
3270	1989	QRNational	In service	-
3271	1989	QRNational	In service	-
3273	1989	QRNational	In service	-
3274	1989	QRNational	In service	-
3275	1989	QRNational	In service	-
3277	1989	QRNational	In service	-
3280	1989	QRNational	In service	-
3283	1989	QRNational	In service	-
3284	1989	QRNational	In service	-
3285	1989	QRNational	In service	-

3700 Class

Road #	Original #	Built	Owner	Status
3701	3226	2005	QRNational	In service
3702	3213	2006	QRNational	In service
3703	3217	2006	QRNational	In service
3704	3205	2007	QRNational	In service
3705	3266	2007	QRNational	In service
3706	3223	2007	QRNational	In service

(continued)

Road #	Original #	Built	Owner	Status
3707	3233	2007	QRNational	In service
3708	3225	2007	QRNational	In service
3709	3249	2007	QRNational	In service
3710	3262	2007	QRNational	In service
3711*	3246/3279	2007	QRNational	In service
3712	3272	2008	QRNational	In service
3713	3276	2008	QRNational	In service
3714	3210	2008	QRNational	In service
3715	3281	2008	QRNational	In service
3716	3206	2008	QRNational	In service
3717	3286	2008	QRNational	In service
3718	3245	2008	QRNational	In service
3719	3265	2008	QRNational	In service
3720	3269	2008	QRNational	In service
3721	3738	2008	QRNational	In service
3722	3250	2008	QRNational	In service
3723	3259	2008	QRNational	In service
3724	3257	2008	QRNational	In service
3725	3242	2008	QRNational	In service
3726	3235	2008	QRNational	pending
3727	3215	2008	QRNational	pending
3728	3234	2008	QRNational	pending
3729	3278	2008	QRNational	pending
3730	pending	pending	QRNational	pending
3731	pending	pending	QRNational	pending
3732	pending	pending	QRNational	pending
3733	pending	pending	QRNational	pending
3734	pending	pending	QRNational	pending
3735	pending	pending	QRNational	pending
3736	pending	pending	QRNational	pending
3737	pending	pending	QRNational	pending
3738	pending	pending	QRNational	pending
3739	pending	pending	QRNational	pending
3740	pending	pending	QRNational	pending
3741	pending	pending	QRNational	pending
3742	pending	pending	QRNational	pending
3743	pending	pending	QRNational	pending
3744	pending	pending	QRNational	pending
3745	pending	pending	QRNational	pending
3746	pending	pending	QRNational	pending
3747	pending	pending	QRNational	pending
3748	pending	pending	QRNational	pending

** 3711 was built using parts from both 3246 and 3279, both heavily damaged in separate derailments.*

(continued)

Road #	Original #	Built	Owner	Status
3749	pending	pending	QRNational	pending
3750	pending	pending	QRNational	pending
3751	pending	pending	QRNational	pending
3752	pending	pending	QRNational	pending
3753	pending	pending	QRNational	pending
3754	pending	pending	QRNational	pending
3755	pending	pending	QRNational	pending
3756	pending	pending	QRNational	pending
3757	pending	pending	QRNational	pending
3758	pending	pending	QRNational	pending
3759	pending	pending	QRNational	pending
3760	pending	pending	QRNational	pending
3761	pending	pending	QRNational	pending
3762	pending	pending	QRNational	pending
3763	pending	pending	QRNational	pending

Above: Having just arrived in Australia from Siemens, Germany, 3801 and 3802 wait at the Port of Brisbane (Fisherman's Island) Thursday 10 July 2008. Shawn Stutsel

3800 Class

Road #	Built	Owner	Status
3801	2008	QRNational	pending
3802	2008	QRNational	pending
3803	2008	QRNational	pending
3804	2008	QRNational	pending
3805	2008	QRNational	pending
3806	2008	QRNational	pending

(continued)

Road #	Built	Owner	Status
3807	2008	QRNational	pending
3808	2008	QRNational	pending
3809	2008	QRNational	pending
3810	2008	QRNational	pending
3811	2008	QRNational	pending
3812	2008	QRNational	pending
3813	2008	QRNational	pending
3814	2008	QRNational	pending
3815	2008	QRNational	pending
3816	2008	QRNational	pending
3817	2008	QRNational	pending
3818	2008	QRNational	pending
3819	2008	QRNational	pending
3820	2008	QRNational	pending
3821	2008	QRNational	pending
3822	2008	QRNational	pending
3823	2008	QRNational	pending
3824	2008	QRNational	pending
3825	2008	QRNational	pending
3826	2009	QRNational	pending
3827	2009	QRNational	pending
3828	2009	QRNational	pending
3829	2009	QRNational	pending
3830	2009	QRNational	pending
3831	2009	QRNational	pending
3832	2009	QRNational	pending
3833	2009	QRNational	pending
3834	2009	QRNational	pending
3835	2009	QRNational	pending
3836	2009	QRNational	pending
3837	2009	QRNational	pending
3838	2009	QRNational	pending
3839	2009	QRNational	pending
3840	2009	QRNational	pending
3841	2009	QRNational	pending
3842	2009	QRNational	pending
3843	2009	QRNational	pending
3844	2009	QRNational	pending
3845	2009	QRNational	pending

86 Class

Builder:	*Comeng (Granville)*	Model:	*CL627A*
Type:	*Co-Co electric*	Traction motors/voltage:	*Mitsubishi 1500 DC*
Power:	*2700 kW (3620 hp)*	Length:	*18.73 m*
Weight:	*118.3 tonnes*	Gauge:	*1435 mm*

Left: 8622 (and 8601) in storage at Chullora on Monday 19 February 2007. At the time, 8622 was in private hands and (along with 8609 at Eveleigh and 8649 at Werris Creek), was later sold to NREC. 8609 and 8622 were transferred to storage at Lithgow on 26 August 2008, however it is believed that 8649 remained at Werris Creek. 8601 has been acquired by the Dorrigo Steam Railway & Museum, and was subsequently transferred to Kooragang Island.
Chris Walters

The era of electric locomotives on NSW main lines came to end in late June 2002, and since that time, the dwindling numbers of 85 and 86 Class unit have performed no function other than infrastructure trains (particularly Bondi Junction Turnback and AK inspection train duties) and enthusiast tours. In fact, the ten 85 Class themselves have not run at all since 1998. Four of the once fifty-strong 86 Class fleet now remain in the hands of commercial operators (including 8619, which for a time was under consideration for rebuild as an SCT-owned driving-cab unit/crew van), but the likelihood of a return to service for any of them in the foreseeable future appears very slim.

Road #	Built	Owner	Status
8609	1983	NREC	Stored Lithgow
8619	1983	SCT	Stored Islington
8622	1984	NREC	Stored Lithgow
8649	1985	NREC	Stored Werris Creek

XP Class

Builder:	*Comeng (Granville)/ASEA Brown Boveri (Dandenong)*		
Type:	*Bo-Bo diesel-electric*	Engine:	*Paxman 12VP185 V12*
Gross power:	*1480 kW (1980 hp)*	Length:	*17.34 m*
Weight:	*74.0 tonnes*	Gauge:	*1435 mm*

Above: XP2007 *City of Albury* leads the Sydney to Melbourne Daylight XPT service through Menangle on Friday 8 August 2008. Most XP units have, over the years, worn names based on some of the locations they have serviced. However, these are slowly being removed as the fleet is repainted. Trent Nicholson

Amongst the most iconic and well known trains covered in this book are the nineteen locomotives employed by NSW Government-owned, rural and interstate rail passenger provider CountryLink, for its intensive XPT services radiating out from Sydney. Ten XP Class locomotives (or power cars, as they are perhaps better known) formed the core of the first Comeng order for XPT (eXpress Passenger Trains), but were soon followed by five additional units (with an accompanying batch of additional carriages). The final four were delivered in 1992 by ASEA Brown Boveri (or ABB) in Dandenong, Victoria, due to the winding up of the Comeng rolling stock business a few years earlier. The XPT trains are amongst the most highly utilised long-distance rail vehicles in the world, and for a long time, these trains were also holders of Australia's rail speed record (a crown since wrested by QR's electric tilt trains).

Commencing with XP2016 in 2000, a program was undertaken to re-engine the XP fleet with a new Paxman 12VP185 engine replacing the original 12RP200L (although power output remained unchanged). More recently the fleet has been progressively undergoing crew-cab upgrades and a fleet-wide repaint in CountryLink's darker 'Phase 3' three livery of two-tone blue, yellow and white. All 19 continue in regular traffic as of late 2008, with XPT services presently serving Melbourne, Brisbane, Casino and Dubbo 7-days a week.

Road #	Built	Owner	Status
XP2000	1981	CountryLink	in service
XP2001	1981	CountryLink	in service
XP2002	1981	CountryLink	in service
XP2003	1982	CountryLink	in service
XP2004	1982	CountryLink	in service
XP2005	1982	CountryLink	in service
XP2006	1982	CountryLink	in service
XP2007	1982	CountryLink	in service
XP2008	1982	CountryLink	in service
XP2009	1982	CountryLink	in service
XP2010	1984	CountryLink	in service
XP2011	1984	CountryLink	in service
XP2012	1984	CountryLink	in service
XP2013	1984	CountryLink	in service
XP2014	1984	CountryLink	in service
XP2015	1992	CountryLink	in service
XP2016	1992	CountryLink	in service
XP2017	1992	CountryLink	in service
XP2018	1992	CountryLink	in service

Above: XP2017 leads ST24, the northbound Melbourne to Sydney Daylight XPT, through Bomen (just north of Wagga Wagga) on Sunday 15 June 2008. XP2017 illustrates the newest iteration of the CountyLink livery. Stephen Karas

3300/3400 Class

Builder:	*Clyde/Hitachi (Kelso): 3301–3304, 3405, 3415* *Clyde/Hitachi (Somerton): 3316–3319, 3419–3422*	Model:	*JAE30B-3B*
		Type:	*Bo-Bo-Bo electric*
		Traction motors/line voltage:	*Hitachi 25 kV*
Power:	*3000 kW (4020 hp)*	Length:	*20.55 m*
Weight:	*113.0 tonnes*	Gauge:	*1067 mm*

Above: 3414 between rosters at the extensive locomotive workshops at Jilalan (near Sarina) on Sunday 23 September 2002. Chris Walters

Clyde, who had been involved in the earlier 3500/3600/3900 Class order, was tasked with building 15 (later increased to 22) electric locomotives, which they assembled in their Kelso (Bathurst, NSW) and Somerton (in the northern suburbs of Melbourne) plants before shipment north. The class was plagued by a number of problems that significantly delayed their commissioning (and which continue to see them restricted to trailing-unit status). Eventually they did settle down into service, and became attached to the Goonyella network where they would work with the older 3100/3200 Class Comeng/Hitachi units.

Road #	Builder's #	Built	Owner	Status
3301	93-1282	1994	QRNational	In service
3302	93-1283	1994	QRNational	In service
3303	93-1284	1994	QRNational	In service
3304	93-1285	1995	QRNational	In service
3405	94-1286	1995	QRNational	In service
3406	94-1287	1995	QRNational	In service
3407	94-1288	1995	QRNational	In service
3408	94-1289	1995	QRNational	In service
3409	94-1290	1995	QRNational	In service
3411	94-1292	1995	QRNational	In service
3412	94-1293	1995	QRNational	In service
3413	94-1294	1995	QRNational	In service
3414	94-1295	1995	QRNational	In service
3415	94-1296	1995	QRNational	In service
3316	94-1366	1995	QRNational	In service
3317	94-1367	1995	QRNational	In service
3318	94-1368	1995	QRNational	In service
3419	94-1369	1995	QRNational	In service
3420	94-1370	1995	QRNational	In service
3421	94-1371	1995	QRNational	In service
3422	94-1372	1995	QRNational	In service

X200 Class

Builder:	*NSWGR (Chullora)*	Model:	*n/a*
Type:	*0-4-0 diesel-hydraulic*	Engine:	*Cummins NHRS-6B1 4-stroke 6-cylinder*
Traction power:	*190 kW (260 hp)*	Length:	*6.32 m*
Weight:	*30.5 tonnes*	Gauge:	*1435 mm*

Above: SCT's X107 at Parkes Loco on Saturday 17 May 2008. Chris Walters

The first six X200 Class (described as rail tractors, but effectively locomotives) were built at the Plant and Equipment Section of the Water Supply workshops at Chullora during 1963 and 1964, and were a development of two X100 Class units delivered a year earlier. Twelve further X200 Class units arrived during 1967 and 1968, although the design of these was heavily refined. Employed as yard shunters and light branch line power, the X200 Class have endured despite dwindling numbers and a lack of suitable work. Many were modified with the removal of their train brake to enable 'non loco crew' staff to operate them (being renumbered into the X100 Class series as a result) and most of those still owned by commercial operators today are actually stored. Only Xt106i, owned by RailCorp and employed by Rail Fleet Services (a division of UGR) at Chullora, and SCT's X107 and X209 (employed at Parkes and Laverton respectively) are actually used in service.

Road #	Original #	Builders #	Built	Owner	Status
Xt106i	X206	8	1964	RailCorp	In service—RFS Chullora
X107	X207	10	1967	SCT	In service—Parkes
X208	X208	11	1967	CRT	Stored Port Kembla
X209	X209	12	1967	SCT	In service—Laverton
X101	X212	15	1967	CRT	Stored Port Kembla North
X216	X216	19	1968	SCT	Stored Laverton
X118	X218	21	1968	CRT	Stored Port Kembla

Tulloch 0-4-0

Builder:	*Tulloch Limited (Rhodes)*	Model:	*DSL 120/15*
Type:	*0-4-0 diesel-mechanical*	Engine:	*Mercedes Benz, 4 cylinders inline*
Traction power:	*90 kW (120 hp)*	Length:	*5.41 m*
Weight:	*?*	Gauge:	*1435 mm*

Above: The original Tulloch, 1 *Thomas* at Bullock Flat in 2008. Darren Teasdale

Other

The unit was builders number 001—the first locomotive built by Tulloch. Like Comeng, the company had a stronger reputation as a rolling stock builder, and as the few entries in this book will indicate, Tulloch did not produce fleets anywhere near the size of the Clydes or Goodwins. Tulloch locomotive 001 was built originally for Simsmetal, Mascot and eventually formed part of a small fleet of five shunters on site (a 1968 Yorkshire-built 0-6-0, two Ruston 165DSG units built in 1952, and former Australian Iron & Steel B-B diesel-electric D11). The Skitube operation was setting up in the NSW Snowy Mountains between Bullock Flat and Mount Blue Cow in the mid-1980s (the first stage opened 22 July 1987). The steep rack railway was suitable only for the dedicated EMU trains bought new for the line, however the little Tulloch was purchased and overhauled (gaining a new, larger engine at some point) for use as a depot shunter at Bullock Flat. Delivered around 1986, it has been there ever since. Of the other Simsmetal shunters, only D11 has survived, preserved with the Dorrigo Steam Railway & Museum in 1998. The remaining locomotives have been scrapped.

Road #	Builder's #	Built	Owner	Status
1 *Thomas*	001	1958	Skitube, Bullock Flat	In service

W Class

Builder:	*Tulloch Limited (Rhodes)*	Model:	*n/a*	
Type:	*0-6-0 diesel-hydraulic*	Engine:	*Mercedes-Benz MB 820B V12*	*W260*
			GM Detroit Diesel 12V149 V12	*W241, W244*
Traction power:	*485 kW (650 hp)*	Length:	*8.18 m*	
Weight:	*48.8 tonnes*	Gauge:	*1600 mm*	

Above: W244 at Newport on Wednesday 27 December 2006. Bernie Baker

Numbering 27 units, the former Victorian Railways W Class diesel-hydraulic shunters were the most numerous class constructed by Tulloch. That 27 included one (W266) which actually operated for the NSWGR as a demonstrator unit (number 7101) during 1961 prior to delivery to Victoria, both it and sister unit W267 have operated on the standard gauge (with W266 being reported as hauling the first 1435 mm-gauge train in Victoria, a ballast special on 6 July 1961), but generally the W Class became broad-gauge specialists. They were used in yard shunting and small transfer runs until withdrawal during the 1980s. A number were preserved, and from this collection, relative newcomer El Zorro has obtained three examples (including W260, previously displayed at Tocumwal for many years) for track work and infrastructure trains on the broad-gauge Melbourne suburban network. W260 possesses a Mercedes-Benz engine, however both W241 and W244 were among those members of the class re-engined during 1973 with a GM Detroit prime mover.

Road #	Builder's #	Built	Owner	Status
W241	006	1959	El Zorro	In service
W244	009	1960	El Zorro	In service
W260	026	1960	El Zorro	Restoration

other

TA Class

Builder:	*Tulloch Limited (Rhodes)*	Model:	*2-CS*
Type:	*0-6-0 diesel-hydraulic*	Engine:	*Cummins VT 17 10L turbo-charged V12*
Traction power:	*450 kW (600 hp)*	Length:	*7.58 m*
Weight:	*38.0 tonnes*	Gauge:	*1067 mm*

Above: TA1807 in the Boyanup Transport Museum on Friday 21 March 2003. Sister unit TA1813 continues in service with United Group Rail (formerly Goninan) at Bassendean, in Perth. Chris Walters

The ten members of the Western Australian Government Railways TA Class, built by Tulloch in 1970/1971, were a development of the five T Class units delivered by the same firm three years earlier. All fifteen locomotives were used for narrow gauge yard and wharf shunting until their numbers started to dwindle during the 1980s. Although only one T Class now remains (T1804 at Northampton), four TA Class locomotives survive, including TA1807, TA1808 and TA1814, all preserved. For a time, TA1807 was employed by the State Energy Commission at Bunbury, until vested in the Boyanup Transport Museum in 2000, however sister unit TA1813 continues to this day as the United Group Rail (former Goninan) workshops shunter at Bassendean, in the eastern suburbs of Perth.

Road #	Builder's #	Built	Owner	Status
TA1813	062	1970	UGR Bassendean	In service

Sugar Cane

No. 7 *Morrison*, at Babinda Mill on Tuesday 17 September 2002. Chris Walters

Bundaberg Foundry/Hunslet

Above: *Elliott* leads a loaded train at the Burnett Heads Road level crossing, on approach to Millaquin Mill late on Friday 1 August 2008. Rod Milne

Formed in 1888, Bundaberg Foundry entered the era of dieselisation with a remarkable career of cane field machinery production behind them. As late as 1952-53 the company built under license (to well known United Kingdom firm John Fowler) eight highly successful steam locomotives, some of which remained in service for decades. However, the onset of change was swift and the company wisely sensed that a start on diesel locomotive development would be timely.

Another licensing deal was stitched up with Austrian industrialists Jenbacher Werke for supply of locomotive propulsion packages, and in 1953 the first of three diesel prototypes was completed at the works. Although Bundaberg Foundry received some work repairing and rebuilding locomotives over the ensuing years, the three prototypes did not prove to be competitive with the Comeng and Clyde production models. Thus the trio were to remain the only new sugar industry diesel locomotives constructed by Bundaberg Foundry for almost forty years.

In 1990 the facility was purchased by Bundaberg Sugar and shortly afterwards another licensing deal was reached with an overseas manufacturer. The company in question was Hunslet-GMT, who supplied components (including bogies) for the construction of two 465 kW, model SDH650 B-B diesel hydraulic locomotives for the parent company Bundaberg Sugar. Mill staff were consulted during the locomotive's design and construction, with the final result proving radically different from contemporary designs.

Unusually, draw gear was located on the bogies and, like the four Eimco built Generation 4 locomotives constructed the year before, the two Bundaberg/Hunslet units were fitted with the Detroit 12V-92TA engines and a similar microprocessor package that monitored start up power.

The first unit completed was issued to Fairymead Mill as replacement for a rejected Eimco unit, itself on-sold to Mackay Sugar. Meanwhile the second Bundaberg/Hunslet was soon after delivered to Babinda Mill. Initially known as *Bundaberg* and *Babinda* respectively, the former locomotive was subsequently renamed *Booyan*, while the latter was transferred south to Millaquin in 1999 and re-named *Elliott*. They continue to haul Bundaberg district cane to this day.

Any hopes for subsequent deliveries of the Bundaberg/Hunslet design were dashed by the proliferation of rebuilt, ex-government Walkers diesel hydraulic locomotives. However the company was soon heavily involved in the rebuilding of these units. Between 1995 and 2004 the Bundaberg foundry rebuilt eight former Queensland Railways (QR) DH Class locomotives, ten former NSWSRA 73 Class, and both members of the former Westrail M Class. These nineteen units were delivered to Mulgrave (2), Tully (1), Victoria (2), Invicta (5), Kalamia (1), Proserpine (2), Mackay Sugar (2) and Plane Creek Mill (4) with Bundaberg Sugar themselves only taking delivery of *Kolan* (former DH51) for Bingera Mill, rebuilt at the works in 1996. Three other ex-government units, DH41, DH47 and 7336 are stored at the site by various mills pending a decision on their future.

Above: *Booyan* has just crossed over the QR North Coast Line at Meadowvale with a load of cane from Fairymead Yard bound for Bingera Mill, on Sunday 10 August 2008. Rod Milne

Road #	Type	Builder's #	Built	Owner	Status
Booyan	B-B DH	001	1991	Bundaberg Sugar (Bundaberg)	In service
Elliott	B-B DH	002	1991	Bundaberg Sugar (Bundaberg)	In service

Clyde Engineering

Above: Mackay Sugar's rebuilt DHI-71 'slave unit' 11 *Marian* leading standard DHI-71 4 *Habana*, permanently coupled in multiple-unit operation, approach Mirani with a load of cane bound for Marian Mill on Friday 11 July 2008. John Hoyle

Perhaps the best-known Australian builder involved in the supply of sugar cane diesel locomotives was the Clyde Engineering Company. Despite their substantial success in the cane field market, Clyde was perhaps better known as a builder of main line locomotives and rolling stock. Although the company's history can be traced back to 1855, the firm was actually formed in 1898 and built its first locomotive, a 2-8-0 standard goods steam engine, for the NSW Government Railways in 1907. In 1950 the company negotiated the Australian license for the US firm General Motors (Electro-Motive Division) and in September the following year, supplied historic A1A-A1A diesel-electric unit GM1 to the Commonwealth Railways. In the fifty-four years since that delivery, Clyde (later absorbed into EDI Rail, now known as Downer-EDI Rail) has produced over 1700 new and rebuilt diesel locomotives for local and international buyers.

Clyde also initiated the first successful incursion into the cane fields market by an Australian builder offering diesel locomotives with a number of contracts secured in 1953. The first went to Hambledon Mill as No. 1 in March of that year. The locomotive was a 0-6-0 diesel-hydraulic, model DHI powered by a GM engine. This model, shortly thereafter upgraded to classification DHI-71 (following the arrival of the model DH-110 locomotives in 1956), and with occasional design enhancements, was to remain the staple Clyde sugar cane product until 1961. Unlike Comeng, who quickly established themselves as Clyde's main competitor, Clyde were not inclined to veer significantly from the standard package in response to customer needs, and were only interested in the promotion and supply of GM powered products. Although gearing variations were also offered, it appears that although Clyde was keen to establish themselves in the market, they were not of a mind to commit any more resources to the task than was really necessary.

Right: Macknade Mill's DHI-71 No. 18 inside the locomotive shed on the evening of Wednesday 18 September 2002.
Chris Walters

Right: Mourilyan Mill's No. 14 shunting just south of the mill on the afternoon of Tuesday 17 September 2002.
Chris Walters

Right: Mulgrave Mill's No. 14 stabled outside the loco depot on the afternoon of Monday 16 September 2002.
Chris Walters

Given the success of the DHI-71, this approach seems to have stemmed just as much from confidence in the product as much as reasons of economy. On the other hand, it would have been interesting to see what would have eventuated had Clyde adhered to a similar philosophy as Comeng, who were quite willing to vary and adapt their products in response to customer requirements.

In addition to the fall out of the 'off the shelf' approach, smaller builders such as E M Baldwin & Sons and the mills themselves later tackled some of the repair and upgrade services of Clyde (and Comeng) units that the larger firms were unable or unwilling to provide.

The competition between the two larger firms of Clyde and Comeng seems to have been at its most intense in the 1954–1965 period. However, an interesting trend was for many mills to invest primarily in one or the other and few were the companies investing in both Clyde and Comeng products. Despite the race with Comeng, and the later entry into the market of E M Baldwin, Clyde does not seem to have exhibited too much concern over its competitors in this arena. It is known, however, that some hesitation on Clyde's part during the 1960s allowed Baldwin to snap up smaller contracts they might not have otherwise received. One such contract, the rebuild of the historic 1937 built Fowler 0-6-0 diesel-mechanical from Tully, resulted in Baldwin being able to negotiate a deal to source GM engines, which were not covered by the Clyde-EMD licensing agreement.

Clyde did however respond to a call for a heavier, higher powered product when it unveiled the model HG3R unit in 1961. Although not delivered in numbers anywhere as impressive the DHI-71, the new model was also a success.

Above: CSR's Clyde HG3R locomotive *Lucinda* at Victoria Mill, near Ingham, on Thursday 19 September 2002. Chris Walters

Right: Pioneer Mill possesses the only 1067 mm gauge network, and as such its DHI-71 units are wider than the 610 mm examples. Here we see *Colevale, Airdale* and *Maidavale* at the mill on Friday 20 September 2002.
Chris Walters

Right: Proserpine Mill's DHI-71 locomotive No. 7 shunting at the mill on Saturday 21 September 2002. Many of the DHI-71 units right around the state have received new and/or rebuilt cabs over the years.
Chris Walters

Right: Mackay Sugar DHI-71 locomotive No. 53 *Munburra* approaches Racecourse Mill on the morning of Sunday 22 September 2002.
Chris Walters

Sugar cane

Above: Macknade No. 11 at the mill during shunting on Thursday 19 September 2002. This unit is one of two HG3R units in the Macknade fleet. Chris Walters

The HG3R was similar in appearance to the standard DHI-71, although due to the larger engine and wider canopy, did appear a bulkier unit, particularly when observed from head-on. The first deliveries of the HG3R were made to Mackay area mills, with three going to Farleigh's north coast railway operation and a fourth to Marian Mill.

It was with two DHI-71 and three HG3R units built for Hambledon Mill that Clyde relented and made a significant customisation to their product. Hambledon's branch lines to the farming areas located north and east of Redlynch could only be accessed by a line that dipped under the Queensland Railway's Cairns–Kuranda line; unfortunately the structure clearance at this location was quite low, and to avoid costly earth works the mill requested that the five units be modified with a fold-down cab roof to enable passage under the bridge. 1956-built DHI-71 No. 6 was the initial unit to be so treated, while fellow DHI-71 No. 5 followed in 1958. The first modified HG3R arrived as No. 3 in 1964, with numbers 8 and 9 following soon afterwards. The resulting design was practical, yet could not be considered much of an aesthetic success. Compared to cab designs applied to other Clyde units, the five Redlynch units, by necessity of function, left crews rather vulnerable to the climate. The three HG3Rs were eventually fitted with sound-proofed, fully-enclosed low-profile cabs in 1979–1980, while the two DHI-71 locomotives were given standard height cabs from 1980 when it was decided that the three larger units could cope with the traffic levels north of Redlynch. With the closure of Hambledon in 1991, all five locomotives, and the responsibility for hauling cane in the Redlynch district, fell to Mulgrave Mill at nearby Gordonvale. The low cab HG3Rs continue to work Redlynch trains today as Mulgrave 13, 18 and 19 respectively, while the DHI-71 pair are now known as 15 and 16. Mulgrave 15 is now in dismantled form while 16 remains in service.

Another novel variation, this time applied to the standard DHI-71, was the efforts of Isis Central Mill in converting three units into cab-less slave units during the 1980s. This trio were then each modified for multiple-unit operation with a companion cab unit. However, this unique modification was rather short lived as Isis began taking delivery of a series of Walkers rebuilds from 1991 and the Clyde slave units were eventually retro-fitted with cabs and sold to Fijian sugar mills along with their three standard DHI-71 partners.

Mackay Sugar eventually took a leaf from the Isis story, when they converted 1956-built DHI-71 No. 11 *Marian* into a cab-less 'B' unit (see page 210). Their intent was to operate the rebuilt slave unit in multiple unit capacity with 4 *Habana*, a similar unit built in 1960, in the same manner to the earlier Isis pairs.

Despite the success of the heavier HG3R unit, investors still showed keen interest in the DHI-71. A standard HG3R weighed in at around 24.5 tonnes, while the DHI-71s ranged from 14.3 tonnes up to 18.4 tonnes. As for rated power, the HG3R with its GM Detroit primer mover produced 201 kW against the DHI-71 127 kW with its GM 71 series engines. While the DHI-71 model was snapped up by a number of mills the HG3R was purchased primarily by the Mackay and Herbert River mills, with the only other interested parties being Hambledon (with the earlier mentioned retractable cab units), Plane Creek and Isis.

It was Isis in fact that obtained Clyde's last cane field locomotive in HG3R unit 9. The last DHI-71 (actually a DHI-71HS, see page 216) was delivered to Racecourse Mill in 1971. By this time Clyde had shifted construction of sugar mill locomotives to its Eagle Farm plant in suburban Brisbane. However, only four cane fields units were ultimately constructed at Eagle Farm: the aforementioned Isis and Racecourse Mill units, and two previous HG3R locomotives for Pleystowe and Plane Creek in 1970.

Above: Mulgrave 16 rolls through Kamma on its way to the mill with a load of cane on Monday 16 September 2002. All three of Mulgrave's HG3R locomotives are equipped with low-profile cabs in order to clear the QR Kuranda Line overbridge at Redlynch. Chris Walters

It is worth mentioning at this point the curious step that Clyde took in constructing its 1971 Racecourse unit. As built, the locomotive (known originally as 7, and today as *Broadsound* on the mill roster) was fitted with a hydrostatic transmission and was listed as a model DHI-71HS. This type was relatively rare in Australia, and although theoretically more efficient, like the similarly fitted 1990 Professional Engineering B-B unit for South Johnstone, 7 was not a success. The unit was retrofitted with a hydraulic transmission in 1974 and has since operated relatively satisfactorily. The original disposition for the DHI-71 and HG3R, as constructed and delivered to the Australian sugar industry was as follows:

	DHI-71	***HG3R***
Hambledon Mill (610 mm)	*7*	*3*
Goondi Mill (610 mm)	*3*	*0*
Mourilyan Mill (610 mm)	*5*	*0*
Tully Mill (610 mm)	*1*	*0*
Victoria Mill (610 mm)	*5*	*5*
Macknade Mill (610 mm)	*0*	*2*
Pioneer Mill (1067 mm)	*5*	*0*
Inkerman Mill (610 mm)	*1*	*0*
Proserpine Mill (610 mm)	*8*	*0*
Marian Mill (610 mm)	*3*	*2*
Farleigh Mill (610 mm)	*0*	*5*
Pleystowe Mill (610 mm)	*2*	*2*
Racecourse Mill (610 mm)	*7*	*0*
Plane Creek Mill (610 mm)	*2*	*2*
Fairymead Mill (610 mm)	*3*	*0*
Millaquin Mill (610 mm)	*2*	*0*
Isis Mill (610 mm)	*6*	*1*
Moreton (610 mm)	*1*	*0*
Totals	***61***	***22***

Most of these mills (or at least, those that still operate—many locomotives from closed mills have since been passed on) continue to use Clyde units in regular service, and thanks to the simplicity of components and endurance of the technology it is likely they will be around for some time yet.

DHI-71

Road ID	Builder's #	Built	Original owner	Current owner	Status
16	DHI.1/010	1954	Hambledon Mill	CSR Macknade Mill	In service
Iona	DHI.2/011	1954	Inkerman Mill	CSR Macknade Mill	Stored derelict
18	DHI.5/014	1955	Hambledon Mill	CSR Macknade Mill	Stored
55 *Tantitha*	DHI.6/015	1955	Fairymead Mill	Bund. Sugar (Bundaberg)	In service
2 *Goondi*	55-056	1955	Hambledon Mill	Bund. Sugar (Innisfail)	In service
17	55-057	1955	Goondi Mill	Bund. Sugar (Innisfail)	In service
50 *Homebush*	55-058	1955	Racecourse Mill	Mackay Sugar	In service
12	55-060	1955	Goondi Mill	Bund. Sugar (Innisfail)	In service

(continued)

Road ID	Builder's #	Built	Original owner	Current owner	Status
11	55-064	1955	Mourilyan Mill	Bund. Sugar (Innisfail)	In service
18	56-083	1956	Mourilyan Mill	Bund. Sugar (Innisfail)	Stored
14	56-086	1956	Hambledon Mill	Mulgrave Mill	In service
56 Hinkler	56-089	1956	Fairymead Mill	Bund. Sugar (Bundaberg)	In service
3 Daradgee	56-090	1956	Hambledon Mill	Bund. Sugar (Innisfail)	In service
2	56-091	1956	Proserpine Mill	Proserpine Mill	Stored
16	56-093	1956	Goondi Mill	Bund. Sugar (Innisfail)	In service
16	56-096	1956	Hambledon Mill	Mulgrave Mill	In service
D1	56-101	1956	Plane Creek Mill	CSR Plane Creek Mill	In service
28 Te Kowai	56-103	1956	Pleystowe Mill	Mackay Sugar	In service
11 Marian	56-104	1956	Marian Mill	Mackay Sugar	In service (slave)
2	57-147	1957	Plane Creek Mill	CSR Plane Creek Mill	Stored derelict
Margam	57-159	1957	Millaquin Mill	Bund. Sugar (Bundaberg)	In service
41 Sunnyside	57-160	1957	Racecourse Mill	Mackay Sugar	In service
12 Nellie	58-188	1958	Marian Mill	Mackay Sugar	In service
15	58-190	1958	Hambledon Mill	Mulgrave Mill	In service
3	58-195	1958	Proserpine Mill	Proserpine Mill	In service
43 Chelona	59-201	1959	Racecourse Mill	Mackay Sugar	In service
4	59-202	1959	Proserpine Mill	Proserpine Mill	Stored
13	59-203	1959	Mourilyan Mill	Bund. Sugar (Innisfail)	In service
4 Habana	60-215	1960	Pleystowe Mill	Mackay Sugar	In service (control)
5	60-218	1960	Proserpine Mill	Proserpine Mill	In service
60 Waimea	60-219	1960	Fairymead Mill	Bund. Sugar (Bundaberg)	In service
Maidavale	62-266	1962	Pioneer Mill	CSR Pioneer Mill	In service *
6	62-272	1963	Proserpine Mill	Proserpine Mill	In service
Pioneer	63-287	1963	Pioneer Mill	CSR Pioneer Mill	In service *
14	63-288	1963	Mourilyan Mill	Bund. Sugar (Innisfail)	In service
20	63-289	1963	Moreton Mill	Bund. Sugar (Innisfail)	In service
45 Rosella	64-317	1964	Racecourse Mill	Mackay Sugar	In service
Airdale	64-318	1964	Pioneer Mill	CSR Pioneer Mill	In service *
Colevale	65-438	1965	Pioneer Mill	CSR Pioneer Mill	In service *
52 Racecourse	65-440	1965	Racecourse Mill	Mackay Sugar	In service
Ashfield	65-441	1965	Millaquin Mill	Bund. Sugar (Innisfail)	In service
7	65-442	1965	Proserpine Mill	Proserpine Mill	In service
8	65-443	1965	Proserpine Mill	Proserpine Mill	In service
15	66-491	1966	Mourilyan Mill	Bund. Sugar (Innisfail)	In service
13 Devereaux	67-568	1967	Marian Mill	Mackay Sugar	In service
53 Munbura	67-570	1967	Racecourse Mill	Mackay Sugar	In service
42 Broadsound	70-710	1971	Racecourse Mill	Mackay Sugar	In service

** 1067 mm gauge for service on CSR's Pioneer Mill rail network.*

Above: Even sugar cane trains have to shunt sometimes! Clyde HG3R locomotive 8 *Palms* is undertaking such mundane work near the Pleystowe Mill, near Mackay, on Tuesday 7 October 2008. Pleystowe Mill closed three weeks later. Ken Date

HG3R

Road ID	Builder's #	Built	Original owner	Current owner	Status
30 *Conningsby*	61-232	1961	Farleigh Mill	Mackay Sugar	In service
31 *Seaforth*	61-233	1961	Farleigh Mill	Mackay Sugar	In service
32 *St Helens*	61-234	1961	Farleigh Mill	Mackay Sugar	In service
14 *Alexandra*	61-235	1961	Marian Mill	Mackay Sugar	In service
9 *Palmyra*	63-273	1963	Pleystowe Mill	Mackay Sugar	In service
13	64-316	1964	Hambledon Mill	Mulgrave Mill	In service
2 *Pleystowe*	64-321	1964	Pleystowe Mill	Mackay Sugar	In service
15 *Melba*	64-377	1964	Marian Mill	Mackay Sugar	In service
Rebuilt by E M Baldwin in 1985 (builders number 12512.1 7.85)					
18	64-379	1965	Hambledon Mill	Mulgrave Mill	In service
Centenary	64-381	1964	Victoria Mill	CSR Victoria Mill	In service
Ingham	64-382	1964	Victoria Mill	CSR Victoria Mill	In service
11	65-383	1965	Macknade Mill	CSR Macknade Mill	In service
Canberra	65-433	1965	Victoria Mill	CSR Victoria Mill	In service
12	65-434	1965	Macknade Mill	CSR Macknade Mill	In service
19	65-435	1965	Hambledon Mill	Mulgrave Mill	In service

(continued)

Road ID	Builder's #	Built	Original owner	Current owner	Status
Lucinda	65-436	1965	Victoria Mill	CSR Victoria Mill	In service
27 *Lacy*	65-439	1965	Farleigh Mill	Mackay Sugar	In service
29 *Victoria Plains*	66-490	1966	Pleystowe Mill	Mackay Sugar	In service
10	67-569	1967	Plane Creek Mill	CSR Plane Creek Mill	In service
26 *Bassett*	67-596	1967	Farleigh Mill	Mackay Sugar	In service
Perth	69-682	1969	Victoria Mill	CSR Victoria Mill	In service
8 *Palms*	70-708	1970	Pleystowe Mill	Mackay Sugar	In service
Dalrymple	70-709	1970	Plane Creek Mill	CSR Victoria Mill	In service
9	75-812	1975	Isis Central Mill	Isis Central Mill	In service

Above: *Centenary* (with navvy crew/line side tree-chopping framework attached to the hood) at Victoria Mill on Saturday 15 December 2001. Although Mackay Sugar own more (for service at Marian, Farleigh and Racecourse) Victoria Mill possesses the largest single fleet of HG3R units for a single mill. Chris Walters

Comeng

Above: Babinda Mill's *Russell* and 1 *Josephine* at the mill workshop late in the afternoon of Monday 16 September 2002. Both locomotives sport modern, retrofitted cabs. Chris Walters

The Commonwealth Engineering Company (known as Comeng) was formed in 1937 and entered the sugar cane locomotive market in 1955, only a few months behind competitors Clyde Engineering. However, unlike Clyde, Comeng was not a firm noted for an extensive history of locomotive building. Prior to their entrance into the cane fields market, Comeng's only noteworthy involvement in diesel locomotive production had been the assembly of eight English Electric kit units imported from the United Kingdom. The completed units were delivered to Australian Iron & Steel at Port Kembla from April 1950. These Bo-Bo diesel-electric units (see page 174) had pre-empted the Tasmania Government Railways by several months in being the first Australian main line diesel locomotives.

With plants eventually springing up in Brisbane, Perth, Sydney, Adelaide and Melbourne (among other locations), Comeng was at this time better known for rolling stock and equipment production, although their move into the cane fields locomotive market yielded immediate dividends. Their initial product was a rather plain 0-6-0 design dubbed the A Series, based somewhat on the earlier Baguley, Gardner-motored locomotives. Six units were initially constructed and five of these went to Mulgrave Mill, with the sixth going to South Johnstone. Mulgrave's units completed the mill's dieselisation program begun with Baguley diesel No. 1 in 1953, and were numbered 2 through to 6. Most of these vintage machines continue to be used for cane haulage in 2005, however No. 4 was noted out of service as a spare unit in 2002. The South Johnstone unit was originally numbered 16, and is today used by the mill as 36.

Right: Sugar Terminals Limited's Comeng locomotive (with brake wagon) at the western end of Lucinda Yard on Wednesday 18 September 2002.
Chris Walters

Right: Mackay Sugar's *Carlisle*, stabled in the navvy equipment area at Farleigh Mill on the afternoon of Sunday 22 September 2002.
Chris Walters

These early locomotives, and a number of those that soon followed, were simple diesel-mechanical units. However, Comeng soon began to refine the A Series with hydraulic transmission and a variety of prime mover and final drive options. The A Series unit, a direct competitor to Clyde's successful model DHI-71, was over the years delivered with a high variance of equipment types and performance characteristics. The series had a weight range of 14.3 tonnes up to 18.4 tonnes (similar to the Clyde DHI-71), with a power rating of anything between 112 kW and 153 kW. Varieties of Gardner, Rolls Royce, Caterpillar and General Motors engines were used in both these units and later models. Unlike the Clyde locomotives, Comeng built these units (and the subsequent F Series) with the cab and hood sections sitting forward of the gearbox on the frame. Depending on who you talk to, this rendered them too 'front heavy' in appearance or very well balanced. One reason for this was to avoid having the cab sitting above the gearbox, thus providing better access to this equipment and less cab vibration.

However, many units of Comeng, Clyde and Baldwin manufacture were later retrofitted with completely new cab structures. As part of a drive by the mills and sugar industry to improve crew conditions, many locomotives were fitted with replacement compartments isolated from the frame by anti-vibration pads. Air-conditioning and improved window and door seals were also commonly used in some upgrades, and these improvements better protected crews from excessive noise, vibration and climatic conditions. Unfortunately, most of the vintage Comeng units were fitted with rather simple cabs that were not completely sealed from the elements. Bingera Mill's Comeng unit *Invicta* was in fact given a completely new cab as recently as 2001 following collision damage sustained the season before. Some of those units that have not been given new cabs, have received heavy modification to improve crew comfort, including a few of the Bundaberg and Mackay based locomotives, which have been modified with new side doors.

By 1959, Comeng was almost exclusively delivering diesel-hydraulic units, and additionally, many of the earlier diesel-mechanical units were eventually converted over. Oddly, Queensland Railways (QR) continued to invest in 0-6-0 diesel-mechanical Comeng locomotives for its 610 mm gauge Innisfail Tramway operation as late as 1975.

Left: The unique model CA 0-4-0 unit, *Invicta*, at its namesake mill near Giru on Friday 20 September 2002. Chris Walters

Left: Mossman Mill's Comeng units *Douglas* and *Faugh-A-Balaugh*, with a loaded train approaching Mossman from Cassowary on the morning of Tuesday 3 July 2007. Joanne Stratton

Above: Comeng F Series unit 54 *Oakenden*, at Mackay Sugar's Marian Mill on the afternoon of Saturday 21 September 2002. Chris Walters

As stated, unlike Clyde, Comeng was willing to customise their orders to better suit customer's requirements and budgets, and a variety of different engine and major component types and brands were offered depending on the needs of the clients. Comeng also pre-empted Clyde when a heavier, more powerful model was called for. In 1958 Comeng began to deliver the F Series cane field locomotives when it delivered new unit number 3 to Plane Creek Mill for use on the Koumala Line. Akin to a comparison between the original Clyde DHI-71 and later HG3R type, the F Series was a leap ahead compared to the lighter A Series. The F Series offered a power range of 187 kW to 207 kW, and weighed in at between 19.4 tonnes and 25.6 tonnes. However, both models continued to be offered by Comeng, and such was the variation in engine, drive and transmission packages that it was almost a case of no two locomotives being the same.

Comeng also developed some smaller designs, and the result was a small number of 0-4-0 units designed for lighter duties. Clyde had no such product and Comeng must have figured that diversity would bring extra reward. The first of these was a solitary CA Series 0-4-0 diesel-hydraulic unit built for Invicta Mill in 1960. Although it outwardly resembled a fairly standard 1960s vintage A Series locomotive, No. 1 *Invicta* (as it was named) was designed for cane haulage on the mill's then small tramway system. Subsequent to the development and improvement of the Invicta Mill system, in addition to the later arrival of larger locomotives, *Invicta* is these days employed on lighter duties and more often than not is called upon to haul weed spray and navvy trains.

The other two four-wheeled units that found their way into the sugar industry were even smaller model GA locomotives. One was built in 1960 for Kalamia Mill as a light duties unit, while the second was originally delivered in 1961 to the Commonwealth Department of Supply at St Marys, before being purchased second-hand by Fairymead Mill in 1971. This pair were the result of a direct effort by Comeng to emulate Malcolm Moore products, but whether by design or demand, no further GA locomotives resulted. Although *Invicta* is still in service at its namesake mill, both of the GA units are now withdrawn from service with the Kalamia unit, known as *Ivanhoe* now preserved with the Illawarra Light Railway Museum Society at Albion Park, NSW. The Fairymead unit was rebuilt by the mill upon delivery (and is these days numbered 72), however it is now stored out of use.

Although Comeng locomotives were selling well, they could not quite match Clyde for sheer numbers of units delivered. Demand for new locomotives began to slacken off once the 1960s wound down and the industry's efforts to replace steam traction with diesel began to approach completion. In fact Comeng failed to sell a single sugar-cane locomotive between 1966 and 1975.

The entry into the market of E M Baldwin & Sons from 1961 also began to have an impact. This smaller firm's willingness and capability to take on smaller orders, such as rebuilding older locomotives, began to make inroads into the market. With Baldwin later proving the worth of their bogie locomotive designs, Comeng (and Clyde) began to see their cane fields sales results drop sharply.

To stay competitive with Baldwin, Comeng developed their own bogie B-B locomotive in the form of the NA type. Unfortunately for Comeng, only one example of this model was successfully marketed, with the solitary unit going to Cattle Creek Mill as their No. 4 in 1977. However, the unit had insufficient weight to effectively use the power it provided, and Comeng's version of the bogie locomotive design failed to find much industry support. Despite this, the unique locomotive remains in service today as 51 *Finch Hatton*, nominally working out of Mackay Sugar's Racecourse Mill.

Left: 19, a former QR Innisfail and Babinda unit, stored at Bingera Mill on Tuesday 24 September 2002. Locomotive transfers between various Bundaberg Sugar and CSR mills are reasonably common, irrespective of distance.
Chris Walters

Demand was down and Comeng could not compete effectively with Baldwin. With the delivery of A Series 0-6-0 unit Tully 18 later in 1977, Comeng out-shopped their last locomotive for the sugar industry from the Rocklea works.

In spite of this loss of work, the end of the cane field production era coincided with a heavy increase of orders for Comeng locomotives destined to enter government and heavy industrial employment. Despite a large number of locomotive and rolling stock contracts, Comeng (by then a part of the Australian National Industries group) folded altogether with the onset of the 1990s. The company's catalogue of locomotive designs are today in the hands of Bombardier Transportation at Dandenong. However it is very unlikely that any new sugar-cane locomotives will appear from this source any time soon.

The disposition for the Comeng A and F Series units, as originally constructed and delivered to the Australian sugar industry were as follows:

	A	***F***
Mossman Mill (610 mm)	*5*	*0*
Mulgrave Mill (610 mm)	*7*	*1*
Babinda Mill (610 mm)	*7*	*0*
South Johnstone Mill (610 mm)	*7*	*0*
Tully Mill (610 mm)	*8*	*0*
Invicta Mill (610 mm)	*4*	*0*
Kalamia Mill (610 mm)	*4*	*1*
Inkerman Mill (610 mm)	*3*	*1*
Cattle Creek Mill (610 mm)	*2*	*0*
Farleigh Mill (610 mm)	*4*	*0*
North Eton Mill (610 mm)	*1*	*3*
Plane Creek Mill (610 mm)	*0*	*4*
Bingera Mill (610 mm)	*4*	*2*
QR Innisfail Tramway (610 mm)	*6*	*0*
Aramac Shire Tramway (1067 mm)	*1*	*0*
Lucinda Sugar Terminal (610 mm)	*1*	*0*
Totals	***64***	***12***

Additionally, Comeng also supplied the following units:

- 1 x model GA to Kalamia Mill as *Ivanhoe*,
- 1 x model GA to Commonwealth Department of Supply (later to Fairymead Mill),
- 1 x model CA to Invicta Mill as *Invicta*,
- 1 x model NA to Cattle Creek Mill as No. 4 (later Mackay Sugar 51 *Finch Hatton*),
- 2 x other 0-6-0 designs similar to the A/F Series for the 1067 mm Townsville and Mackay sugar terminals (the Mackay unit is now preserved at SDSRA Warwick).

Each locomotive's series or model type is normally recorded in the unit's builder's number, although a number of early A Series locomotives possess builders numbers beginning with a B or a C prefix.

Road ID	Builder's #	Built	Type	Original owner	Owner	Status
2	A1001	1955	0-6-0 DM	Mulgrave Mill	Mulgrave Mill	In service
36	A1102	1955	0-6-0 DH	South Johnstone Mill	Bund. Sugar (Innisfail)	In service
3	A1003	1955	0-6-0 DM	Mulgrave Mill	Mulgrave Mill	In service
4	A1004	1955	0-6-0 DM	Mulgrave Mill	Mulgrave Mill	In service
5	A1005	1955	0-6-0 DM	Mulgrave Mill	Mulgrave Mill	In service
6	A1006	1955	0-6-0 DH	Mulgrave Mill	Mulgrave Mill	In service
Thistle	A1207	1955	0-6-0 DH	Bingera Mill	Bund. Sugar (Innisfail)	In service
49 *Richmond*	A1308	1955	0-6-0 DM	Farleigh Mill	Mackay Sugar	In service
Kalamia	A1409	1955	0-6-0 DH	Kalamia Mill	CSR Kalamia Mill	Stored
7	B1010	1956	0-6-0 DH	Mulgrave Mill	Mulgrave Mill	In service
Jamaica	B1112	1956	0-6-0 DH	QR Innisfail (DL14)	Bund. Sugar (Bundaberg)	Stored
Invicta	A1513	1956	0-6-0 DH	Bingera Mill	Bund. Sugar (Bundaberg)	In service
Ashburton	A1614	1956	0-6-0 DM	Farleigh Mill	Mackay Sugar	Stored
Mossman	B1719	1957	0-6-0 DH	Mossman Mill	Mossman Mill	In service
1 *Josephine*	A1821	1957	0-6-0 DH	Babinda Mill	Bund. Sugar (Innisfail)	In service
Dunethin	H1022	1958	0-6-0 DH	ASC Aramac	Bund. Sugar (Bundaberg)	In service
-	G1023	1958	0-6-0 DH	Lucinda Terminal	Sugar Term. Ltd	In service
1 *Cattle Creek*	B1724	1957	0-6-0 DH	Cattle Creek Mill	Mackay Sugar	In service
31	C1125	1957	0-6-0 DH	South Johnstone Mill	Bund. Sugar (Innisfail)	In service
8	A1926	1958	0-6-0 DH	Mulgrave Mill	Mulgrave Mill	In service
10 *Russell*	A2027	1958	0-6-0 DH	Babinda Mill	Bund. Sugar (Innisfail)	In service
3 *Septimus*	A2128	1958	0-6-0 DH	North Eton Mill	Mackay Sugar	In service
Chiverton	C1030	1958	0-6-0 DH	Kalamia Mill	CSR Kalamia Mill	In service
Keebah	C2231	1958	0-6-0 DH	Inkerman Mill	CSR Inkerman Mill	In service
6 *Allison*	C2234	1959	0-6-0 DH	Babinda Mill	Bund. Sugar (Innisfail)	In service
Sharon	A1935	1959	0-6-0 DH	Bingera Mill	Bund. Sugar (Bundaberg)	In service
3	FA1036	1959	0-6-0 DH	Plane Creek Mill	CSR Plane Creek Mill	Stored
4	FA1037	1960	0-6-0 DH	Plane Creek Mill	CSR Plane Creek Mill	In service
4 *Harvey*	AD1138	1960	0-6-0 DH	Babinda Mill	Bund. Sugar (Innisfail)	In service
7 *Morrison*	AD1239	1960	0-6-0 DH	Babinda Mill	Bund. Sugar (Innisfail)	In service
Invicta	CA1040	1960	0-4-0 DH	Invicta Mill	CSR Invicta Mill	In service
Tully 10	AD1341	1960	0-6-0 DH	Tully Mill	Tully Mill	In service
8 *Mirriwinni*	AA1543	1960	0-6-0 DH	QR Innisfail (DL16)	Bund. Sugar (Innisfail)	In service
28	AA1544	1960	0-6-0 DM	QR Innisfail (DL17)	Bund. Sugar (Innisfail)	In service
Tully 11	AD1347	1960	0-6-0 DH	Tully Mill	Tully Mill	In service
72	GA1148	1961	0-4-0 DM	Com. Dept. Supply	Bund. Sugar (Bundaberg)	Stored
22 *Pinnacle*	AA1549	1961	0-6-0 DH	Cattle Creek Mill	Mackay Sugar	In service
Tully 12	AD1351	1961	0-6-0 DH	Tully Mill	Tully Mill	In service
23	AD1452	1961	0-6-0 DH	South Johnstone	Bund. Sugar (Innisfail)	In service
21	AD1453	1962	0-6-0 DH	South Johnstone	Bund. Sugar (Innisfail)	In service
47 *Pioneer*	AI2358	1962	0-6-0 DH	Farleigh Mill	Mackay Sugar	Stored

(continued)

Road ID	Builder's #	Built	Type	Original owner	Owner	Status
19	AJ2359	1962	0-6-0 DH	QR Innisfail (DL18)	Bund. Sugar (Bundaberg)	Stored
5 *Bramston*	AH2460	1962	0-6-0 DH	Babinda Mill	Bund. Sugar (Innisfail)	In service
Douglas	AL2562	1963	0-6-0 DH	Mossman Mill	Mossman Mill	In service
Tully 14	AK2663	1963	0-6-0 DH	Tully Mill	Tully Mill	In service
Osborne	AH2866	1963	0-6-0 DH	Inkerman Mill	CSR Inkerman Mill	In service
Burnett	AH2967	1963	0-6-0 DH	Bingera Mill	Bund. Sugar (Bundaberg)	In service
Airdmillan	AH3068	1963	0-6-0 DH	Kalamia Mill	CSR Kalamia Mill	In service
54 *Oakenden*	FB3169	1963	0-6-0 DH	North Eton Mill	Mackay Sugar	In service
25 *Eton*	FB3170	1963	0-6-0 DH	North Eton Mill	Mackay Sugar	In service
48 *Carlisle*	AI3271	1963	0-6-0 DH	Farleigh Mill	Mackay Sugar	Stored
Cook	AI3372	1964	0-6-0 DH	Mossman Mill	Mossman Mill	In service
9	FC3473	1964	0-6-0 DH	Mulgrave Mill	Mulgrave Mill	In service
Tully 15	AK3574	1964	0-6-0 DH	Tully Mill	Tully Mill	In service
22	AK3675	1964	0-6-0 DH	South Johnstone Mill	Bund. Sugar (Innisfail)	In service
7	FC3776	1964	0-6-0 DH	Plane Creek Mill	CSR Plane Creek Mill	In service
D8	FC3777	1964	0-6-0 DH	Plane Creek Mill	CSR Plane Creek Mill	In service
Haughton	AH3878	1964	0-6-0 DH	Invicta Mill	CSR Invicta Mill	In service
9	AH3979	1964	0-6-0 DH	Babinda Mill	Bund. Sugar (Innisfail)	In service
Ivy	AL4181	1965	0-6-0 DH	Mossman Mill	Mossman Mill	In service
46 *Barcoo*	FB4383	1965	0-6-0 DH	North Eton Mill	Mackay Sugar	In service
Tully 16	AH4484	1965	0-6-0 DH	Tully Mill	Tully Mill	In service
39	AH4688	1965	0-6-0 DH	South Johnstone Mill	Bund. Sugar (Innisfail)	In service
Wattle	FD4789	1965	0-6-0 DH	Bingera Mill	Bund. Sugar (Bundaberg)	In service
Faugh-A-Balaugh	AL4190	1965	0-6-0 DH	Mossman Mill	Mossman Mill	In service
Northcote	AH4091	1965	0-6-0 DH	Invicta Mill	CSR Invicta Mill	In service
23 *Dalrymple*	AL4892	1965	0-6-0 DH	Cattle Creek Mill	Mackay Sugar	In service
Koolkuna	AH4993	1965	0-6-0 DH	Inkerman Mill	CSR Inkerman Mill	In service
Delta	FD5094	1965	0-6-0 DH	Kalamia Mill	CSR Kalamia Mill	In service
38	AH4695	1965	0-6-0 DH	South Johnstone Mill	Bund. Sugar (Innisfail)	In service
Barratta	AH4098	1965	0-6-0 DH	Invicta Mill	CSR Invicta Mill	In service
Tegege	FD4799	1966	0-6-0 DH	Bingera Mill	Bund. Sugar (Bundaberg)	In service
Tully 17	AH52100	1966	0-6-0 DH	Tully Mill	Tully Mill	In service
Alma	FE56110	1975	0-6-0 DH	Inkerman Mill	CSR Inkerman Mill	Stored
27	AI57111	1975	0-6-0 DM	QR Innisfail (DL20)	Bund. Sugar (Innisfail)	In service
51 *Finch Hatton*	NA59112	1977	B-B DH	Cattle Creek Mill	Mackay Sugar	In service
Tully 18	AO60113	1977	0-6-0 DH	Tully Mill	Tully Mill	In service

Above: The sole NA-type Comeng bogie unit, 51 *Finch Hatton*, on approach to Racecourse Mill on Sunday 21 September 2002. Chris Walters

Below: Tully Mill Comeng locomotives 11 and 16 outside the mill complex on Wednesday 18 September 2002. Chris Walters

E E Baguley Limited (UK)

Above: South Johnstone 10 (now known as 30) at the mill on Wednesday 18 September 2002. This unit started life as QR Innisfail Tramway unit DL12 *Mourilyan*. Chris Walters

Although many 'sister' units are now preserved (including two returned to United Kingdom), this locomotive is the only example of the 15 Baguley units delivered to the Australian sugar cane industry, still available for service. These 15 locomotives were delivered between 1951 and 1954—ordered through one of two agencies (Railway, Mine & Plantation Equipment Limited or the Drewry Car Company, both of London)—and were the forerunners to the ensuing Clyde and Comeng 0-6-0 locomotives that came to dominate the market later that decade. Now known as South Johnstone 30 (previously No. 10), this unit was originally built as DL12 *Mourilyan*, for the QR Innisfail Tramway operation, and along with now-scrapped sister unit DL13 *Innisfail*, was the last Baguley delivered to Australia in 1954. The tramway was sold by QR 1977, at which time DL12 passed into South Johnstone ownership. It has been a long time since 30 was used in cane haulage service, and the locomotive is only used very intermittently as a shunting and navvy (track maintenance) unit.

Road #	Builder's #	Built	Type	Owner	Status
30	3390	1954	0-6-0 DM	Bundaberg Sugar (Innisfail)	Operational

Eimco/Professional Engineering

Above: 33 *Nyleta* races upgrade at Mena Creek with a loaded train from Japoonvale bound for South Johnstone Mill on Tuesday 17 September 2002. Chris Walters

In 1989 South Johnstone Mill, in collaboration with Eimco (who were responsible for the unit's design), imported a 32-tonne, model PSL26 prototype diesel-hydrostatic B-B locomotive from Professional Engineering of Harare in Zimbabwe. The new unit was initially fitted with a Cummins KT19 diesel engine but was troublesome from the outset and in 1993 the mill opted to withdraw the unit and rebuild it. Fortunately the result was satisfactory and the locomotive was placed into service shuttling cane from the Japoonvale sub-depot over the range to the mill. The unit operates today as 33 *Nyleta*.

Eimco's first locally produced unit for the cane field locomotive market was to be employed at Fairymead Mill. The result was a down-rated model PSL27 B-B diesel-hydraulic locomotive unit fitted with a Detroit Diesel 12V-92TA, which departed the company's Alexandria (an inner southern suburb of Sydney) plant on 6 June 1990. However, upon arrival at Fairymead a few days later, tests proved that the unit actually weighed 38 tonnes (as opposed to the specified 32 tonnes), and despite successful trials, the mill opted to sideline the unit temporarily due to the axle load being considered too heavy for several rail bridges on the network. However, Mackay Sugar intervened, and negotiated for the unit to be transferred, and later sold for use out of Farleigh Mill. Mackay Sugar eventually named their new heavyweight *Farleigh* (although today it is also numbered 36).

At around this time, Eimco was also well under way in constructing three slightly more powerful PSL27 B-B diesel-hydraulic units for Mackay Sugar's nearby Marian Mill.

Despite being ordered in late 1989, Eimco were able to put into effect the lessons learnt from both *Farleigh* and *Nyleta*, and the new units proved a success following commissioning from October 1990. The trio were each fitted with the same Detroit prime mover as *Farleigh*, although rated at 537 kW, with each locomotive weighing in at 41 tonnes. These characteristics combined to ensure that the three locomotives were the most powerful 610 mm-gauge locomotives in the world at that time. Designed and built to augment an aging and underpowered fleet, the trio were also purchased to operate over part of the former Queensland Government Railways Finch Hatton Line to the farms once served by the now closed Cattle Creek Mill. Known as 18 *Gargett*, 19 *Narpi* and 20 *Boonganna*, they continue to bring the cane into Marian to this day. Due to the influx of cheaper Walkers rebuilds shortly thereafter, no more Eimco units ensued.

Above: Mackay Sugar's Eimco-built 19 *Narpi* crosses Eungella Road at Gargett, en route to Marian Mill with a loaded cane train on Friday 11 July 2008. Mackay Sugar own three of these B-B DH locomotives for service out of Marian Mill, in addition to a similar, slightly lighter Eimco unit nominally based at Farleigh Mill. The train is working along part of the former QR Mackay to Netherdale branch, re-gauged to form part of Mackay Sugar's extensive 610 mm network. John Hoyle

Road #	Builder's #	Built	Type	Owner	Status
33 *Nyleta*	P.S.L.25.01/L253	1990	B-B DH	Bundaberg Sugar (Innisfail)	In service
36 *Farleigh*	L254	1990	B-B DH	Mackay Sugar	In service
18 *Gargett*	L255	1990	B-B DH	Mackay Sugar	In service
19 *Narpi*	L256	1990	B-B DH	Mackay Sugar	In service
20 *Boonganna*	L257	1990	B-B DH	Mackay Sugar	In service

E M Baldwin

Left: Mackay Sugar's historic E M Baldwin unit *Allandale*, in under-cover storage at North Eton on Saturday 21 September 2002. Chris Walters

E M Baldwin's efforts to compete with the larger firms in the sugar cane locomotive market started slowly, yet through perseverance, inventiveness and a willingness to take on work other companies were reluctant to pursue, the firm soon reaped the reward of success. The company had begun some years before as almost literally a backyard operation based in Castle Hill, in the north western suburbs of Sydney. Unlike Clyde and Comeng, the firm did not enter the cane field market with a standard product to offer customers. Instead, Baldwin's earliest sugar cane locomotive deliveries were a mixture of light duties units, and one-off rebuilds; both of which were jobs the larger firms were normally reluctant to pursue.

The company's first entry into the market was in response to a contract offered by South Johnstone Mill in 1960. Completed early the following year, the result was a tiny, five-ton, four-wheeled diesel-mechanical locomotive based in design on a similar Tulloch Limited-built diesel-mechanical unit built for the Mount Lyell Mining & Railway Company in 1959 (and which is believed to still exist in private ownership in Hobart). Subsequently numbered 18 on the mill roster, little is known of the locomotive's career, except that it was eventually scrapped during 1976. Perhaps not a noteworthy success for the firm, yet it was a start.

Baldwin's next job was the rebuild of a Tulloch Limited 0-4-0 diesel-hydraulic mining locomotive originally built for, yet rejected by Coal Cliff Colliery during 1957. In its new, radically different form, the unit was delivered in 1962 to Millaquin Mill. Like South Johnstone 18, not much of this unit's career was reported, and the locomotive was eventually retired and placed on display in Apex Park, West Bundaberg. Unfortunately it was later removed during the mid 1980s, when the park was redeveloped and its subsequent whereabouts and condition are unknown, although it too is believed to have been cut up for scrap.

Right: Macknade 17, stabled at the mill on the night of Wednesday 18 September 2002.
Chris Walters

Right: Tully 3 on a small navvy train in a siding just north of Tully township on Wednesday 18 September 2002. Tully owns three of these locomotives for the purpose of running navvy specials such as this.
Chris Walters

Several further rebuilds were undertaken by the company, including the unique task of reconstructing a pioneering 1937-built Fowler 0-6-0 diesel-mechanic locomotive Tully 8, for Tully Mill in 1963. This relic exists today with the Illawarra Light Railway Museum Society at Albion Park in NSW and is named *Shellharbour*.

Some of these rebuild projects were the result of Baldwin themselves purchasing redundant equipment and rebuilding them for customers in order to provide a cheaper alternative to construction involving new components. In this way Baldwin began a slow, yet steady stream of production for customers who had particular needs and budgetary constraints that rendered these contracts not really worth the effort of the larger firms. Baldwin was soon earning a healthy reputation among the various sugar companies.

Baldwin's third sugar industry locomotive was another small, four-wheeled diesel-mechanical, this time built for Pleystowe Mill in 1963. With this locomotive Baldwin introduced model numbers to its products, and gave the Pleystowe four-wheeled diesel-mechanical the classification of DM3. The unit, often mistaken as Baldwin's first cane field locomotive, eventually came into the ownership of Mackay Sugar with amalgamation of Marian, Racecourse, Pleystowe and Farleigh Mills in the 1990s.

Above: Bundaberg Sugar's Perry works along Faggs Road at Gooburrum with a loaded cane train bound for Millaquin Mill on Tuesday 12 August 2008. Rod Milne

Following this, the locomotive was subsequently named *Allandale.* Several similar units soon followed this locomotive out the Castle Hill factory, including one for Farleigh Mill (now also owned by Mackay Sugar) and another for Mulgrave, which although similar, was slightly larger. Both were believed to be still in use as of 2008.

From these tiny units, Baldwin eventually developed the model DH8 locomotive and variants. Designed for use on light cane haulage and navvy duties, both Tully (three units) and Moreton Mill (two units) took an interest in the product, while Condong Mill in far north-eastern NSW, also later picked up a variant. The Tully trio (numbered 1, 2 and 3) continue in service, however the Moreton 'Twins' (as staff called them) of *Maroochy* and *Valdora* (modified in recent years for use as a multiple unit pair), were sidelined due to the closure of the mill in 2003, and both were sold into preservation the following year. Condong Mill no longer maintains a rail network, and its DH8 unit is these days based at Macknade as their No. 17, however it was stored defective as of 2008 and does not appear likely to operate again any time soon.

In 1964 Baldwin developed the larger DH15 model, a 0-6-0 diesel-hydraulic designed for general cane haulage and capable of competing with the popular Clyde and Comeng production units. Moreton was again the willing customer, and they invested in an example they christened *Bli Bli* (later modified to *Bli-Bli*). Although the unit was later plagued by a long run of bad luck, suffering a number of serious accidents and derailments, it was at least an operational success and Moreton subsequently purchased another the following year.

This second DH15—later named *Petrie*—was different in that it was one of three Baldwin units constructed in 1965 using the remains of former 915 mm gauge, model 100DLU Ruston & Hornsby diesel locomotives. The other two rebuilds were unique designs for the Gin Gin and Plane Creek Mills. In approaching the construction this way, Baldwin was able to cut production costs and pass savings on to customers.

Although these DH15 locomotives did not exactly set the market alight, they created enough of an interest such that when Baldwin began to offer more powerful variants in the form of a more powerful model DH18, the sugar companies could not help but notice. Macknade Mill took the plunge and bought a DH18 in the form of their No. 14, while others companies such as Hambledon and Victoria Mills quickly followed suit. Baldwin continued to produce smaller locomotives and rebuilds on demand, however they now had a product that was proving itself against the competition, and orders began to increase.

It was at around this time that Baldwin began to experiment with the concept of a bogie sugar cane locomotive. Although overseas manufacturers (notably UK firm, the Hunslet Engine Company) had previously produced lightweight bogie industrial diesel locomotives, the idea was new in Australia. The design would eliminate the hammer-blow effect on rails caused by rigid-framed/rod-coupled locomotives. Meanwhile, further benefits would result from better weight distribution, allowing the option of applying a more powerful propulsion package. During the late 1960s and early 1970s, Baldwin continued to develop the design in conjunction with the Sugar Research Institute, however they initially had difficulty selling the product. The concept required a customer adventurous enough to try on the new design, and despite interest from several parties, it was not until 1972 that a contract was signed.

Above: Macknade 12 loads an export sugar train, bound for Lucinda, at the mill on the evening of Wednesday 18 September 2002. Chris Walters

The customer in question emerged as Kalamia Mill at Ayr. Their requirement was for a locomotive that would perform the work of a Comeng F Series unit (such as that recently obtained by the mill), yet with a lighter axle load and the elimination of the hammer-blow forces of the rigid 0-6-0 design. The result was the pioneering Baldwin B-B diesel-hydraulic unit *Kilrie* that was delivered to the mill during 1972. Although the locomotive itself was subject to a number of teething problems early on, the advantages of the design were immediately obvious. Bingera and South Johnstone quickly placed orders for similar locomotives and many other mills soon followed.

Between 1972 and 1983, the success of the bogie cane field locomotive soon pushed both Clyde and Comeng out of the market by the close of 1977 (although both investigated their own bogie locomotive designs). Over time, Baldwin began to offer larger and more powerful variants of the design, peaking with the model DH32, purchased by a number of mills during the late 1970s and early 1980s. Their last cane field locomotive, a DH32B constructed for Tully Mill (Tully 7), was delivered in 1983. The need for new locomotives had dried up; such was the effect of the completion of the sugar industry steam to diesel transition, and Baldwin's involvement particularly. In 1985 the Castle Hill works were closed, and although the driving forces behind the company continued to remain involved in the industry, E M Baldwin & Sons ceased to be.

The solitary 1435 mm-gauge Baldwin unit included here is the former Tubemakers (Newcastle) 0-6-0 DH unit *Worimi*, now in the care of GrainCorp at nearby Carrington. Pending withdrawal and preservation, *Worimi* plays backup to a pair of tiny remote-controlled shunting units.

Road#	Builder's #	Built	Type	Original owner	Current owner	Status
Allandale	4/473.1 3.63	1963	0-4-0 DM	North Eton Mill	Mackay Sugar	Stored
-	5/774.1 2.64	1964	0-4-0 DH	Farleigh Mill	Mackay Sugar	In service
10	6/881.1 6.64	1964	0-4-0 DH	Mulgrave Mill	Mulgrave Mill	In service
3	6/1082.1 2.65	1965	0-4-0 DH	Tully Mill	Tully Mill	In service
2	6/1082.2 2.65	1965	0-4-0 DH	Tully Mill	Tully Mill	In service
1	6/1082.3 2.65	1965	0-4-0 DH	Tully Mill	Tully Mill	In service
Bli-Bli	6/1257.1 7.65	1965	0-6-0 DH	Moreton Mill	Bund. Sugar (Bundaberg)	In service
17	6/1446.1 9.65	1965	0-4-0 DH	Condong Mill	CSR Macknade Mill	In service
Perry	6/1576.1 8.66	1966	0-6-0 DH	Fairymead Mill	Bund. Sugar (Bundaberg)	In service
Albany	6/1792.1 11.66	1966	0-4-0 DH	Condong Mill	CSR Victoria Mill	In service
St Kilda	6/2179.1 6.67	1967	0-6-0 DH	Gin Gin Mill	Bund. Sugar (Bundaberg)	In service
Petrie	6/2300.1 6.68	1968	0-6-0 DH	Moreton Mill	Bund. Sugar (Bundaberg)	In service
14	6/2490.1 7.68	1968	0-6-0 DH	Macknade Mill	CSR Macknade Mill	In service
Carstairs	6/2715.1 9.68	1968	0-6-0 DH	Inkerman Mill	CSR Inkerman Mill	In service
Rubyanna	3406.1 7.70	1970	0-6-0 DH	Fairymead Mill	Bund. Sugar (Bundaberg)	In service
Manoo	3875.1 7.71	1971	0-6-0 DH	Bingera Mill	Bund. Sugar (Bundaberg)	In service
Hobart	4413.1 7.72	1972	0-6-0 DH	Victoria Mill	CSR Victoria Mill	In service
11	4413.2 8.72	1972	0-6-0 DH	Hambledon Mill	Mulgrave Mill	In service
Iona	4498.1 7.72	1972	B-B DH	Kalamia Mill	CSR Inkerman Mill	In service
Worimi	4877.1 9.73	1973	0-6-0 DH	Tubemakers	GrainCorp	Standy-by
Calavos	4983.1 7.73	1973	B-B DH	Bingera Mill	Bund. Sugar (Bundaberg)	In service
Vulcan	5317.1 11.73	1973	B-B DH	Millaquin Mill	Bund. Sugar (Bundaberg)	In service
Norham	5383.1 7.74	1974	B-B DH	Kalamia Mill	CSR Kalamia Mill	In service

Top right: Diesel-hydraulic Mulgrave 11 approaches the mill with a loaded cane train Wednesday 4 July 2007. Chris Stratton

Middle right: Bundaberg Sugar's *Moorland* (formerly Moreton Mill's *Coolum*) alongside Zandes Lane, north-west of Bundaberg on the former Fairymead Mill system, Wednesday 6 August 2008. Rod Milne

Below: Mackay Sugar E M Baldwin locomotive 7 *North Eton* is on the approach to Racecourse Mill on Sunday morning 22 September 2002. Chris Walters

Above: E M Baldwin's standard-gauge *Worimi*, originally built for Tubemakers (Newcastle), now works for the nearby GrainCorp Grain Terminal at Carrington, as seen here on Tuesday 1 May 2001. Leon Oberg

Above: E M Baldwin's last locomotive, Tully 7, on approach to the mill from the south near Murray River Siding on Wednesday 18 September 2002. Chris Walters

(continued)

Road#	Builder's #	Built	Type	Original owner	Current owner	Status
Brisbane	5423.1 9.74	1974	B-B DH	Victoria Mill	CSR Victoria Mill	In service
24	5477.1 8.74	1974	B-B DH	South Johnstone Mill	Bund. Sugar (Innisfail)	In service
Moorland	5565.1 10.74	1974	B-B DH	Moreton Mill	Bund. Sugar (Bundaberg)	In service
Oakwood	5800.1 5.75	1975	B-B DH	Bingera Mill	Bund. Sugar (Bundaberg)	In service
Givelda	5800.2 6.75	1975	B-B DH	Bingera Mill	Bund. Sugar (Bundaberg)	In service
Delan	5800.3 7.75	1975	B-B DH	Bingera Mill	Bund. Sugar (Bundaberg)	In service
Bucca	6104.1 8.75	1975	B-B DH	Millaquin Mill	Bund. Sugar (Bundaberg)	In service
Darwin	6171.1 9.75	1975	B-B DH	Victoria Mill	CSR Victoria Mill	In service
Barolin	6456.1 11.75	1975	B-B DH	Millaquin Mill	Bund. Sugar (Bundaberg)	In service
Homebush II	6400.1 4.76	1976	B-B DH	Victoria Mill	CSR Victoria Mill	In service
Townsville II	6400.2 4.76	1976	B-B DH	Victoria Mill	CSR Victoria Mill	In service
Wallaman	6400.3 4.76	1976	B-B DH	Victoria Mill	CSR Victoria Mill	In service
25	6470.1 1.76	1976	B-B DH	South Johnstone Mill	Bund. Sugar (Innisfail)	In service
Iyah	6558.1 6.76	1976	B-B DH	Inkerman Mill	CSR Inkerman Mill	In service
9	6626.1 7.76	1976	B-B DH	Proserpine Mill	Proserpine Mill	In service
34 Hampden	6706.1 5.76	1976	B-B DH	Farleigh Mill	Mackay Sugar	In service
Selkirk	6750.1 8.76	1976	B-B DH	Invicta Mill	CSR Invicta Mill	In service
7 North Eton	6780.1 8.76	1976	B-B DH	North Eton Mill	Mackay Sugar	In service
D12	6890.1 10.76	1976	B-B DH	Plane Creek Mill	CSR Plane Creek Mill	In service
Maitland	7070.1 3.77	1977	B-B DH	Victoria Mill	CSR Victoria Mill	In service
Adelaide	7070.2 4.77	1977	B-B DH	Victoria Mill	CSR Victoria Mill	In service
19	7070.3 4.77	1977	B-B DH	Macknade Mill	CSR Macknade Mill	In service
20	7070.4 4.77	1977	B-B DH	Macknade Mill	CSR Macknade Mill	In service
5 Shannon	7126.1 5.77	1977	B-B DH	Pleystowe Mill	Mackay Sugar	In service
Gowrie	7135.1 7.77	1977	B-B DH	Victoria Mill	CSR Victoria Mill	In service
33 Foulden	7220.1 6.77	1977	B-B DH	Farleigh Mill	Mackay Sugar	In service
(11)	7240.1 5.78	1978	B-B DH	Labasa Mill (Fiji)	Proserpine Mill	Stored
26	7244.1 8.77	1977	B-B DH	South Johnstone Mill	Bund. Sugar (Innisfail)	In service
10	7267.1 6.77	1977	B-B DH	Isis Central Mill	Isis Central Mill	In service
Bojack	7280.1 9.77	1977	B-B DH	Kalamia Mill	CSR Inkerman Mill	In service
Daintree	7303.1 7.77	1977	B-B DH	Mossman Mill	Mossman Mill	In service
Hambledon	8002.1 8.78	1978	0-4-0 DH	Goondi Mill	CSR Victoria Mill	Stored
(12)	8290.1 4.79	1979	B-B DH	Rarawai Mill (Fiji)	Proserpine Mill	Stored
10	8860.1 8.79	1979	0-4-0 DH	Roberts Construction	Mackay Sugar	Stored
Beetle	8860.2 8.79	1979	0-4-2 DH	Roberts Construction	Bund. Sugar (Bundaberg)	Stored
Miara	8988.1 6.80	1980	B-B DH	Fairymead Mill	Bund. Sugar (Bundaberg)	In service
Sugarworld Shuttle	9109.1 9.80	1980	0-4-0 DH	Goondi Mill	CSR Victoria Mill	In service
16 Charlton	9562.1 6.81	1981	B-B DH	Marian Mill	Mackay Sugar	In service
17 Langdon	9562.2 6.81	1981	B-B DH	Marian Mill	Mackay Sugar	In service
6 Mia Mia	9815.1 10.81	1981	B-B DH	North Eton Mill	Mackay Sugar	In service
10	9816.1 10.81	1981	B-B DH	Prosperine Mill	Proserpine Mill	In service
Fairydale	10048.1 6.82	1982	B-B DH	Fairymead Mill	Bund. Sugar (Bundaberg)	In service
35 Inverness	10123.1 5.82	1982	B-B DH	Farleigh Mill	Mackay Sugar	In service
11	10130.1 6.82	1982	B-B DH	Isis Central Mill	Isis Central Mill	In service
Burdekin	10215.1 7.82	1982	B-B DH	Invicta Mill	CSR Invicta Mill	In service
32 Liverpool	10385.1 8.82	1982	B-B DH	South Johnstone Mill	Bund. Sugar (Innisfail)	In service
Tully 7	10684.1 4.83	1983	B-B DH	Tully Mill	Tully Mill	In service

Malcolm Moore

Above: ***Stumpy*** **at the Mossman Mill Visitor's Centre Monday 11 August 2003. This unit seems to spend most of its time parked here as part of an industry display.** Chris Walters

It is astonishing just how far and wide Malcolm Moore-built locomotives have been dispersed over the years, without raising a great degree of attention among enthusiasts and historians. The Melbourne-based firm produced a diverse range of locomotives for numerous industries and constructed a number of units that eventually worked in the cane fields (although most entered this market via previous service in other commercial and governmental endeavours). Generally all began life as four-wheeled petrol-mechanical locomotives, however several were converted to diesel over the years. While the general design of these cane fields units varied to some degree, most were small, narrow shunting units suitable only for yard/depot shunting, and light navvy duties. The company produced only one locomotive specifically for the sugar industry; this was a 1956-built 0-4-0 DH simply named *Moore* (now preserved), that was delivered to Victoria Mill. Today, only two Malcolm Moore units are available for mill use, and neither is frontline power or used extensively. These are *Stumpy* at Mossman Mill and *Hydro* at Bingera Mill. Many similar units have been preserved in private collections over the years, while several more were scrapped as work for them dried up.

Road #	Builder's #	Built	Type	Owner	Status
Hydro	1025	1943	0-4-0 DH	Bundaberg Sugar (Bundaberg)	In service
Stumpy	1042	1943	0-4-0 DM	Mossman Mill	Operational/Display

Currently available for Mossman service, however usually held on display at the visitor's centre.

Mulgrave Mill

Above: *Pie Cart* at Mulgrave Mill on Monday 16 September 2002. Chris Walters

Very little is known about this tiny four-wheeled diesel-mechanical locomotive, other than it was built 'in-house' at Mulgrave Mill during 1962, and primarily used as a navvy/track maintenance unit ever since. Just how much 'field' service it sees today is debatable for it never seems to stray too far from the mill.

Road #	Built	Type	Owner	Status
Pie Cart	1962	0-4-0 DM	Mulgrave Mill	In service

Walkers Limited

Above: ISIS 1 leads an outbound empty rake of cane bins along Mill Road, between Isis Central Mill and Cordalba township, on Saturday 23 August 2008. James Chuang

Located in Maryborough, not far south of Bundaberg on the lower portion of the Queensland coast, and having developed a specialty in the design and construction of diesel-hydraulic locomotives, it might surprise some to learn that Walkers Limited constructed only one diesel locomotive for the Australian sugar industry. That 0-6-0 diesel-hydraulic locomotive was built in 1956 in association with the North British Locomotive Company of Glasgow, Scotland, and was delivered to the Mourilyan Harbour for use at the sugar terminal as a shunting locomotive. Used as a demonstrator unit for several years, the locomotive was a satisfactory performer, however when compared to the design, economies and reliability of the similar Clyde and Comeng units coming off the production lines, it just did not measure up. Walkers themselves seemed reluctant to pursue the market with anything resembling true enthusiasm, and so the 0-6-0 was to remain something of an orphan. The locomotive continued to work at the harbour after eventual purchase from Walkers in 1960, until eventually coming into the ownership of Mourilyan Mill in 1992. It remained in service with that mill for several years before being withdrawn towards the end of the decade as their number 11. The locomotive is now based in Victoria for restoration as a preservation project.

In 1968, Walkers constructed their second 0-6-0 diesel-hydraulic unit; this time approximating more of a 'centre-cab' design. This 21.3-tonne, 174 kW locomotive, subsequently named *Mango*, was delivered to the 1067 mm gauge Aramac Shire Council's 68-kilometre tramway operation (which connected to the QR network at Barcaldine) and worked that system until closure in 1976.

That year it was sold to Pioneer Mill at Brandon who maintained the only sugar cane network compatible with *Mango's* track gauge. To look at, the design matches nothing else in the Walkers catalogue. However, the cab and body shape is perhaps vaguely reminiscent of the six larger centre-cab B-B diesel-hydraulic units the firm built for BHP Whyalla from 1962. This fascinating and unique machine continues to haul cane into Pioneer Mill in 2004, and is now known amongst local train crews as *Aramac*.

During the 1960s Walkers started to tap into a siginificant demand for diesel-hydraulic units required for shunting and main line work. First came the earlier mentioned centre-cab shunters for BHP Whyalla, before the company supplied three B-B diesel-hydraulic-type locomotives to the Emu Bay Railway of Tasmania in 1963. In 1966 Walkers adapted the earlier designs into a B-B diesel-hydraulic demonstrator they branded W1. This unit was then issued to the Queensland Railways for trials in yard shunting and transfer operations. QR regarded the unit as a success and subsequently ordered what would ultimately total seventy-two additional units. W1 was renumbered DH1 in 1968 and shortly after the production run of the DH Class commenced.

A heavier, more powerful version appeared in 1969 for the Emu Bay Railway, and this type was soon followed by similar locomotives for the NSW Public Transport Commission (the 73 Class), the Western Australian Government Railways (the M and MA Classes) and a one off unit for Mount Isa Mines (see page 247). All up, between 1962 and 1974 Walkers delivered one hundred and forty five B-B diesel-hydraulic units to these customers (including the six BHP Whyalla locomotives).

Above: The unique, former Aramac Shire Council 1067 mm-gauge 0-6-0 DH, now known as *Aramac*, at Pioneer Mill on Friday 20 September 2002. Chris Walters

Above: Mackay Sugar's 37 *Calen* (ex-7330) leads a rake of bins through the countryside near Kuttabul on Thursday 9 October 2008. Ken Date

The 1980s and 1990s brought with them a major rationalisation of the freight services provided by government railway operators, and part of this was the gradual move to fewer, larger train movements. This trend developed hand in hand with a move away from the carriage of general goods and an increased use of unit trains and bulk haulage. All of these conspired to drastically reduce the need for dedicated, relatively low-powered shunting locomotives, in respect to government service in particular. By the early 1990s, a large percentage of these Walkers locomotives were surplus to requirements. Walkers, in conjunction with the Sugar Research Institute investigated the possibility of rebuilding the B-B diesel-hydraulic hood unit design for use on 610 mm gauge sugar cane haulage. Bundaberg Foundry Engineers, Tulk Goninan at Mackay, and a number of the mills themselves also became involved in the conversion and rebuilding work.

The first unit rebuilt was former QR shunting locomotive DH23, which arrived at CSR's Victoria Mill from Walkers in July 1991, as *Clem H McComiskie*. Compared to later rebuilds the unit was not restructured overtly, although the locomotive had been overhauled, lightened and re-gauged to 610 mm. Both of the original hood sections were still in place, but the cab profile had been modified to be taller than the original configuration. The extra headroom afforded by this increased cab height did cause problems, as the welds were later prone to rust. The newly converted locomotive was commissioned on bulk sugar trains operating from the mill to the nearby port at Lucinda, and was to remain on these services through until the end of the 2003 crush. At that time it was withdrawn for further rebuilding work to bring it into line with subsequent Walkers rebuilds.

The main alteration applied was the removal of the cab and short hood, and the installation of a larger, replacement end-cab. *Clem H McComiskie* had been previously tested on sugar cane haulage, but had proven unsuitable for such work given the poor cab visibility when compared to more recent Victoria Mill Walkers units such as *Herbert II* and *Victoria*. The 2004 rebuild enabled *Clem H McComiskie* to be transferred over to regular sugar cane haulage for the first time since commissioning, although it did not achieve this without several teething problems.

Meanwhile, a similar DH Class rebuild was delivered in August 1991 to Isis Central Mill as ISIS1, and this locomotive was also later rebuilt with a replacement end-cab when inadequacies with the earlier layout were identified. Subsequent rebuilds of Walkers units were given a newly fabricated, larger cab structure located closer to the end of the frame, and aside from Kalamia Mill's *Kilrie*, no other 610 mm locomotives were given a nose or short hood of any kind.

However two DHs were modified for use by Pioneer Mill, and as the Pioneer and QR track gauge is compatible, these two units were not as extensively modified as other rebuilds. The end result was something similar to *Clem H McComiskie* and ISIS1, although perhaps more like the original DH appearance. These rebuilt DH Class locomotives, as have the later 73 and M Class rebuilds, generally employed Caterpillar or Cummins engines connected to the original Voith hydraulic transmission. Although most of the converted locomotives saw original equipment overhauled and re-used as part of the rebuild process, some units have had new common components fitted in cases where the original was unsuitable or unavailable.

Following the success of the rebuilt QR DH Class, Mackay Sugar and CSR then turned to surplus NSWSRA 73 Class and Westrail M/MA Class for further raw materials.

Above: ***Mulgrave*** **at Mohammed Siding, north of Kamma, with a load of cane bound for its namesake mill on Monday 16 September 2002.** Chris Walters

The first 73 rebuilt for sugar cane haulage was 7313, which was rebuilt by Pleystowe Mill as 94 Class unit prototype *Walkerston* in 1994. This unit, as well as the subsequent Mackay Sugar rebuilds were modified to be shorter in frame length and body height than those converted for use at other mills. Thus they have something of a squat appearance, particularly when observed running hood first.

1994 also witnessed the delivery to Queensland of the two M Class locomotives (M1851 and M1852) and two of the three MA Class units (MA1861 and MA1863) from Western Australia. This purchase left MA1862 as the only example of its type in Westrail service. The two M Class units were rebuilt at the Bundaberg Foundry in 1996–97 as *Jourama* and *Cairns* for Victoria Mill, however the MA pair went into storage at Plane Creek Mill and have remained there ever since.

Looking at all of these rebuilt Walkers units, it is generally possible to pick out which locomotives were rebuilt from which type if one looks closely. Some 73 Class units in particular, with the handrails incorporating the sandboxes above the skirting, stand out from the DH and M Class conversions. Some units have had their sand boxes fitted directly onto their bogies in a style similar to the older Baldwin locomotives, while cab and hood shape often belies a particular unit's ancestry.

Mackay Sugar continued to hunt around for surplus Walkers units as late as 2002 when it acquired two DH Class locomotives (CC01 and CC02) previously sold by QR to Cooks Construction for 900 mm gauge brown coal haulage near Yallourn in Victoria. This company had obtained six DH units for the Yallourn (former SEC Victoria) operation—four for service and two for spare parts. With the completion of the Yallourn contract, all six were sold to sugar mills, with Tully having obtained three, Mackay Sugar two (one now sold, see below) and Isis Central Mill one. However, the continued slump in sugar prices has slowed investment and the torrent of Walkers rebuilds from the 1991–98 period has slowed to a trickle in more recent times. Since 1998, two units for Isis and one for Tully are the only rebuilds that have eventuated.

Although further rebuilds for some mills have been mooted, nothing firm has been announced for the immediate future and several companies continue to retain stored, 'untouched' Walkers units pending future opportunities. Between 2004 and 2008 Mackay Sugar managed to sell a number of its stored Walkers units: 7321 (to Patrick PortLink for recommissioning in Sydney), CC02 (ex-DH5, for conversion to 762 mm gauge and restoration by Puffing Billy in Victoria) and DH25 (to provide parts for CC02 and sister unit DH59—numbered DH31—already on site). Despite this, the company still possesses seven Walkers units in store at North Eton (one DH in the form of CC01, and six 73s—two of which, 7327 and 7332, are all but dismantled). At the same time, CSR has three 73s, one DH and the two MAs still in storage, while Mulgrave, Tully and Isis Mills also have a number of unused Walkers units awaiting attention. Many of these are being held for parts, and in particular the industry is keen to keep a supply of spare hydraulic transmissions, as well as Caterpillar engines on hand.

In the short term at least, it is likely that any new locomotives for sugar cane haulage will come from these stored Walkers units, however just how many, and over what time frame this occurs is very much dependant on the state of the industry in years to come.

Top right: Pioneer Mill's 1067 mm *Jardine* at Airdale Loop on Friday 20 September 2002.
Chris Walters

Middle right: *Cairns* (ex-Westrail M1852) at Victoria Mill on Saturday 15 December 2001.
Chris Walters

Below: Mount Isa Mine's 5803 in storage at the mine (before being sold to CSR), on Saturday 9 October 2004.
Danielle Jesser

Amongst all the Walkers diesel-hydraulic variants was a one-off GH500 delivery for Mount Isa Mines. This unit was a look-a-like to the low-nose design pioneered by the EBR 11 Class, although in power and capability, was actually closer to the QR DH Class. Intended for surface shunting at Mount Isa, 303 (as it was initially called) entered service during 1972. By 1991, when it was joined by ex-QR unit DH7 (renumbered 5804), 303 had become 5803 as part of a fleet renumbering. However, within a decade, the need for such shunters had diminished, and eventually 5803 was sold to CSR for use at Pioneer Mill in late 2007 (although it is not believed to have entered service as of October 2008).

DH Class

Road ID	Original #	Builder's #	Built	Owner	Status
CC01	DH4	586	1968	Mackay Sugar	Stored North Eton
5804	DH7	589	1968	Isis Central Mill	Stored Isis Mill
Jardine	DH10	592	1968	CSR Pioneer Mill	In 610 mm service
Giru	DH11	593	1968	CSR Invicta Mill	In 610 mm service
1 *Allan Page*	DH12	594	1968	CSR Plane Creek Mill	In 610 mm service
Gordonvale	DH13	595	1968	Mulgrave Mill	In 610 mm service
ISIS2	DH16	598	1968	Isis Central Mill	In 610 mm service
Victoria	DH17	599	1968	CSR Victoria Mill	In 610 mm service
ISIS3	DH18	600	1968	Isis Central Mill	In 610 mm service
Jarvisfield	DH19	601	1968	CSR Kalamia Mill	In 610 mm service
ISIS1	DH20	602	1969	Isis Central Mill	In 610 mm service
DH22	DH22	604	1969	CSR Pioneer Mill	Stored Pioneer Mill
Clem H McComskie	DH23	605	1969	CSR Victoria Mill	In 610 mm service
TULLY8	DH24	606	1969	Tully Sugar	In 610 mm service
ISIS6	DH28	610	1969	Isis Central Mill	In 610 mm service
DH29	DH29	611	1969	CSR Kalamia Mill	Stored Bundaberg
Herbert II	DH30	612	1969	CSR Victoria Mill	In 610 mm service
Mulgrave	DH31	613	1969	Mulgrave Mill	In 610 mm service
ISIS5	DH35	617	1969	Isis Central Mill	In 610 mm service
DH36	DH36	618	1969	Tully Sugar	Stored Tully Mill
TULLY4	DH40	622	1969	Tully Sugar	In 610 mm service
DH41	DH41	623	1969	Bundaberg Sugar	Stored Bundaberg
Rita Island	DH43	625	1969	CSR Kalamia Mill	In 610 mm service
11	DH46	628	1969	Proserpine Mill	In 610 mm service
DH47	DH47	629	1969	Mulgrave Mill	Stored Bundaberg
2 *Karloo*	DH48	630	1969	CSR Plane Creek Mill	In 610 mm service
Kilrie	DH50	632	1969	CSR Kalamia Mill	In 610 mm service
Kolan	DH51	633	1969	Bingera Sugar	In 610 mm service
CC03	DH56	643	1970	Tully Sugar	Stored Tully Mill
Jerona	DH60	647	1970	Pioneer Sugar	In 610 mm service
TULLY5	DH63	650	1970	Tully Sugar	In 610 mm service
3 *Koumala*	DH64	651	1970	CSR Plane Creek Mill	In 610 mm service
TULLY6	DH66	653	1970	Tully Sugar	In 610 mm service
-	DH67	654	1970	Isis Central Mill	Brake wagon *
Clare	DH68	655	1970	CSR Invicta Mill	In 610 mm service
ISIS4	DH69	656	1970	Isis Central Mill	In 610 mm service
55 *Balberra*	DH70	657	1970	MS Racecourse Mill	In 610 mm service

* *The frame of DH67 is employed as the chassis of a brake wagon, while other components from this unit are held in storage by Isis Mill pending a possible rebuild and recommissioning as a functioning locomotive.*

73 Class

Road ID	Original #	Builder's #	Built	Owner	Status
7304	7304	663	1970	Mackay Sugar	Stored North Eton
38 *Miclere*	7305	664	1970	Mackay Sugar	In 610 mm service
7306	7306	665	1970	Mackay Sugar	Stored North Eton
7308	7308	667	1971	Mackay Sugar	Stored North Eton
7309	7309	668	1971	CSR Plane Creek Mill	Stored Plane Creek
Scott	7310	669	1971	CSR Invicta Mill	In 610 mm service
44 *Walkerston*	7313	672	1971	Mackay Sugar	In 610 mm service
12	7314	673	1971	Proserpine Mill	In 610 mm service
4 *Carmila*	7317	676	1971	CSR Plane Creek Mill	In 610 mm service
Piralko	7318	677	1971	CSR Invicta Mill	In 610 mm service
Hodel	7325	687	1972	CSR Invicta Mill	In 610 mm service
7327	7327	689	1972	Mackay Sugar	Dismantled
40 *Dulverton*	7328	690	1972	Mackay Sugar	In 610 mm service
37 *Calen*	7330	692	1972	Mackay Sugar	In 610 mm service
39 *Cedars*	7331	693	1972	Mackay Sugar	In 610 mm service
7332	7332	694	1972	Mackay Sugar	Dismantled
7336	7336	698	1972	Bundaberg Sugar	Stored Bundaberg
24 *Netherdale*	7337	699	1972	Mackay Sugar	In 610 mm service
14	7339	701	1972	Proserpine Mill	In 610 mm service
7341	7341	703	1972	Mackay Sugar	Stored North Eton
21 *Tannalo*	7343	705	1972	Mackay Sugar	In 610 mm service
Cromarty	7346	708	1972	CSR Invicta Mill	In 610 mm service
7347	7347	709	1973	CSR Plane Creek Mill	Stored Plane Creek
Minkom	7348	710	1973	CSR Invicta Mill	In 610 mm service
7349	7349	711	1973	CSR Plane Creek Mill	Stored Plane Creek

M/MA Class

Road ID	Original	Builder's #	Built	Owner	Status
Jourama	M1851	680	1972	CSR Victoria Mill	In 610 mm service
Cairns	M1852	681	1972	CSR Victoria Mill	In 610 mm service
MA1861	MA1861	713	1973	CSR Plane Creek Mill	Stored Plane Creek Mill
MA1863	MA1863	715	1973	CSR Plane Creek Mill	Stored Plane Creek Mill

Mount Isa Mines GH500

Road #	Original #	Builder's #	Built	Owner	Status
5803	303	682	1971	CSR Pioneer Mill	Stored Pioneer Mill

C250

Road ID	Builder's #	Built	Owner	Status
Aramac	583	1968	CSR Pioneer Mill	In 1067 mm service

Ex-Aramac Shire Council (tramway) *Mango*.

Westfalia Becorit

Above: Invicta Mill's unique Westfalia locomotive, *Strathalbyn*, a few kilometres west of Giru on Friday 20 September 2002. Chris Walters

With the closure of the E M Baldwin's Castle Hill works in the mid 1980s, the company's locomotive manufacturing business was obtained by Hexham Engineering, near Newcastle. Although Hexham did not construct any cane-field locomotives, they retained the rights to build Baldwin units until the firm was taken over by the Australian arm of German industrialists Westfalia Becorit during 1988.

The company promoted new locomotive construction under the Westfalia/Baldwin banner, and some of the staff from the former Castle Hill works joined the new enterprise. However, the collaboration was successful in obtaining only one mill railway locomotive order; a solitary unit for CSR's Invicta Mill at Giru. The 1990 order resulted in a 32-tonne, model DH32C B-B diesel-hydraulic locomotive that the mill christened *Strathalbyn*. The unit was a development of Baldwin's B-B DH unit Tully 7, built seven years earlier at Castle Hill, yet also featured a number of technological and performance enhancements typical of the 'Generation 4' Eimco and Bundaberg Foundry units being built around this time.

Westfalia must have observed Eimco and Bundaberg Foundry Engineers also receiving orders at this time and felt that an increased demand for new sugar cane locomotives was forthcoming. However, as for those other builders, the post-1991 period yielded no further contracts for new locomotives, and thus Westfalia's involvement in supplying locomotives to the sugar industry came to an early end.

In any other mill fleet, *Strathalbyn* would have been a flagship locomotive. However, Invicta Mill actually operates the largest single collection of Walkers rebuilds of any mill, and thus *Strathalbyn*, despite being a success, is somewhat overshadowed by these larger locomotives.

Road ID	Builder's #	Built	Type	Owner	Status
Strathalbyn	13863.1 8.91	1991	B-B DH	CSR Invicta Mill	In service

Preserved Locomotives

Privately-owned 4465 at Werris Creek on the evening of Saturday 24 February 2007.
Dominik Giemza

South Australian Railways

Road #	Builder's #	Built	Owner	Status
350	93	1949	SteamRanger, Mount Barker	Operational (1600 mm)
351	94	1949	NRM Port Adelaide	Display (1600 mm)
507	112	1965	SteamRanger, Mount Barker	Operational (1600 mm)
515	120	1966	NRM Port Adelaide	Operational (1600 mm)
801	A.002	1956	NRM Port Adelaide	Operational (1600 mm)
866	84712	1963	Private (DRR Devonport)	Operational (1067 mm)
900	95/1848	1951	NRM Port Adelaide	Display (1600 mm)
Named *Lady Norrie*.				
907	102/1855	1953	ALRC Tailem Bend	Stored (1600 mm)
909	104/1857	1953	ALRC Tailem Bend	Stored (1600 mm)
930	81885	1955	NRM Port Adelaide	Display (1600 mm)
958	G-3388-01	1965	SteamRanger, Mount Barker	Operational (1600 mm)
963	G-3485-01	1967	SteamRanger, Mount Barker	Stored (1600 mm)

Former South Australian Railway's diesel locomotives in service with SteamRanger.
Below: 507 at Victor Harbor on Sunday 13 July 2008.
Opposite page top, 958 (in a semblance of it's former Australian National livery) at Strathalbyn on Sunday 13 July 2008
Opposite page, bottom: 350 shunts out of the Mount Barker depot on Sunday 5 October 2008.
All three photos by Peter Michalak

Preserved

958
958

350

Western Australian Government Railways and Midland Railway Company of WA

Road #	Builder's #	Built	Owner	Status	Name
A1501	60-216	1960	RHWA Bassendean	Stored (1067 mm)	-
B1601	-	1962	RHWA Bassendean	Operational (1067 mm)	-
B1603	-	1962	Midland Military Markets	Display (1067 mm)	-
B1608	-	1965	Private (Middle Swan)	Stored (1067 mm)	-
B1610	-	1965	BLLPS Boulder	Operational (1067 mm)	-
C1701	A.056	1962	HVTR Pinjarra	Display (1067 mm)	-
C1702	A.057	1962	HVTR Pinjarra	Operational (1067 mm)	-
C1703	A.058	1962	Private (Pinjarra)	Operational (1067 mm)	-
E30	-	1957	RHWA Bassendean	Operational (1067 mm)	-
F41	A.019	1958	Shire of Moora	Display (1067 mm)	-
F43	A.021	1958	RHWA Bassendean	Stored (1067 mm)	-
G50	A.068	1963	RHWA Pinjarra	Stored (1067 mm)	-
RA1918	A.248	1972	RHWA Bassendean	Display (1067 mm)	-
T1804	046	1967	City of Northampton	Display (1067 mm)	-
TA1807	056	1970	BTM Boyanup	Operational (1067 mm)	-
TA1808	057	1970	Merredin	Display (1067 mm)	-
TA1814	063	1970	PCRM Pine Creek	Operational (1067 mm)	-
X1001	830	1954	RHWA Bassendean	Display (1067 mm)	*Yalagonga*
XA1401	862	1955	HVTR Pinjarra	Operational (1067 mm)	*Pendong*
XA1402	861	1955	RHWA Bassendean	Display (1067 mm)	*Targan*
XA1405	864	1955	RHWA Midland	Restoration (1067 mm)	*Warienga*
XA1411	870	1956	Private (Pinjarra)	Display (1067 mm)	*Weedookarri*
XA1415	874	1956	HVTR Narrogin	Display (1067 mm)	*Wurara*
Y1101	1011	1953	RHWA Midland	Restoration (1067 mm)	-
Y1102	1012	1953	Private (Pemberton)	Stored (1067 mm)	-
Y1107	1017	1954	Private (Pemberton)	Stored (1067 mm)	-
Y1108	1018	1954	BLLPS Boulder	Operational (1067 mm)	-
Y1114	1024	1955	PTC Pemberton	Operational (1067 mm)	-
Y1115	1025	1955	PTC Pemberton	Operational (1067 mm)	-
Y1116	1026	1955	BTM Boyanup	Operational (1067 mm)	-
Z1151	7736/2401	1953	Steamtown Peterborough	Operational (1067 mm)	-
Z1152	7737/2402	1953	HVTR Pinjarra	Operational (1067 mm)	-
Z1153	7738/2403	1953	BLLPS Boulder	Operational (1067 mm)	-

Top right: Former Westrail shunter B1603 on display at the site of the Midland Military Markets on Sunday 28 July 2008.
Chris Walters

Middle right: The Pemberton Tramway Company's Y1114 at Pemberton on Saturday 19 July 2008. Four of these British-built Bo-Bo units are on site at Pemberton.
Chris Miller

Bottom right: Former Western Australian Government Railways Metro-Vickers (UK) 2-Do-2 diesel-electric locomotive XA1411 at the Hotham Valley Tourist Railway compound at Pinjarra on Saturday 27 July 2007.
Chris Walters

Opposite page: Shunter Z1152 at Hotham Valley's Dwellingup sheds on Saturday 12 July 2008.
Chris Miller

Commonwealth Railways

Road #	Builder's #	Built	Owner	Status
7921	17939	1943	NSWRTM Thirlmere	Operational (1435 mm)
Ex-United States Army 7921. Operated for Commonwealth Railways as DE90.				
DE91	17933	1943	NRM Port Adelaide	Stored (1435 mm)
Ex-United States Army 7922. Operated for Commonwealth Railways as DE91.				
DR1	327968	1953	RVR Kurri Kurri	Stored (1435 mm)
Ex-Shell Oil, Clyde NSW.				
GM1	ML1-1	1951	Federal Government	Stored (1435 mm)
Named *Robert Gordon Menzies*.				
GM2	ML1-2	1951	NRM Port Adelaide	Display (1435 mm)
GM28	62-268	1963	Port Pirie Council	Display (1435 mm)
On display as GM22 *Sir Hubert Opperman*.				
GM36	66-445	1966	SRHC Seymour	Operational (1435 mm)
Named *C J Storrman*.				
ETSA2	58-192	1958	Homestead Park	Display (1435 mm)
Ex-Commonwealth Railways MDH1 and formerly named *F J Shea*. On display in Homestead Park.				
NB30	-	1957	PRR Quorn	Operational (1067 mm)
NC1	56-95	1956	Steamtown Peterborough	Operational (1067 mm)
Ex-Lakewood Firewood Company No. 2.				
NC2	56-94	1956	PRR Port Lincoln	Display (1435 mm)
Ex-Lakewood Firewood Company No. 1.				
NSU51	DL-1	1954	PRR Quorn	Stored (1067 mm)
Named *George McLeay*.				
NSU52	DL-2	1954	PRR Quorn	Operational (1067 mm)
NSU53	DL-3	1954	OGHRM Alice Springs	Display (1067 mm)
NSU54	DL-4	1954	PRR Quorn	Stored (1067 mm)
NSU55	DL-5	1954	Steamtown Peterborough	Operational (1067 mm)
NSU56	DL-6	1954	MPA Marree	Stored (1067 mm)
NSU57	DL-7	1955	MPA Marree	Display (1067 mm)
NSU58	DL-8	1955	OGHRM MacDonnell	Operational (1067 mm)
Named *Don Williams*.				
NSU59	DL-9	1955	OGHRM MacDonnell	Stored (1067 mm)
NSU60	DL-10	1955	MPA Marree	Stored (1067 mm)
NSU61	DL-11	1955	NRM Port Adelaide	Display (1067 mm)
NSU62	DL-12	1955	Steamtown Peterborough	Stored (1067 mm)
NSU63	DL-13	1955	FNAR Adelaide River	Display (1067 mm)
NSU64	DL-14	1955	OGHRM MacDonnell	Stored (1067 mm)
NT76	53	1968	PRR Quorn	Operational (1067 mm)

Above: In late July 1998, a display of Clyde locomotives was held at Sydney Terminal to celebrate the centenary of the firm. Featured among the locomotives were Q319, AN1, 8162, L262 and classic Commonwealth Railways streamliner GM1—Clyde's first diesel. The five units are seen passing Campsie en route from Delec to Sydney Terminal on Thursday 23 July 1998, with GM1 bringing up the rear. Chris Walters

Above: Ex-Commonwealth Railways NT76 approaches Stirling North with a Pichi Richi Railway special on Sunday 30 May 2004. Greg O'Brien

New South Wales Government Railways

Road #	Builder's #	Built	Owner	Status
4001	77732	1951	NSWRTM Thirlmere	Restoration
4002	77733	1951	PRHS Seven Mile	Operational
4006	77737	1951	City of Wickham	Display as 9401
4102	1003	1953	NSWRTM Thirlmere	Display
4201	55-74	1955	NSWRTM Thirlmere	Operational
4203	55-79	1955	O'Donoghue's Pub, Emu Plains	Display (incomplete)
4204	56-87	1956	LVR Cowra	Operational
4206	56-100	1956	DSR&M Dorrigo	Operational
42101	65-468	1965	Private (Goulburn)	Restoration
42102	66-469	1966	DSR&M Kooragang Island	Operational
4306	2112-16	1957	NSWRTM Thirlmere	Operational
4401	82807	1957	3801 Limited	Operational
4403	82809	1957	SRA NSW/Junee Roundhouse	Operational
4420	82892	1958	DSR&M Dorrigo	Stored Dorrigo
4458	83748	1961	HVRT Branxton	Operational
4461	G-3421-01	1965	HVRT Branxton	Operational
4463	G-3421-03	1965	HVRT Branxton	Operational
4464	G-3421-04	1966	Lachlan ALCo Loco Group	Stored Eveleigh
4465	G-3421-05	1966	Private (Werris Creek)	Restoration
4472	G-3421-12	1966	HVRT Branxton	Operational
4473	G-3421-13	1966	Lachlan ALCo Loco Group	Operational
4486	G-3421-26	1967	Lachlan ALCo Loco Group	Operational
4488	G-3421-28	1967	HVRT Branxton	Operational
4490	G-3421-30	1967	NSWRTM Thirlmere	Operational
4497	G-3421-37	1967	HVRT Branxton	Operational
4498	G-3421-38	1967	HVRT Branxton	Operational
44211	G-6045-11	1971	NSWRTM Thirlmere	Operational
4501	84143	1962	Goodwin ALCo	Operational
4520	84162	1963	NSWRTM Thirlmere	Operational
4521	84163	1963	DSR&M Kooragang Island	Restoration
4601	786	1956	NSWRTM Valley Heights	Display
4602	787	1956	DSR&M Dorrigo	Stored Dorrigo
4615	800	1957	SETS Hornsby	Stored Hornsby
4627	812	1957	HVRT Branxton	Stored Branxton
4638	823	1957	NSWRTM Thirlmere	Display (named *City of Lithgow*)
4701	31	1972	LVR Cowra	Operational
4702	32	1972	LVR Cowra	Restoration
4703	33	1972	LVR Cowra	Operational
4705	35	1972	Werris Creek Council	Display
4706	36	1972	DSR&M Dorrigo	Stored Dorrigo
4707	37	1972	LVR Cooks River	Undergoing restoration
4708	38	1972	LVR Cowra	Operational
4716	46	1973	LVR Cowra	Operational
4719	49	1973	LVR Cowra	Stored as HTV2000
4801	83701	1959	ORH RailCorp	Stored Redfern
4803	83703	1959	NSWRTM Thirlmere	Operational
4805	83705	1959	ORH RailCorp	Stored Redfern
4807	83707	1959	SRANSW/ARHS Canberra	Stored Canberra
4821	83816	1960	GRPS Goulburn	Operational
4822	83817	1960	DSR&M Dorrigo	Stored Dorrigo
4833	84123	1961	Goodwin ALCo	Operational
4916	64-345	1964	NSWRTM Thirlmere	Operational

Right: Former NSWGR A1A-A1A diesel 4006, seen here displayed at Wickham (WA) as Robe River Bo-Bo 9401, on Tuesday 24 July 2007. 4002 and 4006 were used by Robe for railway construction and shunting following their withdrawal from NSWGR service.
Chris Walters

Right: Shunting unit X203 sits within the railway museum at Yass on Sunday 4 July 2004. Chris Walters

Below: 4306 at Thirlmere during a film shoot in October 1998.
Chris Walters

Preserved

(continued)

Road #	Builder's #	Built	Owner	Status
4918	64-347	1964	3801 Limited	Operational
7006	-	1961	NSWRTM Thirlmere	Operational
7007	-	1961	DSR&M Dorrigo	Stored Dorrigo
7008	-	1961	DSR&M Dorrigo	Stored Dorrigo
7010	-	1961	DSR&M Dorrigo	Stored Dorrigo
7100	-	1952	NSWRTM Thirlmere	Stored Broadmeadow
7315	674	1971	ARHS Canberra	Operational
7319	678	1971	ARHS Canberra	Operational
7320	679	1971	Private (Canberra)	Operational
7324	686	1972	Private (Canberra)	Operational
7329	691	1972	DSR&M Dorrigo	Stored Dorrigo
7335	697	1972	DSR&M Dorrigo	Stored Dorrigo
7344	706	1972	SRANSW/3801 Ltd	Operational
7350	712	1973	HVRT Branxton	Stored Branxton
8501	C-7703-01	1979	SETS Werris Creek	Stored
8507	C-7703-07	1980	DSR&M Werris Creek	Stored
8601	-	1983	DSR&M Kooragang Island	Stored
8606	-	1983	SETS Hornsby	Operational
8607	-	1983	Privately owned	Stored
8644	-	1985	Privately owned	Stored Eveleigh
8646	-	1985	NSWRTM Thirlmere	Stored
8650	-	1986	DSR&M Werris Creek	Stored
DP101	-	1937	SSRM Broken Hill	Display
DP103	-	1938	DSR&M Dorrigo	Stored
DP104	-	1938	NSWRTM Thirlmere	Stored
X102	2	1962	DSR&M Dorrigo	Stored
X203	5	1964	Yass Shire Council	Display
X104	6	1964	DSR&M Dorrigo	Stored
X214	17	1968	DSR&M Dorrigo	Stored
X215	18	1968	HVRT Branxton	Stored
X117	20	1968	HVRT Branxton	Stored

Above: 4472 and 4488 at the Hunter Valley Railway Trust site near Branxton on Saturday 26 July 2008. Ross Verdich

Above: Not long after its withdrawal, but before its acquisition by the Dorrigo Steam Railway & Museum, 8501 stands at Lithgow on Friday 28 August 1998. Chris Walters

Above: Privately owned 8644 leads an ARHS tour through Bombo, bound for Kiama, on Saturday 19 February 2006. 8644 is currently stored at Eveleigh, and as of late 2008, this tour was believed to have been its most recent main line run. Chris Walters

Queensland Railways

Road #	Builder's #	Built	Owner	Status
1150	31090	1952	ARHS Townsville	Restoration
1159	31099	1953	QR Heritage Ipswich	Stored
1170	558	1956	QR Heritage	Stored
1172	560	1956	Mount Morgan	Stored
1177	565	1957	ARHS Rosewood	Stored
1179	567	1957	ARHS Rosewood	Operational
1181	569	1958	ARHS/RAILCO Herberton	Stored as 1180
1200	1905/D146	1953	ARHS Redbank	Stored
1225	-	1985	ARHS Redbank	Stored
1262	A.050	1961	QR Heritage, Ipswich	Display
1263	A.051	1961	ARHS Townsville	Stored
1270	A.092	1964	QR Heritage, Mayne	Operational
1281	A.103	1965	QR Heritage, Ipswich	Display
Named *Century*.				
1331	A.224	1971	DRR Devonport, Tasmania	Stored as ZC32
1400	55-55	1955	Private	Restoration
1407	56-131	1957	QR Heritage, Ipswich	Stored
1450	57-172	1957	QR Heritage, Ipswich	Stored
1455	57-181	1958	QR Heritage, Ipswich	Stored
1461	64-349	1964	QR Heritage, Ipswich	Stored
Named *Centennial*.				
1603	A.064	1963	QR Heritage, Mayne	Operational
1604	A.059	1962	ARHS Rosewood	Operational
1613	A.076	1963	Longreach	Display
1614	A.077	1963	ARHS Rockhampton	Display
1616	A.079	1963	QPSR Box Flat	Operational
1620	A.138	1967	QR Heritage	Operational
1632	A.153	1967	MVHR Gympie	Operational
1639	A.160	1967	MVHR Gympie	Stored
1649	A.191	1969	MVHR Gympie	Stored
1650	A.193	1969	ARHS Redbank	Operational
1651	A.194	1969	QR	Operational
1707D	63-282	1963	ARHS Swanbank	Stored
1710D	63-285	1963	QR Heritage Ipswich	Rail simulator (cab only)
DH2	584	1968	QR Heritage	Stored
DH5	587	1968	PBR Menzies Creek	Stored (900 mm) as CC02
DH14	596	1968	OGHRM MacDonnell	Operational
DH25	607	1969	PBR Menzies Creek	Stored
DH38	620	1969	ARHS Rosewood	Operational
DH59	646	1970	PBR Belgrave, Victoria	Operational (762 mm) as DH31
DL1	-	1939	QR Heritage	Operational
Named *Etheridge*.				
DL2	7747/2481	1954	Forsayth	Display
Named *Forsayth*.				
DL3	571	1961	ARHS Rosewood	Operational
Named *Mt Surprise*.				

Right: DH59 now masquerades as 762 mm-gauge DH31 (in VR livery no less!) for the Puffing Billy Railway in Victoria, and it is seen here at Belgrave on Saturday 30 August 2008. Shane O'Neil

Above: QR Heritage locomotive 1620, near Karrabin on return to Ipswich during a trial run on Tuesday 2 September 2008. Peter Reading

Right: Featured within the main pavilion at The Workshops Museum at Ipswich is 1281 *Century*, one of two diesel locomotives given a gold version of the Queensland Railways scheme to commemorate the QR centennial of 1965. Clyde unit 1461 is in a similar scheme, and named *Centennial*. Chris Walters

Victorian Railways

Road #	Builder's #	Built	Owner	Status
B63	ML2-4	1952	Steamrail Newport	Stored (1600 mm)
B64	ML2-5	1952	Steamrail Ballarat	Stored (no bogies)
B72	ML2-13	1953	Steamrail Newport	Stored (1600 mm)
B74	ML2-15	1953	SRHC Seymour	Operational (1600 mm),
Named *John Hearsch*.				
B75	ML2-16	1953	Westerbrook Rail, Seymour	Stored (1600 mm)
B83	ML2-24	1953	ARHS North Williamstown	Display (1600 mm)
C501	76-824	1977	SRHC Seymour	Operational (1435 mm)
Named *George Brown*.				
E1102	-	1928	ARHS North Williamstown	Display (1600 mm)
E1106	-	1929	Steamrail Newport	Stored Newport (1600 mm)
E1108	-	1929	Steamrail Newport	Stored Newport (1600 mm)
E1109	-	1929	Steamrail Newport	Stored Newport (1600 mm)
F202	1755	1951	SRHC Seymour	Operational (1600 mm)
F208	1761	1951	707 Operations Newport	Operational (1600 mm) as F317
F211	1808	1953	ARHS North Williamstown	Display (1600 mm)
F212	1915	1953	VGR Maldon	Operational (1600 mm)
F216	1807	1952	ARHS North Williamstown	Display (1600 mm)
L1150	1884	1953	ARHS North Williamstown	Display (1600 mm)
Named *R G Wishart*.				
L1160	1894	1953	Steamrail Newport	Stored (1600 mm)
L1162	1896	1953	Steamrail Newport	Operational (1600 mm)
L1169	1921	1954	Steamrail Newport	Stored (1600 mm)
M231	-	1959	Steamrail Newport	Operational (1600 mm)
M232	-	1959	Steamrail Newport	Stored (1600 mm)
S303	57-167	1957	SRHC Seymour	Operational (1600 mm)
Named *C J Latrobe*.				
S308	57-179	1958	ARHS North Williamstown	Display (1600 mm) as Sd308
Named *Sir Redmond Barry*.				
S313	60-230	1961	Steamrail	Operational (1600 mm)
Named *Alfred Deakin*.				
T320	55-63	1955	SRHC Seymour	Operational (1600 mm)
T333	56-102	1956	VGR Seymour	Operational (1600 mm)
T334	56-105	1956	MRPS Moorooduc	Operational (1600 mm)
T341	56-120	1956	YVR Seymour	Operational (1600 mm)
T342	56-123	1956	SGTR Seymour	Operational (1600 mm)
T356	59-214	1959	Steamrail Newport	Operational (1600 mm)
T357	61-242	1961	SRHC Seymour	Operational (1600 mm)
T364	62-249	1962	Steamrail Newport	Operational (1600 mm)
T367	64-322	1964	ARHS North Williamstown	Display (1600 mm)
T378	64-333	1964	SRHC Seymour	Operational (1600 mm)
T395	65-425	1965	Steamrail Newport	Operational (1600 mm)
V56	-	1959	ARHS Williamstown	Display (1600 mm)
W243	008	1960	ARHS Williamstown	Display (1600 mm)
W250	015	1960	YVR Healesville	Operational (1600 mm)
W255	020	1960	ARHS Williamstown	Display (1600 mm)
T411	68-627	1968	MRPS Moorooduc	Operational (1600 mm)
T413	56-107	1969	T413 Group	Operational (1600 mm)
Ex-Australian Portland Cement D1 *Wesley B McCann*. Now named *Steve Gibson*.				
Y127	65-393	1965	707 Operations Newport	Operational (1600 mm)
Y133	65-399	1965	SRHC Seymour	Operational (1600 mm)
Y135	65-401	1965	SGTR Korumburra	Operational (1600 mm)
Y137	65-403	1965	ARHS North Williamstown	Static display (1600 mm)
Y159	67-579	1968	DSCR Daylesford	Operational (1600 mm)
Y164	67-584	1968	Steamrail Newport	Operational (1600 mm)

Right: Steamrail's F317 *Dynon Donk*, at Newport Workshops on Saturday 22 September 2001. F317 is the unit's original number, although in the latter part of its career it operated as F208.
Chris Walters

Middle right: Former VR box-cab electric E1102 at the ARHS North Williamstown museum on Sunday 23 September 2001.
Chris Walters

Below: Steamrail's M231 shunts freight vehicles around Newport on Saturday 9 August 2008.
Les Coulton

Tasmanian Government Railways

Road #	Builder's #	Built	Owner	Status
U1	21	1958	DRR Devonport	Stored (1067 mm)
U3	26	1959	Launceston City Council	Static display (playground)
Named *Hutch*.				
U5	32	1960	DVR New Norfolk	Operational (1067 mm)
U6	37	1960	DRR Devonport	Operational (1067 mm)
V2	2228/D61	1948	DRR Devonport	Operational (1067 mm)
V4	2230/D63	1948	HVTR Dwellingup	Operational (1067 mm)
V5	2381/D130	1951	HVTR Dwellingup	Operational (1067 mm)
V6	2382/D131	1951	DRR Devonport	Stored dismantled
V7	2536/D260	1955	DVR New Norfolk	Stored (1067 mm)
V8	2537/D261	1955	BPR Queenscliff	Operational (1067 mm)
V9	-	1959	PBR Menzies Creek	Static display (1067 mm)
V12	-	1968	PBR Belgrave	Operational (762 mm)
VA1	2227/D60	1962	BPR Queenscliff	Operational (1067 mm)
X1	1796/D88	1950	TTM Glenorchy	Static display (1067 mm)
X3	1798/D90	1950	BPR Queenscliff	Operational (1067 mm)
X4	1799/D91	1950	DRR Devonport	Operational (1067 mm)
X10	1805/D97	1951	DVR New Norfolk	Stored (1067 mm)
X18	1813/D105	1951	DVR New Norfolk	Operational (1067 mm)
X20	1815/D107	1952	BPR Queenscliff	Operational (1067 mm)
X30	1830	1952	DVR New Norfolk	Stored (1067 mm)
Y2	-	1961	DVR New Norfolk	Operational (1067 mm)
Named *Henry Baldwin*.				
Y3	-	1962	QVM Launceston	Static display (1067 mm)
Y4	-	1964	TTM Glenorchy	Operational (1067 mm)
Named *Rowallan*.				
Y6	-	1970	DRR Devonport	Operational (1067 mm)
Y8	-	1971	DRR Devonport	Stored (1067 mm)

Above: Y2 and X18 lead a Derwent Valley Railway special west through Hayes bound for National Park on Sunday 4 January 2004. Chris Walters

Right: Malcolm Moore shunter U6 at the Don River Railway museum near Devonport, on Tuesday morning 11 July 2006. The six members of this class were radically rebuilt by the TGR upon acquisition at the end of the 1950s. U6 is now commonly employed as the workshops shunter here. Chris Walters

Right: Former TGR unit V12 is now employed by Puffing Billy (Victoria) as 762 mm-gauge D21, as seen here on a works train at Emerald on Saturday 30 August 2008. Shane O'Neil

Right: The first main line diesel locomotives in government service within Australia were the TGR X Class, as exemplified by X4, seen here at the Don River Railway on Tuesday 7 April 2008. Ross Verdich

Preserved locomotives of Australian private industry

Road #	Builders #	Builder	Built	Owner	Status
007	69214	ALCo USA	1940	PRHS Seven Mile	Operational (1435 mm)
Bo-Bo DE. Originally Spokane, Portland & Seattle 21, later used by HI. Known as *Mabel*.					
1000	3449-01	ALCo USA	1966	PRHS Karratha	Operational (1435 mm)
Bo-Bo DE. Originally ALCo C415 demonstrator in the US, later used by HI.					
2000	3415-01	ALCo USA	1965	PRHS/Rio Tinto Seven Mile	Display (1435 mm)
Co-Co DE. Ex-HI.					
26	391	Andrew Barclay UK	1953	SSRM Broken Hill	Display (1067 mm)
0-6-0 DM. Ex-Zinc Corporation, later used by Silverton Tramway Company.					
Seymour	2392	Baguley/Drewry	1952	ILRMS Albion Park	Operational (610 mm)
0-6-0 DM. Ex-Victoria Mill.					
15	2520	Baguley/Drewry	1954	Loco Function Centre, Mourilyan	Display (610 mm)
0-6-0 DM. Ex-South Johnstone Mill.					
L'il Toot	3354	Baguley/RMP	1951	PBR Menzies Creek	Display (610 mm)
0-6-0 DM. Ex-Inkerman Mill.					
1	3377	Baguley/RMP	1953	ANGRMS Woodford	Stored (610 mm)
0-6-0 DM. Ex-Mulgrave Mill.					
Mowbray	3378	Baguley/RMP	1954	Ballyhooley Railway	Operational (610 mm)
0-6-0 DM. Ex-Mossman Mill.					
Netherdale	13	Bundaberg/Jenbach	1954	ANGRMS Woodford	Operational (610 mm)
0-6-0 DM. Originally North Eton Mill D2, then Marian *Netherdale*, retrofitted with Comeng cab/hood.					
1	DHI.7	Clyde	1955	GDHMM Gympie	Stored (610 mm)
0-6-0 DH. Ex-Proserpine Mill.					
ETSA1	61-237	Clyde	1961	NRM Port Adelaide	Display (1435 mm)
C DE. Ex-ETSA Port Augusta.					
1 *Clyde*	58-187	Clyde	1958	DSR&M Dorrigo	Stored (1435 mm)
0-6-0 DH. Ex-Australian Defence Industries, later used by Mountain High Railway, Tumut.					
3017	WA-135-C-6043-04	Comeng	1985	PRHS Seven Mile	Operational (1435 mm)
Co-Co DE. Rebuilt from Goodwin/ALCo C636.					
-	E1120	Comeng	1956	Collie Station Museum	Operational (1067 mm)
0-6-0 DM. Ex-SEC Western Australia, Bunbury Powerhouse.					

Right: Former Hamersley Iron C628 No. 2000, on display outside the Rio Tinto/Pilbara Iron maintenance facility at Seven Mile on Tuesday 24 July 2007. Chris Walters

Right: A former Inkerman Mill Baguley unit *L'il Toot* on a short section of 610 mm-gauge track at Puffing Billy's Menzies Creek museum on Saturday 30 August 2008. Shane O'Neil

Right: ETSA No. 1 at the National Rail Museum at Port Dock, Port Adelaide on Sunday 8 June 1997. This unit was based on the six MDH Class locomotives built by Clyde for the Commonwealth Railways a year earlier. Chris Walters

Road #	Builders #	Builder	Built	Owner	Status
-	BB1050	Comeng	1961	Pemberton Tramway Company	Operational (1067 mm)
0-6-0 DH. Ex-Bunnings Mill.					
Bob	F1029	Comeng	1958	SDSRA Warwick	Operational (1067 mm)
0-6-0 DM. Ex-Townsville Terminal.					
Ivanhoe	GA1042	Comeng	1960	ILRMS Albion Park	Stored (610 mm)
0-4-0 DH. Ex-Kalamia Mill.					
5802	JA4282	Comeng	1964	ZZR Lithgow	Operational (1067 mm)
0-6-0 DH. Ex-Mount Isa Mines, originally numbered 2, then 302, and then briefly 7302.					
DE10	2118	Davenport/BHP	1966	PRR Quorn	Stored (1435 mm)
Bo-Bo DE. Ex-BHP Whyalla, converted from petrol/electric PE1 (built in 1928) during 1966.					
Shellharbour	590 9.63	E M Baldwin	1963	ILRMS Albion Park	Operational (610 mm)
0-6-0 DM. Rebuilt from John Fowler 21912 of 1937, ex-Tully Mill 8.					
Valdora	6/1258.5 6.65	E M Baldwin	1965	ASCR Bundaberg	Operational (610 mm)
0-4-0 DH. Ex-Moreton Mill.					
5450	8970	EMD USA	1950	PRHS Seven Mile	Operational (1435 mm)
Bo-Bo DE. Ex Western Pacific Railroad, later used by MNM.					
5451	10805	EMD USA	1951	Mining & Machinery Museum (park), Port Hedland	Display (1435 mm)
Bo-Bo DE. Ex Western Pacific Railroad, later used by MNM.					
D1	-	EE UK/Comeng	1950	NSWRTM Thirlmere	Operational (1435 mm)
Bo-Bo DE. Ex-AIS/BHP Port Kembla, first main line diesel locomotive in Australia.					
D7	-	EE UK/Comeng	1951	Private-Canberra	Operational (1435 mm)
Bo-Bo DE. Ex-AIS/BHP Port Kembla.					
D9	A.005	EE Australia	1956	LVR Cowra	Operational (1435 mm)
B-B DE. Ex-AIS/BHP Port Kembla.					
D11	A.009	EE Australia	1956	DSR&M Dorrigo	Operational (1435 mm)
B-B DE. Ex-AIS/BHP Port Kembla.					
D20	A.041	EE Australia	1960	State Mine, Lithgow	Operational (1435 mm)
B-B DE. Ex-AIS/BHP Port Kembla.					
D21	A.042	EE Australia	1960	State Mine, Lithgow	Stored (1435 mm)
B-B DE. Ex-AIS/BHP Port Kembla.					
D23	A.036	EE Australia	1960	State Mine, Lithgow	Operational (1435 mm)
B-B DE. Ex-AIS/BHP Port Kembla.					
D24	A.037	EE Australia	1960	State Mine, Port Kembla	Stored (1435 mm)
B-B DE. Ex-AIS/BHP Port Kembla.					

Right: Ex-Mount Isa Mines Comeng unit 5802, then recently arrived at the Zig Zag Railways' Clarence Yard, on Saturday 5 July 2008. Shane O'Neil

Right: Originally built by Fowler in 1937, and then radically rebuilt by E M Baldwin in 1963, Tully 8 is now known as *Shellharbour*, and is owned by the Illawarra Light Railway Museum Society at Albion Park, where it is seen in December 2002. Chris Walters

Right: Former Mount Newman Mining (and before that Western Pacific USA) 5450, at the Pilbara Railway Historical Society compound near Seven Mile, on Wednesday 25 July 2007. Chris Walters

Road #	Builders #	Builder	Built	Owner	Status
D25	A.038	EE Australia	1960	ARHS Canberra	Operational (1435 mm)
B-B DE. Ex-AIS/BHP Port Kembla.					
1	A.104/A.232	EE Australia	1965	PRHS Seven Mile	Operational (1435 mm)
Bo-Bo DE. Ex-GML and BHPIO. Rebuilt with new frame and body in 1970 following collision damage.					
2	A.105	EE Australia	1965	Mining & Machinery Museum (park), Port Hedland	Display (1435 mm)
Bo-Bo DE. Ex-GML and BHPIO.					
Planet 1	2150	F C Hibberd	1939	BBR Whiteman Park	Operational (610 mm)
0-4-0 DM. Ex-Lake View and Star Gold Mine, Kalgoorlie.					
Planet 2	3996	F C Hibberd	1962	BBR Whiteman Park	Operational (610 mm)
0-4-0 DM. Ex-Great Boulder Mine, Lake View and Star Gold Mine, (both Kalgoorlie), then Boulder Loop Line.					
51 Planet	3570	F C Hibberd	1952	DSR&M Dorrigo	Stored (1435 mm)
0-4-0 DM. Ex-Metropolitan Water, Sewerage & Distribution Board (Warragamba Dam construction then West Ryde pumping station).					
52	3575	F C Hibberd	1952	LVR Cowra	Operational (1435 mm)
0-4-0 DM. Ex-Metropolitan Water, Sewerage & Distribution Board (Warragamba Dam construction then West Ryde pumping station).					
53	3715	F C Hibberd	1954	RVR Kurri Kurri	Operational (1435 mm)
0-4-0 DM. Ex-Metropolitan Water, Sewerage & Distribution Board (Warragamba Dam construction then Maritime Services Board, Coffs Harbour Wharf).					
Gemco	-	Gemco	1965	ANGRMS Woodford	Operational (610 mm)
0-4-0 DH. Ex-Lake View and Star Gold Mine, Kalgoorlie, later used by Marian Mill.					
PW27	-	Gemco	1964	BBR Whiteman Park	Operational (610 mm)
0-4-0 DH. Ex-Public Works Department, Wyndham. Named *Wyndham*.					
32	8585 1/S1001	Goninan/GE	1954	BHP Museum (Newcastle)	Display (1435 mm)
Bo-Bo DE. Ex-BHP Newcastle.					
34	8585 3/S1003	Goninan/GE	1954	RVR Kurri Kurri	Operational (1435 mm)
Bo-Bo DE. Ex-BHP Newcastle.					
42	3456-10/60-006	Goninan/GE	1960	Private-RVR Kurri Kurri	Stored (1435 mm)
Bo-Bo DE. Ex-BHP Newcastle.					
43	3456-10/60-007	Goninan/GE	1960	RVR Kurri Kurri	Stored (1435 mm)
Bo-Bo DE. Ex-BHP Newcastle.					
47	3456-12/60-011	Goninan/GE	1960	DSR&M Dorrigo	Stored (1435 mm)
Bo-Bo DE. Ex-BHP Newcastle.					
52	4970-12/61-016	Goninan/GE	1961	DSR&M Dorrigo	Stored (1435 mm)
Bo-Bo DE. Ex-BHP Newcastle.					
53	9211-04/64-018	Goninan/GE	1964	RVR Kurri Kurri	Stored (1435 mm)
Bo-Bo DE. Ex-BHP Newcastle.					

Right: Once employed by the Metropolitan Water Sewerage & Distribution Board in the construction of Warragamba Dam, Planet/Hibberd unit 53 now operates with RVR Kurri Kurri, where it is seen on Sunday 14 September 2008. Fred Sawyer

Right: The former Public Works Department, Gemco-built PW27 is seen here in operation on the Bennett Brook Railway on Sunday 23 March 2003. Chris Walters

Right: The former Townsville Harbour Comeng-built shunting unit, now known as *Bob*, at the Southern Downs Steam Railway Association museum at Warwick, on Saturday 13 January 2007. Chris Stratton

Road #	Builders #	Builder	Built	Owner	Status
54	3835-12/65-020	Goninan/GE	1966	RVR Kurri Kurri	Stored (1435 mm)
Bo-Bo DE. Ex-BHP Newcastle.					
JL3	17	Goninan/GE	1963	DSR&M Dorrigo	Stored (1435 mm)
B-B DE. Ex-John Lysaghts, Port Kembla. Named Helen Mary.					
-	1874-11/64-019	Goninan/GE	1964	DSR&M Dorrigo	Stored at Dorrigo
Bo-Bo DE. Ex-Sulphide Corporation, Cardiff.					
D1	6626-06/67-023	Goninan/GE	1967	GRPS Goulburn	Stored (1435 mm)
Bo-Bo DE. Ex-Blue Circle Southern Cement, Marulan South.					
5497	C-6096-02	Goodwin/ALCo	1975	Mining & Machinery Museum (park), Port Hedland	Display (1435 mm)
Co-Co DE. Ex-MNM/BHPIO.					
5499	C-6096-04	Goodwin/ALCo	1975	RHWA Bassendean	Display (1435 mm)
Co-Co DE. Ex-MNM/BHPIO.					
5502	C-6096-07	Goodwin/ALCo	1976	PRHS Seven Mile	Operational (1435 mm)
Co-Co DE. Ex-MNM/BHPIO.					
125	102	Hitachi Japan	1968	Powerworks, Morwell	Display (900 mm)
Bo-Bo electric. Ex-SEC Victoria.					
-	16830	John Fowler UK	1926	MNGR Menangle Park	Stored (610 mm)
0-6-0 DM. Ex-Childers, Condong and Goondi Mills.					
-	18801	John Fowler UK	1927	MNGR Menangle Park	Operational (610 mm)
0-4-0 DH. Ex-Plane Creek Mill.					
1	18260	John Fowler UK	1929	ANGRMS Woodford	Stored (610 mm)
0-6-0 DM. Ex-Childers and Goondi Mills.					
Isis 2 *Rosalie*	4110019	John Fowler UK	1950	BBR Whiteman Park	Operational (610 mm)
0-6-0 DM. Ex-Isis Central Mill.					
14	4210051	John Fowler UK	1954	WGR Walhalla	Operational (762 mm)
0-6-0 DM. Ex-SEC Victoria, named Spirit of Yallourn.					
The Pioneer	4271	Kelly & Lewis	1935	ATT Alexandra	Operational (610 mm)
0-6-0 DM. Ex-Clark & Pearce, Rubicon.					
Paul Simpson	5957	Kelly & Lewis	1936	ATT Alexandra	Operational (610 mm)
0-6-0 DM. Ex-Clark & Pearce, Rubicon.					
37	-	Kelly & Lewis	1942	ARHS North Williamstown	Display (900 mm)
Bo-Bo Electric. Ex-SEC Victoria.					
Joe	811	Malcolm Moore	1942	NDM Nambour	Display (610 mm)
0-4-0 DM . Ex-Imperial Chemical Industries, Dry Creek, later used by Moreton Mill.					

Right: Former BHP Newcastle GE Bo-Bo locomotive No. 34, in operation at the Richmond Vale Railway, near Kurri Kurri, on Sunday 16 April 2005. Chris Walters

Right: Ex-Mount Newman Mining and BHP Iron Ore M636 locomotive 5499, at the RHWA museum at Bassendean on Tuesday 27 July 2008. Chris Miller

Right: One of only two surviving SEC Victoria electric locomotives, No. 37 is now an exhibit within the ARHS North Williamstown Museum, where it is seen on Sunday 23 September 2001. Chris Walters

Road #	Builders #	Builder	Built	Owner	Status
-	1013	Malcolm Moore	1943	PBR Menzies Creek	Display (610 mm)
0-4-0 DM. Ex-Dept Supply & Shipping, later used by Inkerman Mill.					
KMR 2	1039	Malcolm Moore	1943	KMR Kerrisdale	Operational (610 mm)
0-4-0 DM. Ex-Dept Supply & Shipping, later used by Mourilyan Mill.					
-	1049	Malcolm Moore	1943	ATT Alexandra	Operational (610 mm)
0-4-0 PM. Ex-Dept Supply & Shipping, later used by SEC Victoria.					
Jimpy	1051	Malcolm Moore	1943	ANGRMS Woodford	Stored (610 mm)
0-4-0 DM. Ex-Australian Army.					
84001	1032	Malcolm Moore	1943	ANGRMS Woodford	Stored (610 mm)
0-4-0 PM. Ex-Australian Army.					
84002	1035	Malcolm Moore	1943	ANGRMS Woodford	Stored (610 mm)
0-4-0 PM. Ex-Australian Army.					
RT3	1961	Malcolm Moore	1961	DSCR Daylesford	Operational (1600 mm)
0-4-0 DHS. Ex-Massey Ferguson, Sunshine.					
Maylands	-	Maylands Brickworks	c.1960	BBR Whiteman Park	Operational (610 mm)
0-4-0 PM. Ex-Maylands Brickworks.					
SEC1	-	Metro Vickers UK	1924	RHWA Bassendean	Display (1067 mm)
Bo-Bo (600 volt DC) electric. Ex-State Electricity Commission of WA, East Perth.					
E1	-	Metro Vickers UK	1928	NRM Port Adelaide	Display (1067 mm)
Bo-Bo electric. Ex-BHP Iron Knob/Iron Monarch/Rapid Bay.					
21	27084	North British	1953	DVR New Norfolk	Operational
0-8-0 DH. Ex-EBR.					
E7	5999-54-1	Perry SA	1954	Town of Iron Knob	Display (1067 mm)
Bo-Bo electric. Ex-BHP Iron Knob/Iron Monarch					
-	235667	Ruston & Hornsby	1945	DRR Devonport	Display (1067 mm)
0-4-0 DM. Ex-Cornwall Coal (Fingal), earlier used by Melbourne & Metropolitan Board of Works					
-	279571	Ruston & Hornsby	1949	DRR Devonport	Operational (1067 mm)
0-4-0 DM. Ex-Cornwall Coal (Fingal), earlier used by Marine Board of Burnie					
-	284836	Ruston & Hornsby	1950	TTM Glenorchy	Operational (1067 mm)
0-4-0 DM. Ex-Emu Bay Railway, earlier used by Electrolyte Zinc, Rosebery/Risdon					
W L Raws	304475	Ruston & Hornsby	1951	NRM Port Adelaide	Stored (1600 mm)
0-4-0 DM. Ex-Imperial Chemical Industries, Osborne.					
5	279567	Ruston & Hornsby	1949	ANGRMS Woodford	Operational (610 mm)
0-4-0 DM. Ex-Titanium Alloy P/L Cudgen NSW, later used by Condong Mill.					

Right: The former Plane Creek Mill 0-4-0 DH Fowler locomotive, between shunts at the Menangle Narrow Gauge Railway, near Campbelltown on Sunday 16 May 2004. Chris Walters

Right: The first diesel locomotive built in Victoria entered service in 1935, and survives today as *The Pioneer*. It is one of two such units in operation on the Alexandra Timber Tramway, where it is seen in this view from Sunday 27 March 2005. Ewan McLean

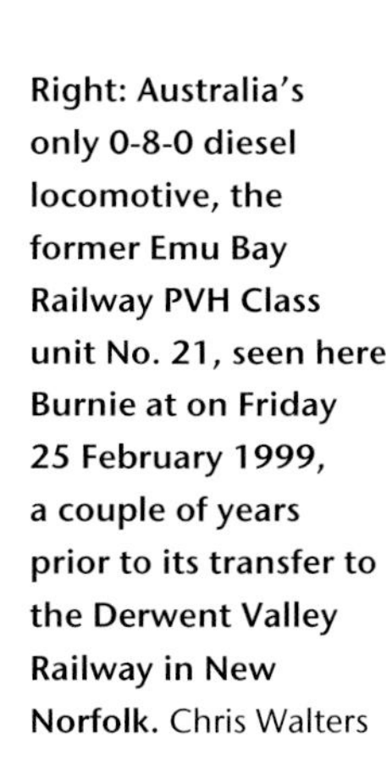

Right: Australia's only 0-8-0 diesel locomotive, the former Emu Bay Railway PVH Class unit No. 21, seen here Burnie at on Friday 25 February 1999, a couple of years prior to its transfer to the Derwent Valley Railway in New Norfolk. Chris Walters

Road #	Builders #	Builder	Built	Owner	Status
1	354040	Ruston & Hornsby	1953	CCBT Korumburra	Operational (610 mm)
0-4-0 DM. Ex-Tivoli Collieries P/L Queensland, later used by Invicta Mill.					
6	371959	Ruston & Hornsby	1953	ILRMS Albion Park	Stored (610 mm)
0-4-0 DM. Ex-Titanium Alloy P/L Cudgen NSW, later used by Condong Mill.					
NRT1	296058	Ruston & Hornsby	1950	PBR Menzies Creek	Operational (762 mm)
0-4-0 DM. Ex-Melbourne and Metropolitan Board of Works. Fitted with original cab from EMB Macknade Mill 14 (see page 235).					
KMR 4	285301	Ruston & Hornsby	1949	KMR Kerrisdale	Operational (610 mm)
0-4-0 DM. Ex-Public Works Department.					
-	187072	Ruston & Hornsby	1937	DRR Devonport	Operational (1067 mm)
0-4-0 DM. Ex-Mount Lyell Mining & Railway Company, later used by Dillingham Constructions, Launceston/Rosebery.					
Ruston	404981	Ruston & Hornsby	1957	BBR Whiteman Park	Operational (610 mm)
0-4-0 DM. Ex-Christiani & Neilsen, later used by Bunnings Brothers at Manjimup.					
1001	576	Walkers	1963	WGR Walhalla	Operational (762 mm)
B-B DH. Ex-EBR.					
1002	577	Walkers	1963	DRR Devonport	Operational (1067 mm)
B-B DH. Ex-EBR.					
1003	578	Walkers	1963	ZZR Lithgow	Stored (1067 mm)
B-B DH. Ex-EBR.					
1004	-	TGR/Walkers	1966	ZZR Lithgow	Operational (1067 mm)
B-B DH. Ex-EBR.					
1101	638	Walkers	1969	CKST Group Cairns	Operational (1067 mm)
B-B DH. Ex-EBR.					
1102	639	Walkers	1969	CKST Group Cairns	Stored (1067 mm)
B-B DH. Ex-EBR.					
1105	642	Walkers	1969	CKST Group Cairns	Operational (1067 mm)
B-B DH. Ex-EBR.					
SEC1	D1041	Vulcan/Drewry	1949	HVTR Dwellingup	Operational (1067 mm)
0-6-0 DM. Ex-SEC Western Australia, South Fremantle tippler shunter. Named *South Fremantle*.					
D1	2405/D193	Vulcan/Drewry	1953	WCWR Queenstown	Operational (1067 mm)
0-6-0 DM. Ex-Mount Lyell Mining & Railway Company, later used by EBR/Pasminco.					
D2	2406/D194	Vulcan/Drewry	1953	WCWR Queenstown	Operational (1067 mm)
0-6-0 DM. Ex-Mount Lyell Mining & Railway Company, later used by TGR/AN Tasrail and ZZR Lithgow.					

Right: Once owned by Electrolytic Zinc and then the Emu Bay Railway and Pasminco, this Ruston model 88DS unit is now both an exhibit, and shunter at the Tasmanian Transport Museum at Glenorchy (Hobart), as seen here on Sunday 13 January 2008. Chris Stratton

Right: Former EBR class leader 1001 is now in the hands of the Walhalla Goldfields Railway at Walhalla in Victoria. For use on the line, the group has re-gauged the unit from 1067 to 762 mm as seen here on Wednesday 11 July 2007. Chris Miller

Right: Former Mount Lyell Mining & Railway Company, Vulcan/Drewry-built locomotive D1 awaits departure from Dubbil Barril with a West Coast Wilderness Train bound for Regatta Point (Strahan) train bound for on Wednesday 9 April 2008. Spencer Ross

Commercial operators fleet list index

Queensland sugar mill fleet list index (north to south)

Acknowledgements, sources and further reading

Special thanks are due to Simon Barber, Jim Bisdee, John Bollans, Michael Bray, Steve Bromley, John Browning, Jim Bruce, Tony Burgess, Barry Burton, Stephen Carr, Peter Chandler, James Chuang, Peter Clark, John Cleverdon, Adrian Compton, Brad Coulter, Les Coulton, Graham Crichton, Ken Date, Melanie Dennis, Michael Dix, Stuart Dix, Ian Dixon, Ted Drake, John Dunn, Roger Evans, Dominik Giemza, Bob Gioia, Bob Grant, Alex Grunbach, Mark Hall, John Hoyle, Julian Insall, Greg Isele, Michael James, Evan Jasper, Danielle Jesser, Scott Jesser, Stephen Karas, Peter Kitcher, Alex Mackay, Tom Marschall, Phil Martin, Ross McClelland, Terry McConnell, Daniel McKee, Ewan McLean, David Melling, Peter Michalak, Chris Miller, Stephen Miller, Rod Milne, Toad Montgomery, Bernie Morris, Steve Munro, Trent Nicholson, Brian Nielson, Leon Oberg, Greg O'Brien, Shane O'Neil, Steve Palmano, David Phillips, David Porter, Greg Pringle, Peter Reading, Roger Renton, Andrew Rosenbauer, Spencer Ross, Robert Rouse, Fred Sawyer, Arthur Shale, Travis Simmons, Damien Smith, Les Straden, Chris Stratton, Joanne Stratton, Shawn Stusel, Darren Teasdale, Allan Tilley, Ed Tonks, Wayne Trowbridge, Darren Tulk, Ross Verdich, Daven Walters, Brian Webber, Doug Williams, Ken Williams, Steve Williams, Steve Zvillis, ARHS Tasmanian Division, ARHS Western Australian Division, Skitube, Ausloco, LocoShed, ALRosters and Tassierailnews yahoogroups

Books

- *Australian Diesel Scene 4* (Eveleigh Press 2000)
- *An Australian Diesel Locomotive Pocket Book*, Peter J Clark (ARHS NSW Division 1973)
- *A History of the BHP Tramways* (BHP)
- *Australian National Locomotives (Tasmania)*, Kenn Pearce (Railmac 1981)
- *BHP Rail*, Don Drysdale (View Prods 1988)
- *BHP Tramways, Centenary History*, David Griffiths (Mile End Railway Museum, 1985)
- *Built by Baldwin*, Craig Wilson (LRRSA 2002)
- *Changing Before Our Eyes*, Simon Barber (SJB Publications 1998)
- *Diesel and Electric Locomotives of the NSWGR—Volume 2*, M Morahan (NSWRTM 1998)
- *Early Diesel and Electric Locomotives of the NSWGR*, M Morahan (NSWRTM 1997)
- *Five Decades of Clyde-GM Locomotives*, Lawrie Gillies (ARHSnsw 1998)
- *Hamersley Iron Railway* (HI 1985)
- *Hotham Valley Tourist Railway*, John Purcell (HVTR)
- *QR Locomotive history—as at 30 June 1999* (QR, 1999)
- *Locomotives of Australia*, Leon Oberg (Rosenberg 2007)
- *Locomotives of Australian National*, Robert Sampson and Ronald E Fluck (Mile End Railway Museum, 1982)
- *Locomotives of the Silverton Tramway*, Steve McNicol (Railmac 1990)
- *Made in Maryborough: A Pictorial Record of the Railway Rollingstock Produced by Walkers Ltd*, A M West (ARHS Queensland 1994)
- *The Midland Railway Company Locomotives of Western Australia*, A Gunzburg (LRRSA 1989)
- *New Zealand Railway Motive Power 2002*, David Parsons (NZRLS 2002)
- *Railways In The Pilbara*, John Joyce and Allan Tilley (J & A Publications)
- *Tasmanian Railways 1871–1996: A Pictorial History*, Greg Cooper and Grant Goss (Regal Press 1996)
- *WAGR Locomotives 1940–1968*, A Gunzburg (ARHS WA Division 1968)
- *Westrail's English Electric Experience*, Rod Milne (Railmac 1998)
- *Westrail Locomotives*, Kenn Pearce (Railmac 1981)
- *Working Class Beauty (A tribute to the TGR X and XA classes)*, Rod Milne (Railmac 2000)

Magazines

Australian Locomotive News various issues

Australian Model Railway Magazine various issues

ARHS Bulletin various issues

Catchpoint various issues

Light Railways various issues

MotivePower various issues

Newsrail various issues

Rail Australia various issues

Rail News Victoria various issues

Railway Digest various issues

Sunshine Express various issues

Tasmanian Railway Hobbyist various issues

Tasmanian Railway News various issues

Online resources

- All Time Union Pacific Diesel Roster (last accessed 3 November 2008)
  http://utahrails.net/all-time/all-time-index.php
- Australian sugar industry locomotives—June 2005 (last accessed 3 November 2008)
  http://www.lrrsa.org.au/QLD_locolist_June2005.htm
- CFCLA website (last accessed 3 November 2008)
  http://www.cfcla.com.au/locomotives.htm
- Comrails website, locomotive pages (last accessed 3 November 2008)
  http://comrails.railpage.org.au/cr_locos/index.html
  http://comrails.railpage.org.au/sar_locos/index.html
- Daylesford Spa Country Railway (last accessed 3 November 2008)
  http://www.dscr.com.au/rollingstock.php
- The Workshops Rail Museum (Ipswich), DL Class factsheet
  (last accessed 3 November 2008)
  http://www.theworkshops.qm.qld.gov.au/education/programs/pdf/factsheets/
  factsheet_class_dl_diesel_20071203.pdf
- Don River Railway–locomotives (last accessed 3 November 2008)
  http://www.donriverrailway.com.au/locomotives.html
- EE 12 CSVT website, Australian-built (last accessed 3 November 2008)
  http://www.12csv.com/pages/traction/australian/index.htm
- General Electric Roster (last accessed 3 November 2008)
  http://www.ole.net/~rcraig/GE.HTML
- Hotham Valley Tourist Railway Diesel Locomotives (accessed 3 November 2008)
  http://www.hothamvalleyrailway.com.au/diesel_locomotives.htm
- LocoPage online (last accessed 3 November 2008)
  http://locopage.railpage.org.au/

- MZ Class (Google translation of NOHaB MZ Class pages, last accessed 3 November 2008) http://translate.google.com/translate?hl=en&sl=de&u=http://nohab-gm.de/mzlist/mzlist.php&sa=X&oi=translate&resnum=2&ct=result&prev=/search%3Fq%3DNoHAB%252BMZ%252BClass%252BDSB%252B2858%26hl%3Den%26client%3Dsafari%26rls%3Den
- MZ Class (Google translation of Railorama NoHAB locomotive pages, last accessed 3 November 2008) http://translate.google.com/translate?hl=en&sl=da&u=http://www.railorama.dk/motormateriel/%3Ffid%3D1&sa=X&oi=translate&resnum=4&ct=result&prev=/search%3Fq%3DNoHAB%252BMZ%252BClass%252BDSB%252B2858%26hl%3Den%26client%3Dsafari%26rls%3Den
- National Rail Equipment (NREX) Roster (last accessed 3 November 2008) http://www.ole.net/~rcraig/NRE.HTML
- National Railway Museum—Inventory of all major locomotives (last accessed 3 November 2008) http://www.natrailmuseum.org.au/common/nrm_a03_m03_1.html
- Preserved Australian sugar cane locomotives (last accessed 3 November 2008) http://www.lrrsa.org.au/LRR_SGRc.htm
- Rail Heritage WA, Rail Transport Museum—Diesel Locomotives (last accessed 3 November 2008) http://www.railheritagewa.org.au/museum/museum.htm#diesel
- The Clyde DH-110 Class Diesel Locomotive (CR NC Class) (last accessed 3 November 2008) http://users.chariot.net.au/~nldoncas/nicspages/nc.htm
- The Railways of Canada Archives–Canada Calling (last accessed 3 November 2008) http://www.trainweb.org/canadianrailways/CanadaCalling/January2000.html
- SD40-2 Locomotive Specifications (last accessed 3 November 2008) http://www.highironillustrations.com/railfan_specification/spec_sd40.html
- Steamranger Enthusiast Pages—Diesel Locos and Railcars (last accessed 3 November 2008) http://www.steamranger.org.au/enthusiast/diesel.htm
- Tastrain, Diesel Locomotive Information web pages (last accessed 3 November 2008) http://www.railtasmania.com/loco/locostat.php http://www.railtasmania.com/loco/
- Tasmanian Government Railways U Class Diesel Shunter (last accessed 3 November 2008) http://www.our-australia.com/blog/pages/uclass.html
- Tas Steam Alive Productions–The Queen Victoria Museum at Inveresk (last accessed 3 November 2008) http://www.users.bigpond.com/tassteamalive/qv.htm
- Utah Railway–Roster of Diesel Locomotives (last accessed 3 November 2008) http://www.utahrails.net/utah-ry/utah-ry-diesel-index.php
- The Unofficial EMD homepage (last accessed 3 November 2008) http://www.trainweb.org/emdloco/index.html